COMMUNITY DEVELOPMENT IN AMERICA

Community Development in America

EDITED BY

JAMES A. CHRISTENSON and JERRY W. ROBINSON, JR.

THE IOWA STATE UNIVERSITY PRESS / **AMES,** IOWA

JAMES A. CHRISTENSON is associateprofessor of sociology and director of the Survey Research Center at the University of Kentucky, Lexington, and was formerly extension CD specialist at North Carolina State University. He is associate editor of the *Journal of the Community Development Society* and of *Rural Sociology.* He has written over 50 extension and experiment station publications and has published over 25 articles in the journals of his field.

JERRY W. ROBINSON, JR., is professor of sociology and rural sociology and extension specialist at the University of Illinois, Urbana. He was editor of the *Journal of the Community Development Society* from 1976 to 1979. He has published training materials on conflict management, organization development, human relations, and winning behavior skills; his research has focused on the effects of training programs on the attitudes and behaviors of adult learners.

©1980 The Iowa State University Press
Chapter 6 ©1980 Jerry W. Robinson, Jr.
All rights reserved

Composed and printed by The Iowa State University Press, Ames, Iowa 50010

First edition, 1980
Second printing, 1981

Library of Congress Cataloging in Publication Data
Main entry under title:

Community development in America.

   "This book is the product of cumulative efforts of members of the Community Development Society."
   Includes bibliographies and index.
   1. Community development—United States—Addresses, essays, lectures. I. Christenson, James A., 1944–   II. Robinson, Jerry W., Jr., 1932–   III. Community Development Society.
HN90.C6C6615   307′.0973   80-11046
ISBN 0-8138-1475-8

CONTENTS

PREFACE

THIS BOOK is the product of cumulative efforts of members of the Community Development Society. In 1977 the editors submitted a proposal to the editorial committee of the society to sponsor a publication in celebration of the tenth anniversary of the society's existence. We stated that the proposed book "would attempt to review the state of the art of community development in America." The proposal generated considerable dialogue within the editorial committee, within the society's board of directors, and among the membership concerning the scope of the proposed monograph and who should be contributors. The society's membership is noted for its broad representation of various disciplines and institutions. Thus, the book evolved to represent writings from all segments of the Community Development Society—government; private enterprise; and university teaching, research, and extension.

The preliminary outline for the book grew out of a content analysis of articles (see Chapter 3) published in the first ten volumes of the *Journal of the Community Development Society*. Thus, the major themes and concerns that have appeared in the journal during the past decade are magnified and critiqued in the following pages. The final outline of the book, along with the scope and content of the chapters, was debated by the authors and discussed with the membership of the society at special sessions during the ninth annual meeting of the Community Development Society at the Virginia Polytechnic Institute and State University in 1978. In addition, all chapters were submitted to the same review process that is used to critique manuscripts submitted for publication to the *Journal of the Community Development Society*. Thus, this book, while reflecting the views of the 25 contributors and the organizational decisions of the editors, is also a reflection of the writings, concerns, and inputs of a broad cross section of society members.

OVERVIEW

This book begins with a discussion of major concepts that surround community development, provides a working definition of community development for subsequent chapters of the book, and then describes the growth of community development as a science and profession. The second chapter provides a thorough history of community development in

American society. In this chapter, Phifer, with List and Faulkner, comments on the unique quality of the American spirit that has stimulated people to improve their quality of life—their social, economic, and cultural environment. In many ways community development is the embodiment of democratic society—a system built on checks and balances, public participation, and a restless desire for change and improvement. In Chapter 3, the history of community development is expanded by analyzing the writings of contributors to the *Journal of the Community Development Society* since its inception in 1970. This chapter describes three major themes weaving through the *Journal:* the technical assistance approach, the self-help approach, and the conflict approach. Other issues raised in the content analysis of the society's journal were public participation, the teaching of community development, research in community development, evaluation, and the need for theory. Such issues lay the foundation for the subsequent chapters.

The next three chapters critique three specific approaches to community development. In Chapter 4, Gamm and Fisher describe how the technical intervention approach to community development has evolved into major governmental programs during the past ten years. Both governmental and university programs have provided technical assistance to community groups and governments in the form of grants, education, and information to improve the quality of life in communities. The role of government in community development has far-reaching implications for the future of the profession. It raises the question of whether community development will become a status quo entity, one of action without change. In Chapter 5, Littrell reviews the most commonly used mode of community development: the self-help or the nondirective approach. Littrell questions whether self-help is a viable *modus operandi* in today's highly complex and vertically integrated society. He suggests some new ways of interpreting and initiating such community development efforts. A discussion of conflict in Chapter 6 indicates that the self-help approach to community development may be impossible for people without economic or political resources. Robinson argues that people outside the political process have little influence on and thus derive little from the technical assistance or the self-help approach, so they resort to confrontation. Meaningful change cannot be achieved without a redistribution of benefits and this will not occur without conflict in many communities. Techniques and tactics for using, preventing, and managing community conflict are discussed.

What do community development professionals do? In Chapter 7, Warner presents a framework for interpreting the work of community development practitioners: individual traits, the functions they perform, the institutional setting in which they work, and the clientele they serve. Then a series of authors from very different backgrounds and professional roles comment on their work and perspective of community development. Included are individuals working in government, private enterprise, universities, the Cooperative Extension Service, and institutes; others working with neighborhood organizations and voluntary associations; a community psychologist; and a community planner. Each of these authors provides practical insights into what it means to work in community development from their perspective. For example, McCoy writes that professionals working in the private sector are concerned with doing rather than study, with facts rather than options, and with products rather than process. On the other hand, the publicly oriented community developer tends to view the process and study aspects—that is, group dynamics, citizen involvement, feedback, interaction, and analysis assistance—as the prime goal of community development. Child, when discussing the role of the private consultant in community development, describes the need for a client orientation. A private consultant is in business trying to provide a quality product, a constant market, satisfied customers, reasonable profits, good management, and flexibility. Harris, a trained Alinsky organizer, discusses grass roots community development efforts. M. Cohen reflects on the role of the community psychologist engaged in community development work. Hamilton describes the role of community development specialists in the Cooperative Extension Service; and Melvin gives us the planner's point of view.

Can community development be taught? What should be taught? And how? Lee Cary, first president of the Community Development Society, tackles some of these issues in Chapter 8. Building on historical analysis of the evolution of institutional programs and curricula in the United States, Cary provides a framework for teaching community development. Most important, he suggests some of the concepts and skills that should be provided in a community development educational program.

Reviewing several major research efforts relevant to community development efforts (needs assessment, community services, and industrialization), Garkovich and Stam raise some issues about the relevance of current research for community development in our society. This chapter reviews a wide range of community development research efforts and, in the process, suggests areas of needed research. In Chapter 10, Voth, Bothereau, and R. Cohen discuss the difficult problem of evaluating community development efforts. The authors conclude that much community development work is done in a process framework, helping people to achieve community improvement through their own efforts. Such process efforts are most difficult to evaluate. Some suggestions for evaluating both process and task achievement in community development programs are provided.

Chapter 11 discusses the integration of theory and practice of community development using a grounded theory framework. Blakely suggests how scholars and practitioners might engage in the process of theory building to meet the requirements of the rapidly changing profession called community development. In the final chapter, Spiegel speculates on the future: He asks questions about the role of government in community development, the internal and external pushes and pulls that community development is likely to experience in the 1980s, and trends that community development may take in the future.

ACKNOWLEDGMENTS

The authors of these chapters have benefited considerably from the criticism and suggestions of the reviewers listed below. We would like to extend our appreciation to them for enhancing the quality of the material presented in the book. Special thanks goes to Paul Warner who helped to coordinate, review, and edit parts A–G, Chapter 7, on roles of professionals in community development. We also want to thank the authors of each chapter for reviewing other chapters, helping to provide continuity and flow to this book. We extend our appreciation to the Northeast and North Central Rural Development Centers for providing seed money to help with typing, xeroxing, and other costs incurred in the preparation of this manuscript. We are grateful to Carol Sanderson of Iowa State University Press for her excellent technical editorial assistance. Finally, and most important, we thank the editorial committee for their support and the board of directors and members of the Community Development Society for underwriting this publication. Because of this, all royalties will go to the Community Development Society.

The following individuals reviewed at least one chapter of this book. The authors very much appreciate their help.

Robert Bealer	Donald Johnson	J. Norman Reid
Austin Bennett	Harold Kaufman	Frank Santopollo
Claude Bennett	James Laue	Harvey Schweitzer
Bradley Brown	Huey Long	Bobbie S. Sparks
Rosemary Caffarella	Douglas McAlister	Virginia Purtle
C. Milton Coughenour	Richard Maurer	Willis A. Sutton, Jr.
Lee Day	Gail Metheny	Janice S. Taylor
Don A. Dillman	Kenneth Pigg	Richard Thomas
Glen A. Eyford	Ronald Powers	Raymond Vlasin
Paul Gessaman	Glen Pulver	Henry Wadsworth
Duane L. Gibson	John Quinn	Kenneth P. Wilkinson
Thomas A. Hobgood		

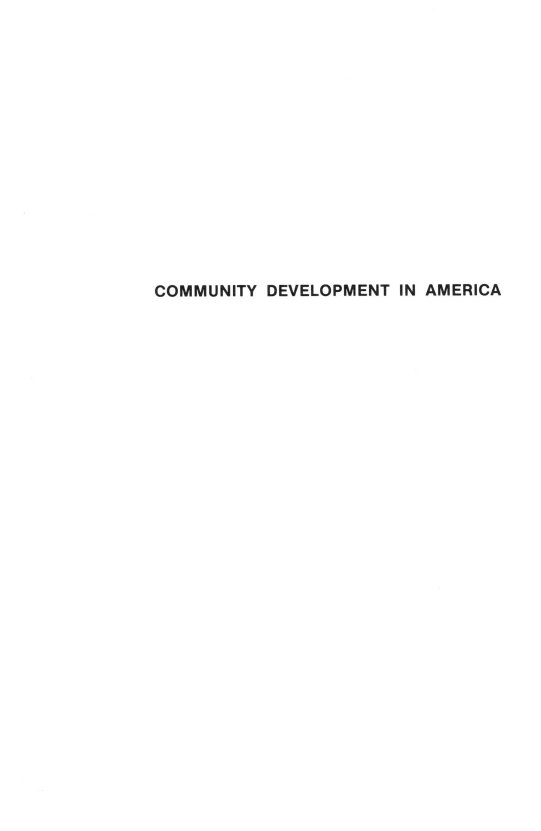

COMMUNITY DEVELOPMENT IN AMERICA

CHAPTER 1

In Search of Community Development

James A. Christenson and Jerry W. Robinson, Jr.

INTRODUCTION

The community development profession is coming of age. While efforts in this area have a long tradition, within the last decade community development has become a major program in thousands of communities and counties across America, in most state governments, in the federal government, and in many nations throughout the world. The Community Development Society celebrated its tenth year of existence in 1979. Universities offering advanced degree programs in this field have multiplied tenfold in the last decade. In the private sector, numerous consulting firms with special units in community development have sprung into existence; and large corporations such as Sears and Exxon and foundations such as Rockefeller, Ford, and Kellogg have initiated educational programs with a community development emphasis.

In spite of recent growth and emphasis, community development remains in search of mature professional identity. Even with all the activity in government, in the private sector, and in professional societies, considerable ambiguity exists as to what community development is. To someone working with the federal government, community development might suggest revenue sharing or community development block grants. A professional working in state government might see it as flood disaster relief, new roads, recreational centers, or comprehensive planning. To a local public official it could suggest industrial growth, community beautification, revitalization of the downtown area, extension of sewer lines, and new schools. To community activists, it may mean job development and housing or health services for the poor and disadvantaged. To specialists in the Cooperative Extension Service it may mean organization of community clubs, leadership training, educational programs on conflict management, or working with local leaders to attract industry. To environmentalists, it may mean slowing economic growth and preserving the desirable attributes of a valley. In short, community development means many things to many people. This diversity is both a strength and a weakness of the field. The

3

profession is so young that very diverse efforts fall under its label. Unfortunately for someone new to the area, it is difficult to grasp all the diverse components of community development.

PURPOSE AND SCOPE

The purpose of this book is to provide a critique of various perspectives, themes, efforts, and orientations that fall in the arena of community development (CD). We also seek to provide an operational synthesis of CD practice. The following chapters provide a brief history and a state of the art of community development efforts in America. Various approaches for initiating CD efforts are discussed. Role expectations for professionals in different settings such as government, private agencies, universities, the Cooperative Extension Service, or as activists in neighborhood settings are presented. We seek to relate theory, research, evaluation, and practice.

This book is limited to community development in America. While trying to make sense out of diversity, we cannot do justice to all aspects of community development throughout the world. We will provide up-to-date assessments of various approaches to community development theory serving the student, the professional, and the lay person. We provide a broad description of the origins of community development, what it is, where it is going, and some insights on the changing scene of community development in America.

MAJOR CONCEPTS

Concepts help us define our perceptions of reality. They exist in our minds as the result of organized or systematic experiences of our senses. Concepts are basic elements of theory and therein define and guide intellectual and research efforts. Community development encompasses a loosely tied group of concepts based on the experiences of CD practitioners. Few will argue with Dunham's (1972, p. 37) conclusion that the term community development is used loosely, ambiguously, and with various meanings in the United States. We take strong exception to Brokensha's (1968, p. 78) description of community development as a knowledge-free area, noted for murky banalities, half-truths, and nonsense. But we agree that clarification of the meaning of community, development, social change, community development, and related concepts is in order before a review of the history, approaches, and roles in the practice of community development is presented.

Community

Community means fellowship in the Greek language. Reflecting on the meaning of the word, Aristotle asserted that people came together in a community setting for the enjoyment of mutual association, to fulfill basic needs, and to find meaning in life. The philosopher, Thomas Hobbes, on the other hand, saw community as the natural process of people coming together to maximize their self-interest. Hobbes felt that self-interest could be best satisfied in a group setting. Community allowed individuals to abandon the many diversified and labor-demanding activities required in subsistence living. By coming together in a community setting, one individual could be a farmer, another a baker, a third a merchant, another a blacksmith or a teacher, and so on. Men and women could pursue, within certain limits as defined by customs and mores, the activities suited to their ability and/or liking.

In primitive societies, communities were relatively easy to identify. They were groups of people living close to one another and isolated from other groups of people. In early American rural society it was easy to identify the boundaries of communities by observing the way wagon ruts from a farmstead turned when they entered the main road. Communities were small and geographically dispersed. For example, in 1790 there was no city in the United States larger than 50,000. By 1840, there were only 5 cities of such size (New York, Boston, Philadelphia, Baltimore, St. Louis). But a century later there were over 200 cities of 50,000 or more.

Today it is more difficult to see and define a community as place. Dirt has given way to asphalt and self-sufficiency of groups has given way to mutual interdependence. The rural-urban cultural and social gap has narrowed. With growth in population and rapid means of transportation, patterns of social interaction have become much more complicated. Places of work, of recreation, and of sleep are often miles apart, perhaps communities apart. Yet no matter how complex communities have become, the need to understand and be able to define community is still of critical importance for community development. Before we can analyze change or development, we have to come to a common understanding of what a community is.

Hillery (1955), Sutton and Kilaja (1960), and Willis (1977) have summarized much of the literature and suggest four main components for defining the concept of community. First and foremost a community involves *people*. There is little debate over this element. Also, few authors deny that *area* or *territory* should be an element of community (Hillery 1955, p. 117). However, not all writers include territory, land, or geographical boundaries in their definitions of community. It seems popular today to describe community as an open system or social system and imply some sort of elastic boundaries (see Willis 1977; Christenson and Warner, in review). But we think that geographical boundaries *are* an integral part of community and consequently it is considered a second component of our definition.

Social interaction is another component of community (Kaufman 1959; Wilkinson 1972, 1979). Social interaction has slightly different meanings to the various writers and researchers. It obviously suggests that people within a defined geographical area in some way relate to or are interdependent on one another. According to Hillery (1955) and Willis (1977), this social interaction suggests a collection of organizations such as businesses, schools, police and fire departments, industries, banks, hospitals, and units of local government to which and with which people relate and on which people depend. Kaufman (1959) writes that these associational networks form a configuration that "holds" communities together. Social interaction suggests the possession of some common norms, customs, and means for obtaining desired ends.

The fourth element of community is the idea of common attachment to or psychological *identification with* a community. Most people are able to give you the name of the community within which they live. People become dependent on a particular locality for shopping, public services, recreation, work, and seeing their friends and neighbors. This locality is what most people *identify with* as community. People may also identify with and have strong ties to a neighborhood, a particular subdivision in a city, or some other geographical referent. If one is visiting New York and a person there asks where you live, you may say Seattle even though you may live in Gig Harbor some 50 miles from Seattle. But no one would recognize Gig Harbor so you give a name that denotes some recognizable location. If you are in Seattle when someone asks where you live, you would say Gig Harbor. And if you are standing in downtown Gig Harbor and are asked where you live, you would probably say Southpoint, a particular subdivision of Gig Harbor. Thus, our identification with a community depends somewhat on who asks, where we are located, and how specific the question is.

In this book we do not consider neighborhoods, subdivisions, or similar entities as communities. While people may have strong ties to their neighborhoods, such entities are, by definition, dependent on the larger community for institutional and public services and for governance. The importance of neighborhoods, however, should not be de-emphasized. They often bring together or encompass groups of people with similar interests, ethnic heritages, and social and economic statuses. As such, neighborhoods are important considerations for understanding the heterogeneous nature of communities and are forces to be reckoned with when attempting to initiate change or to understand forces impeding change within communities.

To facilitate discussion of community development one must be able to analyze and define a community, understand how it functions, and perceive elements stimulating consensus or common interest, while at the same time identifying elements that might divide or polarize a community. From our perspective *a community is defined and best described by the following elements: (1) people (2) within a geographically bounded area (3) involved in social interaction and (4) with one or more psychological ties with each other and with the place they live.*

Development and Social Change

"Perhaps no single word has been more widely and frequently used by such a large number of people in so many countries of the world today than the term development" (Kim 1973, p. 462). Development implies improvement, growth, and change. It is concerned historically with the transition of cultures, societies, and communities from less advanced to more advanced social stages. Such terms as industrialization, modernization, and urbanization have been used interchangeably with the broader concept of development. We imply these changes when we contrast developed and underdeveloped countries. Let us analyze development in terms of improvement, growth, and change.

Development when treated as a normative concept, which is usually the case, is synonymous with improvement. In this context, development means social transformation in the direction of more egalitarian distribution of social goods such as education, health services, housing, participation in political decision making, and other dimensions of people's life chances.

While development as improvement tends to focus more on the social and psychological transformations in societies and communities, development as growth involves the technological and economic transformation. Development as growth focuses on economic prosperity. A common indicator of development as growth would be the expansion of the gross national product (GNP). For example, Portes (1976, p. 565) employs the gross national product (per capita) as an indicator of the relative average growth of both developed and less developed nations between 1963 and 1973. In 1963 the gross national product per capita (in 1972 dollars) was $2,381 for developed nations and $185 for less developed nations. By 1973 the GNP (again in 1972 dollars) for developed nations was $3,561 compared with $252 for less developed nations. Such comparisons indicate a rapidly growing gap between the developed and the less developed nations. Development as growth includes the institutional transformation of structures to facilitate technological advancement and improvements in technology, production, and distribution of goods and services.

Development as change involves a broader perspective. Development has come to be regarded as a type of social change (Kim 1973, p. 463). While social change can be considered as a concept that charts the transformation of societies, states, and communities, development is seen as planned or directed social change. Development does not just happen but entails some deliberate policies that are sustained by those in power (Portes 1976). Development as social change is putting a particular ideological orientation into action to restructure the social normative and economic order for desired ends. Development is based on and grounded in a societal vision. Such a societal vision is not shared by all. For one person the planned transformation of a society or a city would be development; for another person it would be social or economic deprivation. The desire to change the social order, which we call development, is a biased perspective of the person or group desiring such change. No restructuring of benefits in a social order occurs without some cost to a segment of that social order.

Intervention

Development as a form of social change can be seen more easily by presenting two visions of the social order. First is the vision of those who adhere to the law of nonintervention. This perspective has evolved from the natural-law and the ''invisible-hand'' ideology of the laissez-faire doctrine under which western nations, such as the United States, expanded during the eighteenth and nineteenth centuries. It is based partially on economic analysis and partially on ideological beliefs warning that tampering with the natural environment and/or the social order would upset the harmonic forces at work within the universe. It holds that if *homeostatic* forces are left to evolve of themselves, they will bring about the maximum good for both the physical and the social universe.

The idea of development stems from the vision of society in terms of planned intervention, which stresses the utilization of knowledge and technology to help solve the problems of individuals and groups. It is based on the philosophical idea that in applying systematic and appropriate knowledge to the problems confronting the social system, we can facilitate purposefully directed change for the betterment of all. The idea of intervention finds many of its philosophical ideas in the early works of Marx on the inevitable class struggle and the need to facilitate the restructuring of society on more equitable terms.

To facilitate an understanding of development as an intervention perspective, three types of planned community changes are presented in Chapters 4, 5, and 6—the technical assistance, the self-help, and the conflict approaches. An arbitrary and therefore artificial boundary has been established in limiting this discussion to three basic areas of analysis. In reality these three analytical frameworks overlap.

Many other writers have developed trichotomous models of change. Jack Rothman (1974) formulated three models of practice that include locality development, social planning, and social action. Crowfoot and Chesler (1974) formulated the countercultural, the professional-technical, and the political models. Chin and Benne (1976, pp. 22–45) have developed the rational-empirical, the normative-reeducative and the power-coercive models. The three approaches presented in Chapters 4–6 are more closely related to those presented by Chin and Benne than to the other two models.

Community Development

A wide variety of definitions of community development is available in the literature, especially in the *Journal of the Community Development Society* and the *International Community Development Journal*. To provide an overview, we have reviewed these journals and have collated the definitions of community development as follows.

BENNETT 1973, p. 59: "the deliberate attempt by community people to work together to guide the future of their communities, and the development of a corresponding set of techniques for assisting community people in such a process."

DARBY and MORRIS 1975, p. 43: "an educational approach which would raise levels of local awareness and increase the confidence and ability of community groups to identify and tackle their own problems."

DUNBAR 1972, p. 43: "a series of community improvements which take place over time as a result of the common efforts of various groups of people. Each successive improvement is a discrete unit of community development. It meets a human want or need."

FREDERICKSON 1975, pp. 97–98: "finding effective ways of helping and teaching people to adapt new methods and to learn new skills. This process is, however, done in such a way as to retain community control and community spirit."

HAMMOCK 1973, p. 18: "a process of creating special community organizations throughout society which will be responsible for channelling demands to centers of power, to distributors of benefits."

HAUSWALD 1971, p. 96: "a process, as a method, as a program, and as a movement; or as a set of purposes."

HUIE 1976, pp. 14–15: "the process of local decision-making and the development of programs designed to make their community a better place to live and work."

KONEYA 1975, p. 10: "all of the efforts made to establish and maintain human interaction while improving the appropriateness of the physical setting to that interaction. Underlying values to this development are the recognition of the individual's right to select the extent of community or privacy and the group's right to identify its own needs for community development."

LONG 1975, p. 29: "an educational process designed to help adults in a community solve their problems by group decision making and group action. Most community development models include broad citizen involvement and training in problem solving."

LOTZ 1970, p. 67: "the involvement of people and the coordination and integration of all efforts directed at bettering conditions."

MILES 1974, p. 94: "the process which basically initiates and develops structure and facilitates program development that includes users of the program. I identify Community Development in the context of initiating and of developing supportive human relationships."

OBERLE, DARBY, and STOWERS 1975, p. 64: "a process in which increasingly more members of a given area or environment make and implement socially responsible decisions, the probable consequence of which is an increase in the life chances of some people without a decrease in the life chances of others.''

PARKO 1975, p. 46: "facilitating those cultural mechanisms that provide for shared experience, trust, and common purpose.''

PELL 1972, p. 54: "a process. Our concern is with the life process— continuity, adjustment, and fulfillment, and finally the self-sufficiency of people.''

PLOCH 1976, p. 8: "the active voluntary involvement in a process to improve some identifiable aspect of community life; normally such action leads to the strengthening of the community's pattern of human and institutional interrelationships.''

VAUGHN 1972, p. 34: "people who are affected by change participate in making it. . . . A system provides for communication among all groups in the community, including open discussion of issues, feelings, and opinions. The community understands its problem-solving process and needs no further instruction.''

VOTH 1975, p. 148: "a situation in which some groups, usually locality based such as a neighborhood or local community . . . attempts to improve its social and economic situation through its own efforts . . . using professional assistance and perhaps also financial assistance from the outside . . . and involving all sectors of the community or group to a maximum.''

WEAVER 1971, p. 6: "a public-group approach dedicated to achieving the goals of the total body politic.''

WILKINSON 1979, p. 10: "acts by people that open and maintain channels of communication and cooperation among local groups.''

Three other often used definitions that have appeared in major books include those of Roland Warren, Irwin Sanders, and the United Nations. Warren (1978, p. 20) defines community development as "a process of helping community people analyze their problems, to exercise as large a measure of autonomy as is possible and feasible, and to promote a greater identification of the individual citizen and the individual organization with the community as a whole.'' Sanders (1958) presents a fourfold typology of community development: (1) process; (2) method; (3) program; and (4) movement (see Fig. 1.1).

The UN (1963, p. 4) definition of community development has also served as a basis for CD work. Community development is

the process by which the efforts of the people themselves are united with those of governmental authorities to improve the economic, social, and cultural conditions of communities, to integrate these communities into the life of the nation, and to enable them to contribute fully to national progress. This complex of processes is, therefore, made up of two essential elements: the participation by the people

I. A PROCESS

CD as a process moves by stages from one condition or state to the next. It involves a progression of changes in terms of specified criteria. It is a neutral, scientific term, subject to fairly precise definition and measurement expressed chiefly in social relations; e.g., change from state where one or two people or a small elite within or without local community make decision for rest of the people to state where people *themselves* make these decisions about matters of common concern; from state of minimum to one of maximum co-operation; from state where few participate to one where many participate; from state where all resources and specialists come from outside to one where local people make most use of their own resources, etc. Emphasis is upon what happens to *people*, socially and psychologically.

II. A METHOD
(Process and Objective)

CD is a means to an end; a way of working so that some goal is attained. Other methods (such as change by decree or fiat; change by use of differential rewards; change by education) may be supplementary to the CD method which seeks to carry through the stages suggested under *process* in order that the will of those using this method (national government, private welfare agency, or local people themselves) may be carried out. The process is guided for a particular purpose, which may prove "harmful" or "helpful" to the local community, depending upon the goal in view and the criteria of the one passing judgment. Emphasis is upon some *end*.

III. A PROGRAM
(Method and Content)

The method is stated as a set of procedures and the content as a list of activities. By carrying out the procedures, the activities are supposedly accomplished. When the program is highly formalized, as in many Five-Year Plans, the focus tends to be upon the program rather than upon what is happening to the people involved in the program.

It is as a *program* that CD comes into contact with subject-matter specialties such as health, welfare, agriculture, industry, recreation, etc.

Emphasis is upon *activities*.

IV. A MOVEMENT
(Program and Emotional Dynamics)

CD is a crusade, a cause to which people become committed. It is not neutral (like process) but carries an emotional charge; one is either for it or against it.

It is dedicated to *progress*, as a philosophic and not a scientific concept, since progress must be viewed with reference to values and goals which differ under different political and social systems.

CD as a movement tends to become institutionalized, building up its own organizational structure, accepted procedures, and professional practitioners.

It stresses and promotes the *idea* of community development as interpreted by its devotees.

Fig. 1.1. Four ways of viewing community development. (From Sanders 1958, p. 5, and Irwin T. Sanders, 1965, *The Community: An Introduction to a Social system,* Ronald Press, New York. Used with permission from *Rural Sociology.*)

themselves in efforts to improve their level of living, with as much reliance as possible on their own initiative; and the provision of technical and other services in ways which encourage initiative, self-help and mutual help and make these more effective. It is expressed in programmes designed to achieve a wide variety of specific improvements.

Based on an analysis of key aspects in these diverse definitions, we have come to define community development as: *(1) a group of people (2) in a community (3) reaching a decision (4) to initiate a social action process (i.e., planned intervention) (5) to change (6) their economic, social, cultural, or environmental situation.* This definition seems to encompass and synthesize many elements from the definitions presented. We prefer it over Warren's definition because we do not feel that promotion of autonomy and community attachment are crucial elements in defining community development. Sanders's typology provides a more historical and philosophical background for the definition presented, and we see his model as a useful elaboration of our definition. Finally, we chose not to adopt the UN definition because of its emphasis on government control, national progress, and self-help. It excludes any consideration of conflict or dissension. Use of the concept of community development in subsequent chapters of this book is grounded in our six-point definition.

Can community development occur without change? While it is philosophically appealing to talk about community development as improving the life chances for all people in a community, in reality change usually involves a redistribution of goods and resources. No change occurs without some costs, as Littrell discusses (Chapter 5). Does community development have to be grounded in the decisions made by people in a community? Gamm and Fisher (Chapter 4) describe how most technical assistance CD programs initiated by government are unilateral in the decision-making process. Is community conflict a sign of a viable community development effort? This issue is discussed in Chapter 6. In short, definitions of community development are not clear-cut and how one interprets community development affects one's behavior when initiating a development program. Such issues are of crucial importance because they affect our perception of community change.

GROWTH OF COMMUNITY DEVELOPMENT AS A DISCIPLINE

Clinard (1970, p. 117) notes that the term *community development* came into popular use after World War II. This term has supplanted such terms as mass education, village improvement, rural development, community self-help, and community organization. Most of these labels reflected planned intervention strategies through public participation and outside technical assistance to encourage and/or stimulate local community efforts. (For a history of community development, see Chapter 2.)

The term *community development* has acquired a certain "bandwagon" status and it has been used for anything from local self-help efforts to building tracts of low-income homes. This does not mean that attempts have not been made to conceptualize what community development is and to outline, in a theoretical perspective, the ideas of community development. For example, two major journals and a broad range of books have discussed, described, criticized, proposed, and outlined community development. However, many of these definitions and descriptions are conflicting.

Sanders (1958, p. 2) has pointed out that community development evolved from two major forces. On the one hand is economic development from which it takes its surname and on the other hand is community organization from which it takes its first name. Economic development has been chiefly concerned with increasing productivity and efficiency, in spreading forms of economic organizations that multiply and distribute material resources more broadly, and in planning exercises to improve the economic situation of a locality. This type of development may be seen as development *in* the community. From the community organization perspective, community development has evolved out of the early works of the community chest movement, United Community Services, and the United Fund, with their emphasis on public participation and social planning. It is operationalized through associational and group work, community councils, programs in public health education, and community surveys directed at the desires and needs of community residents. Such programs seek to improve the decision-making process *of* the community as well as the quality of local life.

Community development as a discipline within an institutional structure in the United States probably began with the work of William Biddle at Earlham College, Indiana, in 1947. Cary (Chapter 8) discusses how CD programs have developed in many other academic institutions during the last 30 years. Today over 80 universities and colleges offer courses in community development and many have master's programs with a CD option.

The Community Development Society was established in 1970. In less than ten years it has grown to over 1,000 members. The *Journal of the Community Development Society* has celebrated ten years of existence. Thus, the institutional development of curricula in community development, plus the establishment of a professional society and the publishing of a scholarly journal, has brought the discipline to its present state: in search of maturity but well past its early struggling stage.

SOCIAL SCIENCE PERSPECTIVES OF DEVELOPMENT

Each of the social sciences has a slightly different perspective toward development and a unique interpretation of social change. Portes (1976, p. 63), in his review of the sociology of development, summarized the historical evolution of the concept to mean the gradual qualitative passage from less to more differentiated social forms. This transformation occurs through processes of ever more complex specialization and functional interdependence. Through such specialization and differentiation, Portes contends that social roles are transformed to approach modern standards of universalism, specificity, and achievement. Portes (1976, pp. 63–64) suggests that as societal development proceeds, certain adaptive features that increase the capacity of the system to survive in its environment are incorporated. The money economy, formal rationality, administration of justice, and finally the democratic association are among such structural features. A considerable amount of sociological investigation has focused on the polarization of types of development (see Inkeles and Smith 1974). Such polarization can be seen in Ferdinand Tönnies's transformation of societies from *gemeinschaft* to *gesellschaft,* Emile Durkheim's change from mechanical solidarity to organic solidarity, and Robert Redfield's evolution from folk to urban. One of the main problems sociologists have confronted is the determination of functional and structural adaptation of societies and communities to the increased complexity of the developing situation.

Anthropologists view development primarily from cultural and social perspectives. They attempt to build cultural models of society and to view the world through the eyes of members of that society. Anthropologists attempt to view social change from open-minded induction and try not to be prejudiced by a priori theory. Opposite to the anthropological phenomenological approach, economists view the study of social change and development with a priori theories of changes in technology, production, and distribution of goods and services. Economists are particularly concerned about value utilities and the changes that transform cultures, nations, and communities to new levels of productivity.

Historians tend to view development from a social evolutionary perspective. They have aided studies of development by charting and interpreting the stages of development of modern societies in becoming industrialized and urbanized. However, considerable question has been raised as to whether contemporary less developed societies and communities go through the same processes today as did the less developed nations, societies, and communities that have been historically documented. For example, Kim (1973, p. 465) argues that psychological attributes such as achievement, entrepreneurship, and individualism (which were preconditions for development of Western societies) may not be necessary preconditions for modernization of non-Western less developed societies.

The most empirical approach to development today seems to be in the hands of planners. Since Frederick Law Olmstead and Alfred Bettman developed the first master plan of a city in the early 1930s, community planners have worked extensively to meet the needs of governmental decision makers. The master form of planning originally entailed architectural and geographical designs of model cities. Today, planning has expanded to include social, economic, and environmental considerations as well. Although criticisms of the planning ethic have been raised and many evaluative studies have shown comprehensive planning to be rather unsuccessful, the ideas contained in the planning approach offer considerable food for thought (cf. Friedman 1976, pp. 274–77). In summary, these social science disciplines, along with political science, philosophy, geography, psychology, and related disciplines, have different but viable insights when approaching community development. They have influenced the profession and the way community development is practiced.

SCIENCE OR PROFESSION?

Considerable debate occurs among community developers about whether community development is a science or a profession. If community development is a science in and of itself, it moves into territory already occupied by economics, political science, psychology, sociology, and others. Community development as a normative program of change usually assumes conditions of participatory democracy. And what happens if a society makes a decision that democracy is one of its biggest barriers to societal stability and less is best? Democracy seems to work best in an economy with an expanding resource base when everyone gets more, but during a contracting resource base, democracy may well have problems; community development could quickly lose its *raison d'être.*

Perhaps the solution to the debate over whether community development is a science is for community developers to stake a claim on "normative community development" on the one hand or on a group of "scientific principles of community action" on the other. Adherents to normative community development can create philosophical treatises on goals and guidelines for development. These will provide focus for CD efforts, though testing or measurement will be problematic. Adherents to the scientific principles of community action approach can define the variables in change and test carefully constructed propositions; for example, Are the community decision makers more likely to act in desired ways when conflict is intense?

One's definition of community development is influenced by professional orientation, and community developers are a diverse group. They must face up to the dilemma into which they have placed themselves. Theory development and the growth of the profession can go no further than the taxonomy of relevant concepts on which the profession is based. Each community developer must decide which "camp" she or he belongs to if we are to have more than a set of vague principles about community action that combine ideological principles and observations of how people actually behave. In America and in the Community Development Society there is room for adherents to both groups. Constructive change and dialogue require inputs from both the supporters of normative community development and the advocates of scientific principles of community action.

CONCLUSION

Change will occur. Change is a pervasive condition of our times. People have the opportunity to either effect change or be affected by it. The growing complexity of American society makes it almost impossible for an individual, working alone, to initiate change. But a group of people working together can initiate social action to improve their life chances. This is what we call community development, the central thesis of this book. In the following chapters, the authors point out how people have initiated CD efforts in the past, what conditions effect the successful implementation of CD efforts, and what kind of CD intervention strategies are likely to be successful in the future. We hope the many points of view will stimulate, arouse (or provoke), and inform you about community development in America.

REFERENCES

Bennett, Austin. 1973. Professional staff members' contribution to community development. *J. Community Dev. Soc.* 4 (1):58–68.

Brokensha, David. 1968. Comments. *Hum. Organ.* 27 (1):78.

Chin, Robert, and Kenneth Benne. 1976. General strategies for effecting change in human systems. In *The Planning of Change,* 3d ed., W. Bennis, K. Benne, R. Chin, and K. Corey, eds., pp. 13–21. New York: Holt, Rinehart & Winston.

Christenson, James A., and Paul Warner. Application of systems theory to community development. In review.

Clinard, Marshall B. 1970. *Slums and Community Development.* New York: Free Press.

Crowfoot, James E., and Mark A. Chesler. 1974. Contemporary perspectives on planned social change: A comparison. *J. Appl. Behav. Sci.* 10 (3):278–303.

Darby, John P., and Geoffry Morris. 1975. Community groups and research in Northern Ireland. *Community Dev. J.* 10 (2): 113–19.

Dunbar, John O. 1972. The bedrock of community development. *J. Community Dev. Soc.* 3 (2):42–53.

Dunham, Arthur. 1972. Community development in North America. *Community Dev. J.* 7 (1):10–40.

Frederickson, H. George. 1975. Strategy for development administration. *J. Community Dev. Soc.* 6 (1):88–101.

Friedman, John. 1976. The future of comprehensive urban planning. In *Readings in Community Organization Practice,* 2d ed., R. Kramer and H. Specht, eds., pp. 255–74. Englewood Cliffs, N.J.: Prentice-Hall.

Hammock, John C. 1973. Community development: Organization-building and political modernization. *J. Community Dev. Soc.* 4 (2):12–19.

Hauswald, Edward L. 1971. The economically distressed community: A synoptic outline of symptoms, causes, and solutions. *Community Dev. J.* 2 (2): 96–105.

Hillery, George. 1955. Definition of community—Areas of agreement. *Rural Sociol.* 20 (June):111–23.

Huie, John M. 1976. What do we do about it?—A challenge to the community development professional. *J. Community Dev. Soc.* 6 (2):14–21.

Inkeles, Alex, and David H. Smith. 1974. *Becoming Modern: Individual Changes in Six Developing Countries.* Cambridge: Harvard Univ. Press.

Kaufman, Harold. 1959. Toward an interactional conception of community. *Social Forces* 39 (Oct.):8–17.

Kim, Kyong-Dong. 1973. Toward a sociological theory of development: A structural perspective. *Rural Sociol.* 38 (4):462–76.

Koneya, Mele. 1975. Toward an essential definition of community development. *J. Community Dev. Soc.* 6 (1):4–12.

Long, Huey B. 1975. State government: A challenge for community developers. *J. Community Dev. Soc.* 6 (1):27–36.

Lotz, Jim. 1970. Training in community development. *Community Dev. J.* 1 (1):67–75.

Miles, Lewis M. 1974. Can community development education and community education be collaborative? *J. Community Dev. Soc.* 5 (2):90–97.

Oberle, Wayne; James P. Darby; and Kevin R. Stowers. 1975. Implications for development: Social participation of the poor in the Ozarks. *J. Community Dev. Soc.* 6 (2):64–78.

Parko, Joseph E., Jr. 1975. Re-discovery of community: Neighborhood movement in Atlanta. *J. Community Dev. Soc.* 6 (1):46–50.

Pell, Kay. 1972. The role of OEO in community development. *J. Community Dev. Soc.* 3 (2):54–61.

Ploch, Louis A. 1976. Community development in action: A case study. *J. Community Dev. Soc.* 7 (1):5–16.

Portes, Alejandro. 1976. On the sociology of national development: Theories and issues. *Am. J. Sociol.* 82 (1):55–85.

Rothman, Jack. 1974. Three models of community organization practice. In *Strategies of Community Organization,* 2d ed., F. Cos, J. Erlich, J. Rothman, and J. Tropman, eds., pp. 22–39. Itasca, Ill.: Peacock.

Sanders, Irwin. 1958. Theories of community development. *Rural Sociol.* 23 (Spring):1–12.

Sutton, Willis A., Jr., and Jiri Kilaja. 1960. The concept of community. *Rural Sociol.* 25 (June):1974–203.

UN. Ad Hoc Group of Experts on Community Development. 1963. *Community Development and National Development.* New York, p. 4.

Vaughn, Gerald F. 1972. Evaluating a community development institute. *J. Community Dev. Soc.* 3 (1):30–39.

Voth, Donald E. 1975. Problems in evaluating community development. *J. Community Dev. Soc.* 6 (1):147–62.

Warren, Roland. 1977. *Social Change and Human Purpose: Toward Understanding and Action.* Chicago: Rand McNally.

_____. 1978. *The Community in America,* 3d ed. Chicago: Rand McNally.

Weaver, John C. 1971. The university and community development. *Community Dev. J.* 2 (1):5–12.

Wilkinson, Kenneth. 1972. A field theory perspective for community development research. *Rural Sociol.* 37 (Spring):43–52.

_____. 1979. Social well-being and community. *J. Community Dev. Soc.* 10 (1):4–13.

Willis, Cecil W. 1977. Definitions of community II: An examination of definitions of community since 1950. *South Sociol.* 9 (1):14–19.

History of Community Development in America

Bryan M. Phifer, with E. Frederick List and Boyd Faulkner

THIS CHAPTER deals with the emergence of the field of community development from early self-help efforts through community organization and social work thrusts to the field as we know it today. It describes the roles played by individuals, organizations, educational institutions, and government and their influence on community development.

EARLY AMERICAN SELF-HELP

One could argue that community development has been part of our culture since Jamestown. Using the criteria of self-reliance and initiative, one would certainly have some grounds for this argument. On the other hand, the earliest communities in America were often directed in a fairly authoritarian manner and survival was the prime objective. By the time of Alexis de Tocqueville's tour of the country in the 1830s, both democracy and a concern for self-improvement were evident. His book, *Democracy in America,* provides rare insight into what made the country tick, both philosophically and socially. Indeed, he observed that

Americans of all ages, all stations in life, and all types of dispositions are forever forming associations. There are not only commercial and industrial associations in which all take part, but others of a thousand different types—religious, moral, serious, futile, very general and very limited, immensely large and very minute.

Americans combine to give fetes, found seminaries, build churches, distribute books, and send missionaries to the antipodes. Hospitals, prisons, and schools take shape in that way. . . . In every case, at the head of any new undertaking, where in France you would find the government or in England some territorial magnate, in the United States you are sure to find an association. [Tocqueville 1966, p. 485]

The proponents of community development are a varied lot and have established a confusing number of models. Examples include:

1. utopian movements or planned types of religious communities, such as the Shakers, Dunkards, Mennonites, Amish, Hutterites, and Mormons, who formed isolated groups of communities, most of which supported tradition rather than change and were highly authoritarian
2. special movements or settlements, such as Brook Farm
3. cooperatives, credit unions, farm organizations, community organizations, neighborhood councils, and the like, all of which tend to support change
4. civic and service clubs
5. business and industrial groups, such as the Sears Foundation and utility companies, which support community improvement efforts
6. community organizations and health and welfare councils with a strong social work emphasis

DISTINCTION BETWEEN SELF-HELP AND COMMUNITY DEVELOPMENT

It is ambiguous to include all activities based on a self-help concept under the rubric of community development, since community development is holistic and not focused on special interests or piecemeal projects. It goes beyond sporadic joint efforts, such as barn raisings or clean-up, paint-up campaigns; neither is it "social welfare" for others. Self-help has long been a part of the American heritage. Community development as we know it today—a purposeful attempt to improve communities under democratic conditions of participation—did not begin to emerge until the twentieth century. It did not burst on the scene suddenly. Instead, a convergence of a number of influences ultimately grew into the field of community development.

ROOTS OF COMMUNITY DEVELOPMENT

A major recognition of the need to improve rural life came as a result of President Theodore Roosevelt's 1908 Country Life Commission. Many of the concerns recognized by the commission centered on the inadequacies of rural communities. Commission recommendations gave impetus to the growing demand for the U.S. Department of Agriculture (USDA) and the land-grant colleges to take a more active role in the life of rural Americans. Out of this movement arose the Cooperative Extension Service as provided by the Smith-Lever Act of 1914. The report of the House Committee on Agriculture in submitting the bill included these guidelines:

The theory of the bill is to extend this system to the entire country by providing for at least one trained demonstrator or itinerant teacher for each agricultural county, who in the very nature of things must give leadership and direction along all lines of rural activity—social, economic, and financial. . . . He is to assume leadership in every movement, whatever it may be, the aim of which is better farming, better living, more happiness, more education, and better citizenship. [U.S., H. Rept. 110, 63d Congress, p. 5]

This philosophy of extension was in keeping with that proposed by the Committee on Extension Work of the Association of American Agricultural Colleges and Experiment Stations. The association had been working for a number of years to obtain federal support for extension work to help meet the growing demand for such education. In *History of Agricultural Extension Work,* Alfred Charles True states:

During the first decade of the twentieth century, the work connected with farmers' institutes and other forms of agricultural extension work in which the land-grant colleges participated, increased so rapidly in extent and variety that these institutions had great difficulty in meeting the demands on them in this direction without impairing their resident teaching and research. A demand therefore arose for Federal appropriations for extension work, partly to stimulate increased state appropriations for this purpose. [True 1928, p. 100]

At the meeting of the association in Portland, Oregon, in August 1909, the Committee on Extension Work repeated its recommendation for federal appropriations for extension work and developed a proposed plan that:

Defines extension work broadly yet closely. Defines agriculture and rural life so as to include instruction and aid in any phase of this field—in subjects technical and scientific, concerning business management, home making, sanitation; and economic, social, and moral subjects. Indicates that Extension work is for adults and youth and children, and for people in *towns and cities as well as in the open country* [italics in original]. [True, p. 102]

The influence of the Cooperative Extension Service on community development, especially in rural areas, has been widely recognized. In his annual report of extension work for 1923, C. B. Smith, then Director of the States Relation Service of the USDA, stated:

The maxim that all programs of extension work should be based on an analysis of local or community needs has been given increasing support, as shown by the greater number of community programs developed throughout the United States. More than 21,000 communities . . . have local committees or clubs which join with Extension agents in developing and working out local programs of work. [True, p. 175]

Thus it was apparent from early extension workers' experiences that the involvement of local people in identifying needs and developing programs was essential to successful extension work. True points out:

Extension forces were also realizing that they could not reach large numbers of people effectively without the active cooperation of many local leaders. They therefore increased their efforts, to get beyond the county organization supporting their work and to build their programs on a community basis. [True, p. 175]

Whether this philosophy was basically self-serving or whether it truly sought to meet community needs is impossible to determine. Suffice it to say that the successful extension worker had to develop programs *with* people rather than *for* people.

The earliest community clubs under the sponsorship of the Cooperative Extension Service started in the South in the 1920s. This movement for organized communities was directed at improving the welfare of the people not only in communities but also in the surrounding countryside. The community club or organized community movement probably originated in Mississippi (Kaufman 1978), and one such club in Mississippi, Oktec, is still active after more than 50 years. Gradually, the organized community movement spread to other southern states. Although extension work in the South was segregated at that time, community clubs also were widely used in black communities. J. A. Evans of the USDA observed in 1923:

Some form of community organization . . . is utilized in each county that has a Negro agent. Community clubs elect local leaders, help make programs of work, raise funds for club equipment, and for premiums at local fairs and exhibits, provide social entertainment, and assist generally in promoting various phases of the extension program for their community and county. [True 1928, p. 191]

Although the early Cooperative Extension Service centered much attention on community development, not until the mid-1950s did it take formal action to institutionalize community development as a major program effort nationwide.

RURAL COMMUNITY ORGANIZATION

President Roosevelt's Country Life Commission determined that a major problem of rural people was lack of organization. As a result, several states (including Georgia, Kentucky, Mississippi, Missouri, New York, North Carolina, West Virginia, and Virginia) undertook community organization work. Many states used a community scorecard for measuring and scoring community efforts. Much of this early effort was under the direction of rural sociologists from colleges of agriculture and many of these persons were ordained ministers who were sensitive to the need for social improvement in rural areas.

Rural sociologists concentrated on rural community organization in the years following World War I, with much work being stimulated by research grants offered by the USDA. Carl Taylor, a leader in both the area of rural community organization and research related to rural communities, observed in a review of early rural sociology research:

Indeed it is more than possible that the opportunities for these early studies would not have opened if the building of research methodology or social theory, instead of interest in situations, had been insisted upon. [Taylor 1958, p. 188]

One of the first books on community development published in the United States was Frank Farrington's *Community Development: Making the Small Town a Better Place to Live and a Better Place in Which to Do Business,* published in 1915. It is a handbook and guide in community organization that focuses on the economic aspects of community improvement, business and commercial organization, and the role and importance of service clubs. Farrington intended his book to be used by towns of less than 10,000 population, but his ideas also proved useful to larger towns. Although the emphasis of this work is on local initiative, its concept of community development is narrow by today's standards.

EXTERNAL INFLUENCES

In reviewing the history of community development in the United States, one cannot overlook early work overseas and its influence on such efforts at home. In 1908 the Indian poet Tagore urged young people to work together for village welfare. In 1914, with the assistance of Leonard Elmhurst, an Englishman, Tagore founded a rural institute that was associated with his government and had contact with government agencies.

In the early twenties the Indian colonial government introduced its first rural development operation under another Englishman, F. L. Brayne. These individual attempts led to national CD programs in India and other British colonial areas. The Indian government, for example, started the Village Rehabilitation Scheme in 1944.

The emergence of community development in many parts of Africa also had a British colonial influence that existed later than in India. The British and the French both initiated community development in African villages by promoting literacy and self-help in their territories.

To clarify the purpose and meaning of village development work, British colonial officials held the Cambridge Conference on African Administration in 1948 and established community development as an official term. This conference defined community development

as a movement designed to promote better living for the whole community with the active participation, and, if possible, on the initiative of the community, but if this initiative is not forthcoming spontaneously, by the use of techniques for arousing and stimulating it in order to secure its active and enthusiastic response to the movement. Community development embraces all forms of betterment. It includes the whole range of development activities in the district whether these are undertaken by government or unofficial bodies. [*Community Development* 1958, p. 2]

At the Ashridge Conference in 1954 this definition was shortened to a "movement designed to promote better living for the whole community and the active participation on the part of the community" (*Community Development*, p. 2).

Later, the United Nations and the U.S. International Cooperative Administration devised their own definitions; but the essential elements of improvement and local initiative remained, with the addition of external resources including those of government. The UN definition stated:

The term "community development" designates the utilization under one single programme of approaches and techniques which rely upon local communities as units of action and which attempt to combine outside assistance with organized local self-determination and effort, and which correspondingly seek to stimulate local initiative and leadership as the primary instrument of change. [UNESCO, E/2931 1956]

In brief, early efforts by the British and French have influenced the shape and direction of community development in numerous countries.

ROLE OF EDUCATIONAL ASSOCIATIONS

In the United States, various associations and organizations have been involved in community development for several decades. One of the most influential of these is the National University Extension Association (NUEA). At its first conference in 1915, President Charles Van Hise took a firm position on the importance of "informal community service" and in 1919 recognition was given to the "human community," a step away from the limited physical or geographic area. In 1924 the term community development appeared in the NUEA proceedings, while in 1935 a plea was made for university-sponsored CD workers. Through the World War II years the movement in universities was given impetus by NUEA leaders Howard McClusky of the University of Michigan, Jess Ogden of the University of Virginia, and Baker Brownell of the University of Montana.

A community organization committee was established in the NUEA in 1948, followed in 1955 by a Division of Community Development. In 1960 Katharine Lackey wrote an extensive report of the status of community development in member institutions of the NUEA. This report covered the Universities of Michigan, Wisconsin, Indiana, Nebraska, Washington, Utah, Minnesota, Michigan State, Pennsylvania State, Purdue, Kansas State, Northern Michigan, and Southern Illinois.

Another organization that has given support to community development over the years is the Adult Education Association, which has a section for community development in its structure. Membership in this group overlaps considerably with membership in the NUEA Division of Community Development. The 1960 *Handbook of Adult Education* (Knowles 1960) contains a chapter on community development authored by Howard McClusky.

EARLY UNIVERSITY EFFORTS

One of the pioneers in university-sponsored efforts in North America is St. Francis Xavier University in Antigonish, Nova Scotia, which has provided a distinguished CD training program for nearly 50 years. Through its Coady International Institute, the university attracts many foreign nationals seeking training for work in their home countries. The institute emphasizes true grass-roots methods of training, through which students become involved with community residents in dealing with community issues. (See Chapter 8 for more information.)

An interesting event in the history of community development that had far-reaching effects was the Montana study conducted by Baker Brownell in the late 1940s while he was on the staff of the University of Montana. This study was directed at determining the potential for revitalizing dying lumber towns in the northwest. Richard W. Poston (1950) was commissioned to record the activities conducted during this study; the result was a book entitled *Small Town Renaissance,* which gained him a reputation as a student and practitioner of community development. The remarkable phenomenon observed was that although the discussion groups in the various lumber towns were not organized for action, several took significant action that saved their towns from the otherwise inevitable cycle of boom and bust.

After writing about Brownell's Montana study, Poston was invited to the University of Washington to direct the activities of its Bureau of Community Development. There he developed a vigorous field program with a staff of eight consultants working in small communities throughout the state. The Washington approach was oriented toward citizen participation with study committees, town meetings, and action projects dominating community life through the initial period of the effort. Always present was the realization that most communities needed some economic stimulus. Consequently, many projects had economic development overtones. These efforts, combined with more traditional CD approaches, proved to be sound methods of achieving both community and economic development.

Meanwhile, Baker Brownell went to Southern Illinois University at Carbondale in the early fifties to help organize an Area Services Unit, including a Community Development Division, for this fast-growing institution. In 1953 Richard Poston joined the staff to begin a new operation similar to that at the University of Washington. Many of the community problems were similar, but the economic and employment needs in southern Illinois were so great that Poston soon added a factory location specialist to his staff. The activities of this specialist were partially supported by the two major power companies in the region.

A former teachers' college, Southern Illinois University grew from 1,500 students in the late 1940s to 15,000 students by 1960. Its outreach for community development covered the southern 33 counties of Illinois. With a sizable staff of specialists from SIU, this area was well served within a few years.

In 1959 an academic unit, the Community Development Institute, was established at SIU and offered a major in community development at the undergraduate level. A master's program followed in 1962. In 1966 the Community Development Division and the Community Development Institute were combined to form the Department of Community Development. In 1974 a major reduction in total SIU staff reduced the department's functions to teaching and research.

William Biddle's program at Earlham College in Richmond, Indiana, began in 1947. Known as "community dynamics," this effort combined graduate study with community experience in the student's pursuit of the master's degree. The goal was to provide a training program at the graduate level with a democratic philosophy toward community development. The program continued for 13 years until a change in college administration in 1960 established other priorities. Biddle continued his work in community development, however, and became one of the field's most prolific writers. A collection of his writings is now housed in the Department of Regional and Community Affairs at the University of Missouri, Columbia. (See Chapter 8 for more information.)

Since the early 1960s, Springfield College in Massachusetts has offered the degree of Master of Education in Community Leadership and Development. This program emphasizes group work, community organization, and community development.

For many years West Georgia College in Carrollton has used a variety of cultural studies and experiences to broaden the perspectives of adult students. The goal is to promote interest and develop the ability to deal with all aspects of community life.

The University of Missouri's community development program began in the mid-1950s with a dual thrust from the General Extension Service and the Cooperative Extension Service. The first three area rural development agents were placed in the field in 1956 through special funds provided by the USDA. These two extension programs were combined in 1960 and the field staff was expanded to ten CD agents. In the same year, the Center for Community Development was established on the Columbia campus to meet the need for formal training and backup support of field staff. The center became an academic Department of Community Development in 1962 and began offering courses leading to a master's degree. In 1966 the name of the department was changed to the Department of Regional and Community Affairs in the newly formed School of Social and Community Services. In

1975, with further growth of the school and the addition of another unit, it became the College of Public and Community Services. This college has four units: Department of Regional and Community Affairs, Department of Recreation and Parks Administration, Public Safety Program, and School of Social Work.

Over the years, about a third of the master's degree students in the Department of Regional and Community Affairs have been foreign nationals. The department offers both a master's degree and a diploma in community development. The latter is designed for students who either do not qualify for a master's degree because they lack an undergraduate degree or cannot spend the time required for the advanced degree. As of this writing the University of Missouri extension division has 24 full-time area CD specialists throughout the state.

By 1976, some 63 other institutions of higher education offered majors or degrees in community development (Cary 1976), and the field continues to grow in both its quest for knowledge and its application of known principles. The unique contribution of American colleges and universities has been their focus on human development as the means for achieving community development.

COMMUNITY-BASED EFFORTS

City Departments of Community Development

Kansas City, Missouri, was the first city in the United States to have a Division of Community Development. It was established in 1943, primarily to combat wartime juvenile delinquency, but it later grew into a pioneering effort in citizen participation through community and neighborhood organizations. It remains a very active part of Kansas City's life, with an emphasis on community development rather than funding. Today many cities have departments of community development, although most are funding agencies for government programs, such as community development block grants, and are not philosophically or practically oriented toward community development as it is defined by professionals.

"Citizen participation" is a requirement for cities receiving federal funding under the Community Development Act. However, there is a wide variation of interpretations as to what it means. They range all the way from simple legal notices in newspapers and public hearings, to fulfill legal requirements, to true effort to involve citizens in the developmental process. Almost every city receiving community development funds has either a director of community development or a department of community development or both.

Community Education

Community education, stimulated through grants from the Kellogg and Mott foundations, and carried out primarily through school systems, has had a great influence on community development in the United States.

The community education movement has encouraged communities to utilize their schools for a broad range of after-school activities, ranging from
the more traditional adult education and recreation activities to citizen involvement in the resolution of community issues.

Seay and Crawford have observed:

The Community School Service Program was first developed in five small, widely
separated Michigan communities where the people attempted to use the educative
process in solving their problems. They brought together through educational activities their resources—the natural, human, technological, and institutional resources—and applied them to their local problems in health, recreation, agriculture,
and other aspects of community life. Thus, education was seen as a power in the solution to the problems of people. [Seay and Crawford 1954, p. 17]

In June 1945 Eugene B. Elliott, State Superintendent of Public Instruction in Michigan, proposed to the W. K. Kellogg Foundation that it under-
write an experimental community education program. He wrote:

Set down in simple terms, our proposal is this: We want to take all we know about a
community, put it together in a working program of community self-improvement,
and observe the results. We who are in the Michigan State Education Authority feel
that the community school idea, now spreading rapidly in Michigan and in other
states as well, should be put to a rigorous experimental test. [Seay and Crawford, p.
15]

In July 1945, the Kellogg Foundation agreed to subsidize the project.
This research project continued in formal operation until 1953 with Kellogg
Foundation support. The Mott Foundation later underwrote similar highly
successful work in Flint, Michigan. In the same spirit, the National Community Education Development Act was passed in 1974, providing seed
money to state departments of education and local school systems to further
community education.

Community Organization

Community development and community organization likewise have
been closely associated over the years; indeed the terms have been used almost interchangeably by many, as reflected by the literature. For example,
Murray Ross wrote *Community Organization: Theory and Principles* in
1955; and an article, "Community Organization and Community Development: Similarities and Differences" by Tom Sherrard, appeared in 1962 in
the *Community Development Review* published by the Agency for International Development.

While community development and community organization might
share some similar objectives, there are basic differences between them.
"The difference," according to Roland Warren (1963, p. 327), "is in the
kinds of settings and tasks and personnel with which they have been associ-

ated.'' Community organization gives greater attention to the established social service organizations, which deal with a specific clientele. Community development, on the other hand, might involve the establishment of an entirely new organizational structure, using people from all segments of the community, to reach an agreed-upon goal. Community organization is more apt to involve the use of social services *for others.* In the community development context, those involved in the major effort might *themselves* be the beneficiaries of that effort—the result is self-help on an organized, community-wide scale.

DISTINCTIVE CD LITERATURE

A body of literature distinct to community development began to emerge in the 1940s. Ogden and Ogden published *These Things We Tried: A Five-Year Experiment in Community Development* in 1947. In 1953, Ruopp edited *Approaches to Community Development* and Poston wrote *Democracy is You: A Guide to Citizen Action.* In 1955, the United Nations published *Social Progress through Community Development,* which was widely regarded as a cornerstone of community development literature at that time. The first issue of the *Community Development Bulletin* published by the International Cooperation Administration appeared in 1956.

Other literature began to follow, including Batten (1957), Sanders (1958), Mezirow (1962), Warren (1963), Ogden and Ogden (1964), Clinard (1966), Batten (1967), Biddle (1968), and Cary (1970).

The first issue of the *Journal of the Community Development Society* was published in the spring of 1970. Establishment of the society and its journal greatly stimulated the publishing of articles on community development.

ALTERNATIVE APPROACHES

Social Work Approaches

Purists argue that some of the early social movements or projects are really not accurately classified as community development. Others maintain that a significant relationship exists and that these movements deserve mention in a historical context.

One such project in 1917 was known as the Cincinnati Social Service Unit Project (Steiner 1925). It was a city-wide effort to support a demonstration project concentrated in the Mohawk-Brighton district of Cincinnati. The purpose was to develop an ongoing child health program. Organizational units at the neighborhood and block levels worked together to launch and carry out the services as needed. Care was taken to involve the local residents in the decisions and actions required so that the total effort was well distributed throughout the population and was not considered a top-down operation. Not only was the health program very beneficial to the children, but the whole project was a demonstration of democratic community organization.

Settlement Houses

The settlement house movement was more related to community organization and social work than to community development in that its primary focus was to do things *for* people. Settlement houses played a unique role in large American cities around the turn of the century. The first settlement house, founded in a crowded section of London in 1884, was named Toynbee Hall, since it grew out of the work of Arnold Toynbee. In 1887 Stanton Coit founded a settlement house in New York City, and in 1889 Jane Addams and Ellen Gates Starr founded the famous Hull House in Chicago.

Early settlement houses in this country were directed primarily at helping newcomers to large cities adjust to their new environment. One of their highest priorities was the Americanization of immigrants, who generally settled in crowded inner cities, could not speak English, and worked at menial jobs. Courses in the English language were emphasized and other adult eduction classes were provided. Settlement houses also provided day care centers, baths, community centers, and libraries; organized savings banks and community clubs; and provided recreational facilities.

Crusaders such as Jane Addams made a tremendous contribution to the social and economic welfare of newcomers to large cities through the settlement house movement. As the great wave of foreign immigrants began to wane after the turn of the century and other social service agencies arose, settlement houses gradually lost the unique role they once played; although as late as the early 1960s some 200 affiliated groups belonged to the Federation of Settlements and Neighborhood Centers.

Conflict Approach

The Back of the Yards movement, organized by Saul Alinsky (1969) in Chicago in the 1940s, began a social experiment in neighborhood stabilization. The Polish workers, as Alinsky said, were not so much trying to keep blacks out as they were trying to keep their own people in. Gains were slow, but significant progress was made over the years toward a better neighborhood environment for these blue-collar workers. In the early fifties Alinsky set up the Industrial Areas Foundation in Chicago, which (after initial organizational work there) later embarked on major projects in several other cities. Alinsky's purpose was to help the segments of population that had traditionally been without power to develop influence through organized effort. This approach to social change came to be known as a conflict, or confrontation, approach. Much of the support for his activities came through local church-related organizations. All-out effort was made to acquire power for disenfranchised groups of people and to encourage the people to participate in decisions immediately affecting them and their neighborhoods. Over the years Alinsky launched major projects in Chicago, Rochester, and Kansas City and in southern California with the farm workers. His work demonstrated that power and participation could be acquired through intensive organizational effort. The challenge remains, however, of how to channel such power most effectively: whether to get representation within the establishment or to remain highly organized in order to exert pressure from outside the establishment.

URBAN DEVELOPMENT PROGRAMS

Many diverse programs for curing urban ills have been proposed and carried out over the years. Some of these, such as urban renewal, centered on housing and left monuments to ignorance. As Biddle points out, most of these programs did things *to* or *for* people, rather than *with* people (Biddle 1968, p. 184). The result often was huge housing projects resembling up-ended dominos in a barren wasteland, filled to overflowing with people who did not want to be there. The notorious Pruitt-Igoe project built in 1953–1955 in St. Louis earned the infamous distinction of being labeled the worst public housing in the United States by the Secretary of Housing and Urban Development (HUD) before it was razed in the mid-1970s.

Biddle identified the core of the problem when he described the missing elements in many urban development programs, whether in job training, slum clearance, or industrial development:

All these aims are good, but they lack the essential personal development experience. Community development processes are addressed to this essential need. These processes provide, not the answers, but the means by which citizens shall seek the answers. [Biddle 1968, p. 184]

Moreover, many urban programs have been directed at single issues, disregarding the larger community's interests, need, and involvement. "Continuous community improvement," as Hurley H. Doddy observed, "requires the resources and involvement of all types of groups working on many facets of community problems" (Biddle 1968, p. 185). Biddle continues:

The sociologist Morris Janowitz has criticized his fellow sociologists for finding urban society impersonal, self-centered, and barren, because they believed the importance of local community had declined into disorganization and a mass society. According to Janowitz, these sociologists have failed to take into consideration that "impressive degrees and patterns of local community life exist within . . . metropolitan limits" (Janowitz 1952, p. 241). Such patterns of community life are often visible only to those who are especially discerning and compassionate. And when patterns of community have been discovered, the problem is to find ways for utilizing them to expedite development.

Brokensha and Hodge (1969, p. 141) point out that ''often the failure of urban community development is due to the inability of city dwellers to associate with the agency workers; the latter seldom realize that the poor have a visible way of life.'' In this connection, Gans (1962, p. 10) eloquently describes the communication gap in a Boston project:

Their way of life constituted a distinct and independent working-class sub-culture that bore little resemblance to the middle class and the communication between the agency workers and the people is even less perfect, when lower-class, as opposed to working-class, people are involved.

Thus, urban development programs may concern themselves with community development projects and yet fail to meet the democratic participation requirements of true community development.

URBAN INSTITUTES

Urban institutes have emerged as a means of studying and proposing solutions to urban ills and as a way to recruit members of minority groups for civic and political leadership roles. For example, the Urban Institute in Washington, D.C., was organized in 1968 to meet the need for an independent, broadly based research organization to study and propose solutions to a number of urban problems. It works closely with governmental policy-makers and administrators seeking insights about pressing urban problems and alternatives to existing policies, with special emphasis on social and economic aspects of urban problems. The Urban Institute has close links with urban researchers in government, universities, and social and economic research organizations; maintains a large library; issues a bimonthly publication entitled *Search;* and publishes reports, papers, and reprints of relevant articles.

The Urban Affairs Institute (UAI), formerly the Urban Affairs Foundation, was founded in 1967. It was supported by the Ford Foundation. Its objectives were to seek ways to recruit potential political and governmental leaders from minority groups and to increase awareness of urban students on issues affecting education, public affairs, and government. Early programs of the UAI included fellowships and internship training; public services training; New Opportunities Development, which was a means of encouraging and developing interest in public affairs among secondary school students; Higher Horizons, a multifaceted cultural enrichment program for elementary students; a joint program with Occidental College in Los Angeles to award a Master of Urban Studies degree; and urban scholarship assistance. UAI published the *Urban Fellow* newsletter and the *Black Politician* journal.

The Council of University Institutes for Urban Affairs, founded in 1970, is concerned with degree programs, research, and service programs.

By the end of its first decade, it had approximately 65 institutional members plus individual members.

THE PRIVATE SECTOR

A unique effort in the private sector is the community improvement program sponsored by Sears Roebuck and Company and the General Federation of Women's Clubs. This program, now in its twenty-third year, has made use of regular consultation from professionals in various university community development units.

Several public utility companies have sponsored community development activities for more than a quarter of a century. One of these, Planned Progress (sponsored by Union Electric, Missouri Edison, and Missouri Power and Light companies), involved high school students in community study and action projects. This program was organized in the midfifties. Some utility-sponsored programs encourage cooperative efforts among citizens, businesses, and the utilities. Northern Natural Gas Company and United Telecommunications are active in this regard.

As mentioned earlier, many Cooperative Extension Service workers viewed their role as much broader than agricultural production. In addition to their individual work with communities, "organized community" programs were directed at helping communities organize for a variety of self-improvement efforts, including improved agricultural production. Sponsors such as utility companies and chambers of commerce made annual awards much like today's community betterment programs sponsored by some state governments.

RURAL DEVELOPMENT

The mechanization of agriculture and the resultant vast out-migration of farm labor after World War II was a turning point in rural America. As small towns and counties lost population they found it difficult to maintain basic services, and without services they could not attract business and industry. This cycle only compounded the out-migration as people left to seek employment elsewhere. The USDA and the Cooperative Extension Service took official recognition of this dilemma in 1956 with the revision of the Smith-Lever Act. Section 8 of the revised act authorizes rural development, or community development work, as an official extension function.

The first nationwide rural development program was started by the USDA land-grant college extension system in 1956 with the employment of rural development agents in pilot counties throughout the country. Special funds were authorized by the Congress for this purpose.

Rural development was the brainchild of Under Secretary of Agriculture True D. Morse. Before joining the Eisenhower administration, Morse was associated with the Doane Agricultural Service in St. Louis, which had earlier made a study for the Asheville, North Carolina, area. Out of this study grew an effort toward community and area revitalization. Successes from the Asheville experiment gave Morse the incentive to try it on a nationwide scale.

When President John F. Kennedy took office in 1961, his administration looked for a new major thrust for rural America; rural development was that thrust. The name of the program was changed to Rural Areas Development and at the same time the Area Redevelopment Administration came into being. Together, they made a productive marriage of educational resources and money for carrying out community and areawide projects. The Area Redevelopment Administration required that "overall economic development plans" be made by local committees of concerned citizens and governmental officials as a prerequisite for grants. Citizen Rural Areas Development committees were organized and assisted by extension workers throughout the country to facilitate this work; by the midsixties there were active Rural Areas Development committees in more than half the counties in the country.

COMMUNITY RESOURCE DEVELOPMENT

With this effort came reallocation of staff resources among many extension services, with people assigned at both the campus and field levels to provide leadership for rural development. By 1963 the Extension Service, USDA, had established the division of Community Resource Development and the term CRD began to be applied to staff having responsibility for rural and community development. Eventually, many states shortened this designation to community development, and the literature of the USDA Cooperative Extension system began to reflect the broader concepts of community development in contrast to the earlier emphasis on economic development. Today, community development is one of four major programs in the Cooperative Extension Service with 582 full-time and 233 part-time community development positions out of a total of 16,000 in 1978 (Wood 1978).

FEDERAL GOVERNMENT THRUSTS

With the Johnson administration came a flood tide of federal programs offering assistance to communities, beginning with the war on poverty, President Johnson's first major domestic program. Community action agencies were organized nationwide and within two years the Office of Economic Opportunity had a multibillion dollar budget. President Johnson stated in his 1969 budget message that $27 billion would be spent on antipoverty programs in fiscal year 1969 by ten government agencies. This was a big leap—from practically nothing earmarked for antipoverty efforts prior to his inauguration to a vast outpouring of social and community service programs. In his 1969 budget message, President Johnson stated:

In the application of this priority system, my budget provides selective increases for a number of urgent domestic programs, particularly manpower training, model cities, programs to control the rising crime rate, family planning, and health care for mothers and infants, air and water pollution control, and research in better methods of education. . . .

These and other selected programs for which I am recommending increases respond to the most urgent needs of our nation today—the basic problems of poverty, crime, and the quality of our environment. [Budget Message 1969]

As scripture says, "Where the carcass is the vultures will gather" (Matt. 24:28). With such high stakes, not only did interagency fighting over control of programs occur but also many quasi-governmental organizations emerged to take advantage of readily available money. Within two years, most of the Office of Economic Opportunity (OEO) budget was earmarked for specific programs such as Head Start. Moreover, local control was lost by community action agencies and OEO not only lost its grass-roots support but also its federal dominance. Major funding programs were transferred to HEW, HUD, and the Labor Department. Thus, OEO, which started with a meteoric rise, began its not so spectacular demise. Today, OEO's successor, the Community Services Administration, has a range of program efforts not nearly so all-encompassing as that originally envisaged by OEO and local community action agencies are not nearly as visible as in the late 1960s.

One can best appreciate the change in national priorities during the 1960s by looking at federal government outlays during the period 1959–1969. Total expenditures increased from $92 billion to $186 billion. Defense spending did not even double during the period despite the Vietnam war, increasing from $46 to $79 billion. Space exploration and technology peaked during this period with an expenditure of nearly $6 billion in 1966 as compared to $145 million in 1959. *Expenditures for housing and community development jumped from $30 million in 1959 to $1.4 billion in 1969—a 466 percent increase.* This was the era of "big government" spending, which saw the birth of HUD and the emergence of secondary and higher education as major forces in the Department of Health, Education, and Welfare. HUD's forerunner, the Federal Housing Administration, and the U.S. Office of Education were transformed almost overnight from little known agencies with little influence to multibillion dollar operations.

Title I of the Higher Education Act also came into being during the Johnson administration. This act provides grants for community development to institutions of higher education. However, Title I has never been institutionalized within university structures to the extent of Cooperative Extension work, since grants are made only in response to approved proposals and the funding is on a year-to-year basis.

When the first catalog of Federal Domestic Assistance Programs was published in the midsixties, more than 1,100 federal programs were identified. Many of these programs provided funding for community projects. The proliferation of federal grant-in-aid programs of the 1960s almost overwhelmed the capacity of local governments to utilize them effectively. Moreover, restrictive categorical grant programs not only made a science out of "grantsmanship" but also created situations in which local funds that should have been spent on priority needs often were used for match money to get grants for whatever projects were currently being funded. The government's carrot and stick philosophy was so pronounced that local governments and citizen groups began demanding change in funding procedures.

The Revenue Sharing Act of 1972 resulted from increasing demand for more local control over federal funds for community improvements. Special revenue sharing and block grants enabled units of government to concentrate on their own priorities to a greater extent than was possible under the more restrictive categorical grant programs. Today, we find a hodgepodge of programs under the label of community development. Many cities have departments of community development for administering block grant programs, while almost all states have regional planning commissions or councils of government. The range of local, state, and federal efforts runs the gamut from true citizen initiative and effort to those almost wholly directed by governmental units.

THE COMMUNITY DEVELOPMENT SOCIETY

The Community Development Society was organized in 1969 in response to the need of practitioners and others interested in community development to form an organization devoted to continuous study of the field, improvement of practice, and sharing of knowledge and experience. Within ten years it had approximately 1,000 members. Its purpose is to provide:

1. a forum for the exchange of ideas and experiences and the development of common interests

2. for publication and dissemination of community development information to the public

3. advocacy of excellence in community programs, scholarship, and research

4. promotion of citizen participation as essential to effective community development

The first eleven presidents of the Society were Lee J. Cary, University of Missouri, 1969-1970; George Abshier, Purdue University, 1970-1971; Raymond Vlasin, Michigan State University, 1971-1972; John O. Dunbar, Purdue University, 1972-1973; Richard W. Poston, Southern Illinois University, 1973-1974; Duane L. Gibson, Michigan State University, 1974-1975; Bill Beach, Purdue University, 1975-1976; Hugh Denney, University of Missouri, 1976-1977; Glen C. Pulver, University of Wisconsin, 1977-1978; Thomas N. Hobgood, North Carolina State University, 1978-1979; and Gene McMurtry, University of Massachusetts, 1979-1980.

THE CHALLENGE AHEAD

Community development has emerged as a vital force in democratic participation in community self-help during the last fifty years. During this time it moved from primary emphasis on economic development in its embryonic years to a holistic approach toward community capacity building. Whether it retains this emphasis depends largely on the courage, vision, and initiative of citizens and professional practitioners; it is much easier to look to government for solutions than to take the hard road of self-reliance.

In the future more issues, such as energy, inflation, and high interest rates, will be of a public nature; how we decide these issues could determine whether we remain a democracy. Community development can help us realize that these issues have community as well as national and international aspects, and it can provide a means for addressing such issues on both the micro and macro levels.

REFERENCES

Alinsky, Saul D. 1969. *Reveille for Radicals*. New York: Random House, Vintage Books.

Batten, T. R. 1957. *Communities and Their Development*. London: Oxford Univ. Press.

———. 1967. *The Non-Directive Approach in Group and Community Work*. London: Oxford Univ. Press.

Biddle, W. W. 1968. *The Community Development Process: The Rediscovery of Local Initiative*. New York: Holt, Rinehart & Winston.

Brokensha, David, and Peter Hodge. 1969. *Community Development: An Interpretation*. San Francisco: Chandler.

Budget Message to the Congress. 1969. Washington, D.C.: USGPO.

Cary, Lee J., ed. 1970. *Community Development as a Process*. Columbia: Univ. Missouri Press.

———. 1976. Directory: Community development education and training programs throughout the world. Columbia, Mo.: Community Dev. Soc.

Clinard, Marshall B. 1966. *Slums and Community Development*. Glencoe, Ill.: Free Press.

Community Development. 1958. Handbook prepared by study conference at Hartwell House, Aylesbury, Buckinghamshire, Sept. 1957. London: Her Majesty's Stationery Off.

Gans, Herbert J. 1962. *The Urban Villagers: Group and Class in the Life of Italian Americans.* New York: Free Press.

Janowitz, Morris. 1952. *The Community Press in an Urban Setting.* New York: Free Press of Glencoe.

Kaufman, Harold. 1978. (Professor emeritus of rural sociology, Mississippi State University). Conversations with Bryan Phifer.

Knowles, Malcolm, ed. 1960. *Handbook of Adult Education.* Washington, D.C.: Adult Educ. Assoc. U.S.A.

Lackey, Katharine. 1960. Community development through university extension. Community Dev. Publ. 3. Carbondale: Southern Illinois University.

Mezirow, Jack D. 1962. *The Dynamics of Community Development.* New York: Scarecrow Press.

Ogden, Jean, and Jess Ogden. 1947. These things we tried: A five-year experiment in community development. Charlottesville: University of Virginia, Coop. Ext. Serv.

_____. 1964. *Small Communities in Action.* New York: Harper & Row.

Poston, Richard W. 1950. *Small Town Renaissance.* New York: Harper & Row.

_____. 1953. *Democracy is You: A Guide to Citizen Action.* New York: Harper & Row.

Ross, Murray. 1955. *Community Organization: Theory and Principles.* New York: Harper & Row.

Ruopp, Phillips, ed. 1953. *Approaches to Community Development.* The Hague: W. Van Hoeve.

Sanders, Irwin T. 1958. *The Community: An Introduction to a Social System.* New York: Ronald Press.

Seay, Maurice F., and Frank N. Crawford. 1954. The community school and community self-improvement. Lansing, Mich.: Clair L. Taylor, Supt. Public Instr.

Sherrard, Tom. 1962. Community organization and community development: Similarities and differences. *Community Dev. Rev.* 7 (1):11, and AID June.

Social Progress through Community Development. 1955. UN Bureau of Social Affairs, Sales #551U. 18. New York.

Steiner, Jesse F. 1925. *Community Organization: A Study of Its Theory and Current Practice.* New York and London: Century.

Taylor, Carl. 1958. *Adult Education* 8 (3):188. Review of *The Growth of a Science—A Half Century of Rural Sociological Research in the United States* by Edmund Brunner, Harper & Brothers, New York, 1957.

Tocqueville, Alexis de. 1966. *Democracy in America, 1835. A New Translation* by George Lawrence. Edited by J. P. Moyes and Max Lerner. New York: Harper & Row.

True, Alfred Charles. 1928. History of agricultural extension work in the United States: 1785–1923. USDA, Misc. Publ. 15. Washington, D.C.: USGPO.

UNESCO. 1956. E/2931, Oct. *Twentieth Report of the Administrative Committee on Coordination,* Economic and Social Council annex III.

U.S., Congress, House. 1915. Committee on Agriculture, *Cooperative Agricultural Extension Work: Report to Accompany H.R. 7951.* 63d Cong., 2d sess., H. Rep. 110.

Warren, Roland L. 1963. *The Community in America.* Chicago: Rand McNally.

Wood, Emily. 1978. (Program analyst, Extension Service, USDA.) Conversation with Bryan Phifer.

Three Themes of Community Development

James A. Christenson

ON THIS tenth anniversary of the Community Development Society of America (CDSA) it seems worthwhile to review what community development is, where it seems to be going, and why. When a "state of the art" book was proposed to celebrate this anniversary, two questions arose, What is community development? and What content should be contained in a book on community development? Our solution to these questions was to review the few books on the subject and to look at various journals (e.g., *Journal of the CD Society, International CD Journal, Rural Sociology, Journal of Agricultural Economics, Human Organization.*) This review generated some consensus on three major themes: self-help, technical assistance, and conflict. A more systematic assessment was obtained by a content analysis of the major community development journal in America, the *Journal of the Community Development Society.* This analysis is the basis for this chapter and the foundation for this book.

Note that the practice of community development may be somewhat different from its reflection in the *Journal.* The fact that some issues have received more attention than others may be a function of both the interests of editors/reviewers and what contributors choose to write about. However, for ten years the *Journal* has documented the what, where, and why of issues of concern to the membership. It is our chief mode of formal documented communication. Its articles manifest philosophies, strategies, roles, models, research findings, practical insights, and ideological debates. In short, the *Journal* reflects the intellectual, research, and practical concerns of the professional community called the Community Development Society.

This chapter reviews the content of the *Journal* for the past decade, lists some of the major issues, describes the various themes of community development that have evolved, and speculates on future issues to be faced. To do this, more than 200 articles have been reviewed. The following pro-

---

The articles listed in this chapter appeared in the *Journal of the Community Development Society.* Because this chapter is a review of one publication and more than 100 articles are listed in its text, no reference section is included.

cedure was used when reading each article. (1) The general area or issue presented in the article was codified. (2) The developmental or action theme (self-help, conflict, or technical assistance) was recorded. (3) The content of the article was inspected for its inclusion of concepts and/or propositions that were tested or discussed in a theoretical context; if the article contained such, it was labeled as theory. (4) If data were presented and analyzed, the article was labeled as research. (5) The background of the author(s) was documented—academic, extension, government, or private sector affiliation. Most articles were classified along all five of these dimensions. A few defied complete classification but were treated in relevant dimensions. The purpose of this chapter is not to present a catalog or annotated index of the articles (though some counting will be done) but to synthesize the content. While I have tried to be faithful to what has been written, essentially this is my interpretation of major issues, themes, and content areas. It will be ten years of the *Journal* as seen through my eyes.

FIRST IMPRESSIONS

An impressive variety of articles have appeared over the decade. Journals are usually limited to a specific academic area (such as economics, sociology, or political science), or to a substantive area (such as administration or urban affairs). The *Journal* seems to embrace most social science disciplines and to include a wide range of subject matter. This variety of articles is reflected in the diversity of contributors. Although economics, sociology, and community development are the major academic backgrounds of contributors, articles have appeared from writers in such areas as adult education, urban affairs, law, philosophy, geography, political science, psychology, health, and home economics. The majority of writers (close to 90 percent) comes from academic institutions (this includes those with extension appointments). The other 10 percent come from the private sector and government. More than 30 percent are affiliated with the Agricultural/Cooperative Extension Service. The only trend found in this part of the review is a very slight decrease in the number of practitioners (extension, private sector, and government) contributing to the *Journal* in recent years.

Numerically, during 1970–1979, more articles were written on *philosophies toward and/or strategies of community development* than any other content area (see Table 3.1). Several of these articles emphasized a definitional approach (e.g., Lewis 1974; Oberle et al. 1974). The majority of these articles appeared during the first few years of the *Journal*'s existence. Articles published in recent years in this general area have usually been presidential or keynote addresses. This abundance of articles concerning philosophy and strategies of community development reflected the themes of the early national meetings and the CDS Board of Directors decision at that time to publish major papers presented at the national meetings. It also

TABLE 3.1. Decade Summary of Major Content Areas and Contributors to the Journal of the Community Development Society

Content Areas	Contributors
Philosophy toward and/or strategies of community development	Wadsworth 1970; Gibson and Mulvihill 1970; Fanning 1970; Pulver 1970; Beal et al. 1971; Abshier 1971; Evans 1971; Spiegel 1971; Jones 1971; Wortman 1971; Dunbar 1972; Poston 1973; Sargent 1973; Biddle 1973; Batten 1973; Lewis 1974; Oberle et al. 1974; Koneya 1975; Pulver 1977; Arnot 1977; Hobgood 1978; Tichenor 1978; Schaller 1978; Wilkinson 1979
Citizen participation	McClusky 1970; Hahn 1970; Wireman 1970; Anderson 1970; Long 1971; Brooks 1971; McMurtry 1972; Child 1974; Melvin 1974; Pell 1974; Cook 1975; Frederickson 1975; Christenson 1976; Collins and Downes 1976; Nix and Dressel 1978; Koneya 1978; Goudy and Tait 1979; Frazier 1979
Needs assessment	Kilbourn 1970; Basson 1970; Klimoski and Krile 1973; Nix et al. 1974; Christenson 1975; Nix et al. 1976; Dillman 1977; Blake et al. 1977; Goudy and Wepprecht 1977; M. Cohen et al. 1977; Schwebel et al. 1978; Smith 1978; Garkovich 1979; Matthews and Fawcett 1979; Miller and Broom 1979; Sorter and Simpkinson 1979
Roles	Ratchford 1970; Cebotarev and Brown 1972; Cary 1972; Biddle 1973; Hobgood and Christenson 1973; Bennett 1973; Abshier 1973; Winterton and Rossiter 1973; Huie 1975; Oberle et al. 1975; Vaughn 1976; Nicastro 1976; Sorensen and Pfau 1976
Training	Lotz 1970; Santopolo and Johnson 1970; Hanson 1972; Richmond 1972; Cary 1973; Kleinsasser and Slipy 1975; Ritchie 1975; Cary 1976; Gibson 1977; DePuydt and Persell 1978; Smith 1978; Parsons 1978
Evaluation	Thomas 1970; Vaughn 1972; Western Regional CRD Committee 1972; Ellsworth and Snarr 1972; Voth 1975; Macheracher et al. 1976; M. Cohen 1976; Maesen 1976; Burton 1978; Daley and Winter 1978
Conflict	Hunt 1972; Robinson 1972; Hynam 1973; Blizek and Cederblom 1973, 1974; Stewart 1974; Schilitt 1974; Fisher and White 1976; Walker and Hanson 1976
Community services	Napier 1972; Boesch and Heagler 1973; Ching et al. 1973; Blase et al. 1973; Booth 1975; Shaffer 1978; Keith 1978; Murdock and Schriner 1979; Nelson 1979
Ideal types of communities	Warren 1970; Pulver 1970; Poston 1972; Parko 1975; Goudy 1976

reflected the continuing intellectual struggle to identify what community development is, what it should be, and strategies for "doing" community development.

Concern for clientele also has been an area of emphasis during this decade and numerically is the second major content area in the *Journal* (Table 3.1). The key issue in many of the articles on *public involvement* or *citizen participation* centered on working *with* rather than for people, of getting the public involved in the community development process. Many of these articles evolved from the self-help or nondirective CD theme.

The third major area was related to the concern for citizen participation because it focused on survey methods in the context of *needs assessment* or *problem identification*. The articles focused on why people's needs should be identified, how they can be identified, how they can be used, and how this might extend citizen participation. Consideration of how needs can be identified fostered discussion of various survey methodologies.

The fourth major area of emphasis during the decade focused on the various *roles* of community development workers. Some of the commonly identified roles included teacher, facilitator, consultant, enabler, motivator, integrator, critic, and resource channel. In a related content, some recent articles have struggled with the issue of professional certification (Gibson 1977; Parsons 1978). A companion series of articles were written on *training, educating, and evaluating* CD workers or relevant clientele. These articles included academic program outlines, content area schemes, and performance evaluation measures.

Another group of articles investigated community conflict or community crisis. Some of these articles emphasized the normative implications of community development, raised questions of status quo biases, and in general questioned and suggested strategies for effecting change in the distribution of resources in communities and in society.

Other major content areas included evaluation, community services, and ideal types of communities (see Table 3.1). Areas mentioned less frequently included leadership, multicounty or county planning, public policy, industrialization, land use, health, youth, and family.

Another group of articles that should be acknowledged but were difficult to classify concern case or "success" studies. Several involved community development in foreign countries such as the Dominican Republic, Panama, Turkey, Ecuador (Von Lazer and Hammock 1970; Franklin 1971; Suzuki 1975; Daley and Winter 1978; Daley and Lapit 1979); a few program case studies such as OEO (Pell 1972), VISTA (Walker 1971), HUD (Kellams 1977; Ball and Heumann 1979); neighborhood studies in New York (Kurzman 1970); and many "how to do it" case studies such as the initiation of railroad mobile health units (Napier 1972). They show community development in action but are limited in use because of the specific nature of such studies—interesting to read but often hard to generalize about (Daley and Lapit [1979] is a noted exception).

Few articles were found that might be grouped under the heading of theory (perhaps Lewis 1974; Kaufman 1975; Warren 1975; Wilkinson 1979). A few attempted to link theory to community development efforts (cf. Napier and Maurer 1978). Several articles listed concepts (Santopolo and Johnson 1970; Sofranko and Bridgeland 1972; Stanfield and Heffernan 1977) or schemes, such as Long's (1972) Heuristic Development Matrix. And there were two attempts at budgeting models (Shaffer and Tweeten 1974; Darling 1976). Several other articles provided excellent summaries of a particular area that suggested theoretical implications (e.g., Summers's [1977] article on industrialization). But having looked at these, it seems safe to assert that few articles were related to or based on theory during the first ten years of the *Journal*.

Few research articles appeared during the first four years of the *Journal*'s existence. In the first eight issues (volumes 1–4), only 10 percent of the articles could be classified as research. In the next eight issues, approximately 30 percent of the articles could be clasified as research. In the last four issues, the number of research articles made up nearly 45 percent of the total number of articles in each issue.

While a few of the research articles tested community development concepts, many seemed to be discipline oriented (i.e., sociology, economics). Discipline-related material is expected in a journal that tries to encompass the social sciences, but it is the author's opinion that greater effort could be made by researchers to relate their efforts more directly to community development. Some research articles appear to be watered down efforts that probably were prepared for other disciplines. This is particularly evident when authors do not even allude to possible implications of community development and often discuss findings only in a disciplinary context.

While this brief numerical assessment cannot do justice to the variety of articles over the years, it does point out some common areas of emphasis and the intellectual concerns of the contributors to the *Journal*.

THEMES OF COMMUNITY DEVELOPMENT

At the most general level, the majority if not all the articles focus on what Batten (1973, p. 35) calls the "betterment of people." While a wide range of terminology has been employed, most articles imply that community development is people in a community reaching a decision to initiate a social action process to change their situation. People achieve it through cooperation, confrontation, or technical intervention. Most readers will readily agree with "people initiating action to improve the situation in their locality" (for a more complete definition and other definitions see Chapter 1). However, the "how to" generates some debate. In reviewing the articles I found three lines of thought or action themes that seem to differentiate and categorize the articles. These themes can be labeled (1) self-help, nondirective, or cooperative; (2) conflict or confrontation; and (3) technical intervention, planning, or assistance. These three types of "how to do" community development form the developmental themes apparent in the *Journal* over the past ten years. They are discussed in greater detail in the following three chapters. Here we look briefly at how these themes were presented. While overlap exists among these themes, differences rather than similarities are emphasized so that the unique aspects might be more apparent.

Self-Help

More than two-thirds of the articles can be classified as involving the cooperative, self-help, or nondirective theme (see Batten [1973] or Biddle [1973] for definition of nondirective and self-help; also see Chapter 5). The articles are usually descriptive studies of community development in practice. They focus on people and could be classified as more process oriented than task oriented. Cebotarev and Brown (1972) describe process as the approach whereby people arrive at group decisions and take actions to enhance the social and economic well-being of the community. The assumption of the cooperative or self-help theme suggests that by working together people can improve their situation. The process aspect is emphasized over the task aspect because the subject matter is not as important as the process that people go through. Essentially, the self-help theme assists other people in learning how to handle their problems. During the process, they may achieve a task or goal, but it is incidental to the long-range implication of teaching people how to improve their situation. For example, Ploch presented a detailed analysis showing how a small number of volunteers interested in improving the level of health care delivery in their community evolved from an informal group into the nucleus of a board of directors of an incorporated, community-based health center. The creation of the center was an excellent example of the voluntary involvement of community residents in a process to improve some aspect of community life. He noted that the process appeared to strengthen the community's patterns of human and institutional relationships (Ploch 1976).

The role of the change agent in the cooperative or self-help approach is educational and/or organizational. While change agents may advocate the self-help process, they do not advocate particular courses of action. Rather, they help people explore alternatives and reach their own decisions. Batten (1973) argues strongly against advocacy of goals or manipulation toward specific ends. He points out that such manipulation often leads people to undertake tasks for which they do not have the skill, the desire, or the resources and thereby decreases their ability to confront future problems. Only by doing through self-directed decisions can people learn how to improve their community. The role of the agent is to provide people with an understanding of the self-directed educational or decision-making process whereby they can achieve a specific task. Often an agent will contribute to the organizational aspect by helping people learn how groups work and by helping them to work together. But again, the agent serves in an advisory capacity as an unbiased consultant.

The advantage of self-help is that people themselves determine what is to be done and in the process learn both how to achieve this specific task and the process through which they may accomplish future goals. Self-help has been criticized as not achieving meaningful change; Warren (1974) argues that no meaningful change can come without some conflict. He argues that if everybody is satisfied, nothing changes.

Self-help seems to be more a philosophy than a theory based on research-tested procedures. The questions that have to be resolved from a scientific standpoint are whether self-help works, why it works, and when it is most successful. For example, is self-help orientation most appropriate for middle-class neighborhoods and communities? Perhaps it is unrealistic to try it in low-income neighborhoods. The most crucial problem with this theme is that we have little factual information to support or to disprove it. The many descriptive or success studies presented in the *Journal* suggest that most authors think the self-help theme works. The crucial question seems to be how, where, why, and with what results. In the years to come, if this theme is to move from philosophy to theory, it needs to be broken down and tested as to how, where, and why.

Conflict

Over the past ten years a scattering of articles on the conflict or confrontation theme appeared. Most of them were an explication of Alinsky's approach rather than case studies of conflict. The philosophy behind the confrontation theme is a normative emphasis on justice (cf. Blizek and Cederblom 1973, 1974), which stresses that there should be more equal distribution of resources in society and usually focuses on those outside the power structure (e.g., the poor, minorities).

The operational procedure prescribed in the confrontation theme is similar to that of the self-help theme. The procedure is to get people together, to articulate the problems, to develop indigenous leadership, and to help organize viable groups. While the self-help theme emphasizes people working together to achieve their goal, the confrontation theme empasizes polarization of groups based on salient issues and confrontation between opposing sides. Confrontation usually is employed to achieve a particular normative goal such as justice or equality and in the process to achieve specific events such as the alleviation of job discrimination and the provision of job opportunities for minorities. The articles in the *Journal* tended to report the work done by such professional activists as Saul Alinsky and not the work of the contributors. Although confrontation is interesting to discuss, when it comes to practice it seems that most authors who write for the *Journal* do not use it.

The role of the change agent in the confrontation approach is to get people together to show them that they have power in numbers and that an organized voice spoken by an active minority can influence what is done within a community. The role of the conflict agent is not to lead but to help organize. Those using the Alinsky approach strive to polarize the problem into a well-defined issue and then help the people organize to change the situation.

The advantage of the conflict orientation is that it can achieve change in a very short period of time. The problem is whether this change can be sustained. The development of a permanent structure to sustain change is essential. Backlash is an important concern. The backlash of those challenged, particularly the rich and powerful, may place poor people in a worse situation than they were initially. While some detailed studies exist on the conflict orientation, little systematic analysis shows when, how, why, and with what results. This normative theme has been advocated primarily for those outside the power structure; how often can it be used by middle-class segments of a community? These questions need to be systematically studied in the decade ahead.

Technical Assistance

Technical assistance or planning encompasses about one-fourth of the articles that have appeared in the *Journal* over the last ten years. The technical assistance or planning theme philosophy is that structure determines behavior. In most cases, advocates of this theme end up working *for* people rather than *with* them. While planners and technical assistance workers may argue against this characterization, it is fairly well documented that this orientation has largely ignored public input or participation (cf. Melvin 1972; Koneya 1975, p. 8). However, this is not to say that technical intervention or planning orientation has not been successful. It may have had more lasting impact than the other two themes of community development combined.

This theme emphasizes projects such as building bridges, stimulating economic development, establishing new health centers, or creating jobs. For example, Brinkman (1973) and Rogers, Goudy, and Richards (1976) discuss community development from the perspective of attracting and establishing new industries and their subsequent impact on communities. Boesch and Heagler (1973) write about the establishment of a sanitary landfill. Others (Bonner 1972, 1975; Napier 1972; Blase et al. 1973) write about regional health centers, regional planning, and other project-oriented programs.

The role of the technical intervenor or the planner is to assess the situation in a community, county, or region and, based on the best technical information (such as cost-benefit analysis), to suggest the most economically feasible and socially responsible approaches for improving the situation.

Usually some sort of physical intervention is involved, for example, building a convention center, establishing a comprehensive plan, or developing zoning ordinances. Technical assistants and planners are primarily technicians who use professional skills in designing and developing physical projects. Within the last ten years federal legislation has required that greater effort be made to include the public in determining such developments. However, as Koneya (1975) has pointed out, little more than token involvement of the public is manifest in this approach.

Obviously, a new bridge, a new industry, a mobile service center, or a comprehensive plan will have a major impact on a locality. The questions become, Who does this benefit? Who are the clientele? Again, we need to know why, how, and when this orientation works.

In all likelihood, many CD efforts will include elements of or a combination of the self-help, the conflict, and the technical intervention themes. Although practitioners may normally be skilled in one of these themes or strategies, it will probably be helpful for them to develop skills in all three strategies.

IMPLICATIONS

The absence of articles soundly based in a theoretical perspective is particularly apparent. Many schemes, models, taxonomies, and other organizing structures can be found, but most of them deal with a particular substantive area rather than with concepts or the interrelationships of concepts in a theoretical context. While the *Journal* is not devoted primarily to theory, theory should become an important consideration in the decade ahead. We need to organize our insights to see where, when, and why different social action models work. Blakely in Chapter 11 provides some insights to this issue. One reason for this lack of a theoretical construct is that most articles are descriptive studies rather than proposition-testing studies. While descriptive studies manifest different types of community development and are very much needed, we also need some systematic attempts to assess why development occurs and what its effects are on different segments of the population. Special consideration should be given to linking theory and practice. We need to discuss general theories, such as structural functionalism, general systems theory, field theory, and political economy, to mention but a few, and their relationship to or contribution to community development. We need to draw from the best insights of each discipline and adapt it to the practice of community development. Kurt Lewin's oft-quoted phrase sums it up well: A good theory is practical.

Another area of concern is the various roles of those working in community development. While there have been many articles on modes of behavior, more study is needed on the institutionalization of job specialties and what implications it has for conducting community development in the United States. Has the institutionalization of roles placed practitioners in the position of only supporting the status quo rather than pursuing change-oriented, and perhaps conflict-generating, courses of action?

Another area that requires insight involves the range of activities in which CD workers interact. Detailed descriptions of various roles would greatly help. For example, what does a community psychologist do? What does an extension community development agent do? What do planners do? What does a community development–oriented person in industry do? To what extent can community development be taught to undergraduate and graduate students in universities? These questions are dealt with in subsequent chapters.

This raises the issue of the Community Development Society becoming identified with only one type of group or organization. The concern of the early founders that ensured a broad and diverse membership seems also to be of crucial concern today. A concerted effort has to be made to facilitate the involvement of a wide variety of people from different types of job settings. This variety will contribute to the intellectual growth of the society. It also has implications for the *Journal,* since it is our major means of communication; more opportunity must be provided for nonuniversity people to contribute. This review has made it clear that in recent years fewer practitioners inside or outside the university are being involved.

Evaluation has received some emphasis throughout the decade and a few efforts have systematically been made to determine the effects of community development. This concern needs to be amplified in the decade ahead. While the *Journal* has reported large numbers of success stories, it is obvious that the touched-up pictures tend to play down limitations. One of the few articles that has pointed out what can be learned through failure is the article by Cohen (1976). Evaluation must move from descriptive assessment to quantitative documentation. This shift should be of particular concern to practitioners in a period of increased emphasis on accountability. It raises a new challenge to those in community development and will be an issue not easily solved during the next decade but one that must be squarely faced (see Chapter 10).

This review is my assessment and is influenced by my approach to organization and analysis. However, I do feel that the areas outlined and the themes of community development presented capture the different lines of thought winding through the *Journal* these past ten years. I have tried to stimulate a reconsideration of who we are and where we are going. In the chapters that follow, many of these issues, themes, and concerns are discussed in greater detail.

The Technical Assistance Approach

Larry Gamm and Frederick Fisher

TECHNICAL ASSISTANCE is intended to help communities define their problems and needs and potential solutions while allowing for some degree of community autonomy or "ownership" of problem definition and solution. *Technical assistance* might be broadly defined as the provision of "programs, activities, and services . . . to strengthen the capacity of recipients to improve their performance with respect to an inherent or assigned function" (Wright 1978, p. 343). A key ingredient is the application of expertise to aid the recipient in these efforts (Poats 1972).

The numerous forms in which technical assistance might appear are suggested in a U.S. Office of Management and Budget (OMB) bulletin describing technical assistance to state and local governments: "in the form of funds, manpower, . . . training, seminars, workshops, conferences, technology transfer, research utilization, personnel exchange, on-site Federal manpower assistance, information services and dissemination, and other similar activities" (Macaluso 1975, p. 698).

BASIC ASSUMPTIONS

Technical assistance has deep historical roots. Based on technical advice from his father-in-law, Moses established a network of village advisors (technical assistants). It might be said that Plato offered technical assistance to kings. Domergue makes reference to "transfer of skills and know-how" within and between ancient countries and empires (in fields such as animal husbandry, agriculture, building techniques, and town planning) (Domergue 1968, pp. 1–3). Until the present century, transfer of technology occurred predominantly through "natural" means (communication, travel), via exchange (barter or fee-for-service), or by imposition of a conquering state.

Although its ancestry can be traced to these historical examples of technology transfer, the term *technical assistance* (as a unique form of technology transfer) is of recent vintage. Modern-day technical assistance efforts are predominantly associated with the desire of the provider to enable the recipients to do what the recipients are incapable of doing or unwilling to do on their own. That is, the provider is committed to some goal that, if it is to be attained, requires an adoption of particular skills or technologies by the recipient. Additionally, the provider is unwilling to wait for "natural" means of technology transfer to reach the recipient and is unwilling or unable to directly take over the recipients' responsibilities.

The preceding statements do not exclude the fact that technical assistance efforts are often initiated at the request of or welcomed by recipients. Instead, the intent here is to suggest that the recent rapid growth of technical assistance can be most often traced to the interests of the providers.

Several specific assumptions underlie technical assistance relationships: (1) someone knows about something that another does not, (2) someone decides (the provider, the recipient, and/or someone else) that the potential recipient needs assistance, (3) there exists a climate within which a provider-receiver relationship can be established, and (4) someone provides assistance and others receive.

The relatively recent and rapid growth in technical assistance is associated with the fact that all four of these assumptions seem to match evolving conditions in complex societies (national or international). Increased differentiation and specialization among organizations, increasing interdependence among organizations and societies, improved means (and increasing amounts) of communication as well as other factors call for increased integration and predictability of activities. Just as these factors contribute to the need and demand for technical assistance, they constitute conditions that make its provision possible. (Discussion of these general conditions in modern societies may be found in many works, e.g., Bell [1973], Turk [1977], and Aldrich [1979].)

The nature and focus of technical assistance changes both as new problems emerge (or as "old" conditions become defined as problems) and as new technologies that might be applied to problems emerge. The order of events (problem definition and emergence of problem-solving technology) may vary from situation to situation. Technical assistance has evolved with organizations staking a claim to new responsibilities (around some problem or around some technology) and attempting to help other units (nations, organizations, or communities) use technology to help solve problems.

The following section suggests some general directions in this evolution in technical assistance in two arenas—national and international. Also, it provides a historical backdrop against which one can view the various purposes, targets, auspices, and impetuses associated with technical assistance.

RECENT HISTORY

Present-day forms of technical assistance can be traced to the midnineteenth century.[1] Rapid growth in the use of technical assistance is most visible within the last fifty years of the current century.

Technical Assistance at the International Level

During the 1940s a variety of international organizations (special agencies of the United Nations) with some technical assistance responsibilities were launched, such as the International Bank for Reconstruction and Development, the Food and Agriculture Organization, the World Health Organization, the Expanded Technical Assistance Program. The International Development Association has since become another important source of technical assistance within this constellation of UN special agencies. Technical assistance also became a key part of the U.S. aid effort at the international level during this period. The major U.S. initiative occurred with adoption of the Marshall Plan in 1947. Aid programs for European recovery evolved into more widely targeted aid efforts presently administered by the United States Agency for International Development (AID). Supported by international organizations, governmental organizations (such as AID) or private foundations, professional specialists and technical experts are invited into countries to offer technical assistance in defining and solving problems.

Study of and involvement in technical assistance efforts at the international level suggest a variety of motives that might be attributed to providers and to recipients. The provider nation or international organization may seek to promote the development of recipient countries out of altruistic motives. A slightly more self-interested motive is based on the belief that the provider and others are safer or otherwise benefited by assisting countries in their developmental efforts. Another motive might be that technical assistance demonstrates at least a symbolic concern on the part of the provider for interests of other nations. Also, such offerings can be used to counteract demands on the part of recipients for more tangible aid. Finally, aid has been used by providers to win friends and allies and to protect their own national interests (e.g., offering the assistance of military technicians to other countries).

The recipient country may be motivated to accept technical assistance to advance its efforts toward social and economic development for its institutions and people, to advance its own security through economic develop-

---

1. On the international level, professional specialists and technical experts offered assistance to nations via International Telegraphic Union, the Universal Postal Union, and the International Institute of Agriculture during the latter part of the eighteenth century (Claude 1964). Within the U.S. federal system, the land grant and in 1877 the cash grant to finance state-operated agricultural experiment stations were the chief forms of national assistance to the states prior to 1900. Although technology transfer was often an intent of these programs, provisions related closely to technical assistance provisions of modern programs did not enter the picture until the turn of the century. From 1914 to 1921, grants supporting agricultural extension, highway construction, vocational education and rehabilitation, and maternal and child health contained detailed planning and administration provisions (Wright 1978).

ment and military upgrading, or simply to evince a close relationship to a provider country. Another motive may be to increase its own capability for doing for itself and to avoid overdependence on other nations for the provision of its needs.

Political and personal appeal ideologies should not be ignored as a stimulator of technical assistance. The continent of Africa is awash these days with technical assistance from nearly every corner of the globe. Tanzania is a particularly attractive target of many countries, with Sweden leading the list of donor nations. Tanzania's current brand of humanistic socialism (not to mention its attractive landscape) wins sympathy and applause from a wide spectrum of political views.

Technical assistance and other forms of assistance can be and have been used by providers to undercut the independence of the recipient country. In numerous cases, however, the host country has ordered an assistance mission to leave. Implicit in this discussion of technical assistance relationships are the aspects of both voluntaristic and power-dependent relationships between the provider and the recipient and attention to maintenance of some degree of the autonomy or national sovereignty of the recipient country.

Technical Assistance in the United States

The growth of technical assistance activities in the U.S. intergovernmental system is associated with the rapid proliferation of intergovernmental programs over the last several decades. Government involvement in the definition of community problems and in the provision of programs and funds to attack the problems has substantially increased. The roles of national, state, and local governments with respect to these responsibilities have changed markedly. Local units until recent decades have been primarily responsible both for deciding on the allocation of public goods and services for their residents and for their actual delivery. As the overall types and amounts of such goods and services have increased, local units have retained responsibility for delivery but decisions regarding allocation (deciding what will be offered and how to fund it) have shifted in large part to national and state governmental entities (see Schmandt and Goldbach 1969).

The local community today (more than earlier in the century) may be perceived as "a delivery system which must operate within the general framework cast by the larger policy making and resource allocation system." Communities however retain varying degrees of "administrative discretion in policy interpretation and application" and gain access to resources that they may not be able to provide for themselves (Schmandt and Goldbach 1969, pp. 493–94). In such a situation, technical assistance is a means employed by the larger allocation system (e.g., Congress, state administrative agencies) to attempt to keep local discretion within bounds. That is, the provider of technical assistance attempts to ensure that local performance will measure up to the expectations of the provider unit.

The improved climate for technical assistance is depicted in the growth in federal grant-in-aid programs. The 21 major new programs established between 1946 and 1961 nearly doubled the number initiated during the depression era. "By 1969, there were an estimated 150 major programs, 400 specific legislative authorizations, and 1300 different federal assistance activities for which monetary amounts, applications, deadlines, agency contacts, and use restrictions could be identified" (Wright 1978, p. 54).

The amount of federal and state aid to local units increased from a total of $1.8 billion (25 percent of local revenues) in 1942 to $57 billion (43 percent of local revenues) in 1974 (Wright 1978, p. 70). A study by the U.S. Office of Management and Budget (OMB) found that for fiscal year 1974 about $512 million (about 1 percent of total federal grant-in-aid effort) was allocated to technical assistance purposes. Approximately 90 percent was directed toward specific program areas. Only a small portion was directed toward improvement of local management or service delivery capabilities on a more general or multiprogram basis (Higgs 1975).

According to the same OMB study, just over one-half of these funds go directly to specified state and local operating agencies or to agencies designated by the states' chief executives or legislatures. The remainder goes to third parties—mostly to functional areawide agencies (e.g., economic development districts) but also to universities and public interest groups (Higgs 1975).

Two major findings of the OMB study are particularly relevant. Nearly all the federal funds for technical assistance are tied to specific functional programs (e.g., health, law enforcement). And "the elected officials have relatively little control over the majority of technical assistance funds" (Higgs 1975, p. 745).

The preceding statements suggest that the motives of the national government as an initiator and funder of technical assistance activities reflect the following considerations: (1) increasing identification of domestic problems as national responsibilities, (2) expansion of incentives (in the form of funds or regulations) for engaging states and communities in the implementation and maintenance of programs focused on these problems, (3) establishment and maintenance of special agencies (e.g., single function substate regional organizations) to pursue nationally identified goals with minimal interference from general-purpose governments, and (4) developing a modest commitment to improving the overall expertise and abilities of state and communities in the performance of both nationally defined purposes and purposes defined by states and communities themselves.

The motives of recipients might include: (1) receiving national assistance to carry out nationally defined programs that the recipients want but are unable to provide, (2) capturing national resources that they can (by a process of substitution or deflection) use for their own purposes, (3) employing national assistance to respond to management problems created or worsened by the proliferation of intergovernmental programs, and (4) utilizing national resources to respond to political pressures from local residents stimulated by availability of national program support.

How technical assistance relationships are structured depends in large part on their purposes or targets and on the impetuses and auspices for their development in particular situations. It is to these matters, with a primary emphasis on activities within the United States, that we now focus attention.

TARGETS, ELEMENTS, AND EXAMPLES

The three types of targets for technical assistance each relate to community development but in slightly different ways. The broadest target, and the one that seems to best fit the tradition of community development, is termed *community decision making*. Activities aimed at this target aid community organizations and residents in determining the status of their community, the direction they want their community to pursue, and the appropriate means for getting there.

Another target, closely aligned with CD leadership training and organization, is termed *community resource development*. Assistance in this context helps to ensure that the community has the necessary resources, human and material, to guide and sustain it in effectively adapting to changing conditions or in pursuing new courses of action.

The third target is associated with action or program implementation and is labeled *community task performance*. Assistance directed toward this target seeks to ensure that community programs are administered so as to maximize the benefits to clients and to adhere to appropriate administrative and accountability requirements. (These three targets correspond generally to three levels of hierarchy described by Parsons [1960], i.e., the institutional level, the managerial level, and the technical level.)

Decision Making

Efforts of the U.S. Department of Housing and Urban Development (HUD) in the sixties to examine comprehensive land use plans for communities across the nation are a poignant example of technical assistance to enhance community decision making. Unfortunately, too many of these plans ended up on shelves, rarely touched by human hands. We suspect the general impotence of these tomes was due in large measure to the imposition of expertise from the outside by professional consultant planners and the general lack of community involvement (citizens or officials) in the development of the plans. Hoos (1973), in a critique of systems techniques (technical assistance) recalls the creation of the San Francisco Bay Area Transportation Steering Committee by the state legislature to do a master regional transportation plan. Its technical assistance started with data collection; 10 million pieces of information were collected and converted to 1.5 million punch cards and recorded on 1,100 reels of magnetic tape that required one and one-half hours of IBM7094 computer time to reprocess. End result? Ten million pieces of information converted to 1.5 million punch cards, recorded on . . . The results were predictable. Nobody bothered to ask "so what" at an earlier point in the project.

A more optimistic example of technical assistance toward the goal of community decision making is the International City Management Association's (ICMA) effort to transfer technology through peer exchanges. A city manager who is contemplating a major transition in solid waste collection (in this case, the Environmental Protection Agency is financing the technical assistance) can contact ICMA. Project staff then identify several other city managers who have recently carried out similar projects. From that list, a small number are selected to spend a few days on site, reviewing the proposal implementation plan and sharing the problems and successes that they experienced. In effect, the city manager receives consulting services from professional colleagues.

Other examples of technical assistance associated with community decision making include self-studies or needs assessments. For illustrations and further discussions of technical assistance efforts in community decision making see Reeder (n.d.); Community Survey (1964); National Training and Development Service (1974); Town Meeting '76 (1975); Collins and Downes (1976); Keep America Beautiful (1976); Cohen, Sills, and Schwebel (1977); Dillman (1977); Fisher and Wolfe (1977); and Goudy and Wepprecht (1977).

Such programs have no doubt occurred in communities in most states. Their major problems are assuring community involvement and commitment to the process itself and giving adequate attention to follow-through. With respect to the latter point, it is often difficult to determine whether such assistance has actually produced any meaningful action.

Support for these programs has come through sources such as Cooperative Extension programs (Bevins 1978), Community Action, Model Cities, and HUD 701 programs. It is possible that such programs designed for use in conjunction with General Revenue Sharing, Housing and Community Development Act, and Comprehensive Employment and Training Act programs will become more prevalent.

Community Resource Development

Technical assistance associated with community resource development includes such activities as leadership training programs conducted by universities and management training for municipal personnel by state, national, county, and municipal associations; state departments of community affairs; private training consultants; and universities. Many of these organizations and others are involved in community organization development, i.e., in establishment and maintenance of community organizations for advancing community interests.

Technical assistance for community resource development is becoming more popular in federal programs under the heading of *capacity building*. The general intent is to help the community build internal resources to carry on its developmental plans with a minimum of outside assistance. The National Training and Development Service in its early years of operation was oriented toward this approach to technical assistance and community development. Its four-week training program, Managing Change, was designed to help participants develop an understanding of and skills in action research to be applied to their own organizations and communities with a minimum of outside support and involvement. The training of trainers is another example of this approach. The Pennsylvania Energy Extension Service has a pilot project to help communities develop their own capabilities to design and implement comprehensive energy conservation programs. The intent is to assist these communities toward some degree of self-reliance in dealing with the energy crisis.

An office of the federal government has been interested in assessing the results of technical assistance. In August 1974 the OMB initiated an Interagency Study Committee on Policy Management Assistance. It is composed of career executives experienced in working with state and local governments whose agencies are interested in using federal technical assistance to strengthen the core management capabilities of state and local general-purpose governments. This committee came about through the realization that the proliferation of federal programs had imposed heavy demands on management capabilities of state and local governments.

The way to help resolve the problem was technical assistance in the form of a study committee. It was made up of bureaucrats from 17 federal agencies, who produced three volumes on the subject (one volume over 1,100 pages) and a special issue of *Public Administration Review* (December 1975). Little appears to have happened to yet another layer of technical assistance addressing the management dilemma of state and local governments.

Technical assistance in the form of management training for municipal personnel has often failed to diagnose training needs adequately and to involve local personnel in such diagnostic activities. See Janka (1977) and Gamm and Fisher (1978). Similar problems in leadership training and organization development occur in gaining participant involvement in specification of community issues or organization goals, short-run objectives, and action steps that might be pursued. Unless these problems are overcome, CD potential is dissipated in activities that are far removed from the needs of the individual participants and community groups they represent.

The roles of state, national, county, and municipal associations and state departments of community affairs in this area of technical assistance have been supported in large part through HUD 701 and Intergovernmental

Personnel Act funds. The numerous technical assistance activities of the latter agencies are reported in a summary of a survey of these agencies (Council of State Community Affairs Agencies 1978).

Universities have offered assistance through the support of these state, agencies and associations, Cooperative Extension, and National Science Foundation and private foundation monies and with the support of other groups such as labor and business organizations. A directory of university CD programs offering such assistance has been produced by the Department of Regional and Community Affairs at the University of Missouri (1973). See also Cotton and Linder (1977) and National Training and Development Service (1977). For a review of organization development efforts by a Canadian university and by the National Training and Development Service, see Janka (1977) and LGMP (1977).

Other examples that suggest the range of technical assistance efforts toward community organization development might include those by the League of Women Voters (Van Meter 1975); the Community Technical Assistance Program of the American Medical Student Association Foundation; Ralph Nader–initiated Public Interest Research Groups; and ACORN, Arkansas, Institute for Social Justice (1977).

Task Performance

Technical assistance efforts directed toward community task performance are the most numerous. Nearly every community program imaginable (for roads, energy, the elderly, etc.) has a technical assistance support structure funded largely by federal categorical programs. This support structure includes specialized technical assistance providers within state agencies, major universities, and private consulting firms.

The Clean Community System (CCS), developed by Keep America Beautiful (KAB) and designed to help communities gain control of litter, is an example of community task performance (Keep America Beautiful 1976-1979). To date KAB has helped install CCS in more than 150 communities across the country. Many communities have experienced a measurable reduction in litter and uncontained solid waste by adopting this behaviorally based scheme. The program also fits nicely under community resource development technical assistance, since KAB trains community teams who have the responsibility to train others in their community to design and implement the CCS approach.

Task performance technical assistance does not always result in performing the task with any degree of proficiency. A middle-sized midwest city recently decided to apply for an Intergovernmental Personnel Act (IPA) grant to help solve some management problems in one of its major departments. A committee of eight middle management personnel were charged with the task of writing the proposal. An outside (technical assistance) consultant who was working with the group in a management development effort recognized some problems in the group's decision-making process and asked them, individually, to state the problem. They responded with five very different perceptions. As they discussed the confusion they were experiencing, it became increasingly obvious they had been taken away from a task they had originally been assigned to solve and asked to pursue federal funds (technical assistance). The technical assistance (in this case, training) they were seeking might create more problems in the long run than it would solve because of the way it was designed.

Technical assistance that comes in the way of information sharing is often oriented toward task performance. PENNTAP, Pennsylvania Technical Assistance Program of The Pennsylvania State University, is designed to provide information of a specific nature to solve specific problems. Even then, their technical specialists confide that it is often difficult to get at the heart of the problem. Many times persons or organizations requesting assistance cannot articulate the problem with sufficient clarity. Only after careful consideration are they able to cut through the symptoms to get at the real problem.

It is somewhat comical that personnel from different parts of the same university increasingly encounter one another in the offices of the same community agency. Such situations, however, point to a serious problem associated with task-oriented technical assistance. Those persons involved in supporting one task (e.g., development of a management information system) in a community agency are often uninformed of the activities of others providing assistance for other tasks (e.g., services management, transportation services, or information and referral). Thus it is left entirely to community personnel to ensure that these tasks and technical assistance efforts are coordinated. A corollary problem is that many of the tasks needing technical assistance are defined by others (e.g., state agencies, professional groups) instead of by the recipients. If assistance is to be effective in such cases, the provider of the assistance must either build local commitment to the task or help the community organization gain support for assistance on tasks that it deems more important.

Universities have become increasingly involved in all three target areas of technical assistance, in the form of relevant information for use in community decision making, management and organization activities, and task performance. Examples of such efforts are PENNTAP and cooperative extension programs in many states (Purdue University has a very sophisticated community data system).

AUSPICES AND IMPETUSES

There is a great variety of technical assistance activities and of sources of such activities. Examples of the forms that technical assistance might take are presented in Table 4.1.

Technical assistance relationships and decisions to enter into them may vary according to (1) the auspices under which they are organized and (2)

TABLE 4.1. Forms of Technical Assistance According to Auspices and Impetuses

Impetus for Technical Assistance	Legislative (e.g., Congress, state legislature)	Administrative (e.g., national or state agencies)	Educative (e.g., universities, research institutes)	Collaborative (e.g., national or state professional organizations)	Consultative (e.g., private consultants)
Imposed	policies laws programs funds structural changes	evaluation management criteria guidelines			
Negotiated	funds personnel	programs hardware software information training personnel exchange and training management systems	knowledge skills research information personnel training	standards information research personnel training	
Community initiated				(with other communities) personnel exchange task forces knowledge exchange joint data systems	grant writing data systems management systems

the impetuses for undertaking technical assistance. The auspices under which it is provided can be categorized as legislative (those with powers to create, legislate, and appropriate), administrative (the power to manipulate resources, knowledge, and information), educative (knowledge, skills, and processes of a specialized nature associated largely with educational and research institutions), collaborative (mechanisms created, often mutually, for the specific purpose of providing or enhancing technical assistance in the recipients' domain), and consultative (generally performance of specific tasks by private consultants).

The impetus for offering technical assistance—how it finds its way into the recipients' domain—can be categorized in the following ways: imposed (thrust on the recipient unilaterally from the outside), negotiated (arrived at by mutual consent), and community initiated (invited by those who perceive they have such a need). Examples of the substance or form that technical assistance might take according to auspices and impetuses are indicated in Table 4.1.

SOME GUIDES FOR THE FUTURE

The discussion of technical assistance as a resource for community development raises some obvious problems about its potential to deliver the goods effectively and efficiently. It calls to mind a couple of phrases that help to make a point. The first is Charles Hitch's analogy of program budgeting to his response to Wagner's music: "It sounds better than it is." Those of us who have either given or received technical assistance can surely identify with that observation. The second is an old Bostonian gravestone epitaph, *sum quod eris*—"I am what you will be." Too often the giver of technical assistance operates under this assumption, consciously or otherwise. It remains a dilemma for those who worry about the viability of communities.

Given the potential impotency and frequent inappropriateness of technical assistance in the name of community development, it might be helpful to share our ideas about what might or might not work. It seems to us that the more we attempt to impose technical assistance from the outside, the more we come to realize it does not work either as often or as well as those involved had hoped it would. The World Bank is finding this the case in its widespread technical assistance in developing countries. It is realizing the importance of defining projects and improvements (whatever the context) from the point of view of the clients rather than of the technical assistance teams who assess the situation. The international experiences are equally germane in the United States.

A congressional staff report on local energy policies presented in early 1978 concluded "that not only does the Federal Government not help local communities develop sound energy policies, it actually hinders them in many cases" (Energy Planning Report 1978). These experiences in adapting technical assistance to community development prompts us to suggest a return to Kurt Lewin's concept of action research as a ground for technical assistance. Lewin was always clear about his values and their potential impact on the intervention process with the client. He also emphasized the necessity to engage the client—whether an individual, a group, an organization, or a community—in a mutual process of planning and decision making. The mutuality concept is important not only to assure congruence between needs and solutions but also to gain understanding and commitment by those for whom the assistance is intended. It is increasingly clear that commitment is essential to the successful adoption of any technical assistance and that commitment can best be built through active involvement of the user in the process.

While technical assistance will continue to be an important resource in community development, growing evidence shows that the process by which the assistance is carried out is as important as the content of the assistance. The success of such a process obviously depends heavily on the training of those who are administering technical assistance. Effectiveness criteria for leaders of technical assistance teams have been developed by the U.S. Agency for International Development (1973). Eight of these criteria are paraphrased here in question form. We have added a ninth that reflects growing concern for community involvement. Those who would employ the technical assistance approach to community development, whether in American communities or other countries, should be able to answer yes to each.

1. Are the technical assistance givers technically qualified?
2. Can they administer what will probably be a complex task?
3. Do they exhibit decency and sensibility and interpersonal skills?
4. Will they understand and accept their responsibility for the attainment of stated objectives?
5. Can they be relaxed about their own status in the community and willing to share credit for success openly and freely?
6. Will they be able to defend convictions under stress?
7. Will they be perceptive and politically astute in picking up undercurrents and tensions in interpersonal and interagency relations?
8. Will they accept the challenge of development and institution building as primary goals so as to leave behind local skills and resources to carry on?
9. Will they involve the community in each phase of the process in order to gain the community commitment essential to a successful technical assistance effort?

CONCLUDING OBSERVATIONS

The growth of the technical assistance approach to community development has been attributed herein to two general forces. One such force is the increasing complexity and specialization of and interdependence among institutions in modern society. This force or dynamic contributes to the community need for technical assistance in the performance of even those functions traditionally defined as community responsibilities. A second force is the assignment of new or expanded functions to communities by outside organizations. The proliferation of federal grant programs is the major source of assigned functions and associated technical assistance activities.

Of great importance is the maintenance of a strong community role in technical assistance, which should increasingly focus on enabling communities to anticipate needs and problems. Moreover, communities should be given enlarged roles in defining the form and substance of technical assistance.

Providers of technical assistance should demonstrate a greater awareness of the fact that recipients' preferences (preferred targets of technical assistance and preferred providers of technical assistance) vary according to community size and other characteristics (Nix, Brooks, and Courtney 1976; Jones and Doss 1978). Additional research focused on linkages between policy goals and needs and characteristics of communities assigned policy implementation responsibilities would be helpful (Gamm and Hyman 1973; Bunker 1978).

Technical assistance has been described throughout in terms of a relationship. In this relationship, the commitment of both parties—the recipient and the provider—is essential if technical assistance is to advance community development.

REFERENCES

ACORN. 1977. Community organizing: Handbook 2. Little Rock: Ark. Inst. Social Justice.

Aldrich, H. E. 1979. *Organizations and Environments.* Englewood Cliffs, N.J.: Prentice-Hall.

Bell, D. 1973. *The Coming of Post-Industrial Society.* New York: Basic Books.

Bevins, R. J. 1978. Cooperative extension's public affairs traditions and community development. *J. Community Dev. Soc.* 9 (2):76-84.

Bunker, D. R. 1978. Organizing to link social science with public policy making. *Public Adm. Rev.* 38 (3):223-32.

Claude, I. L., Jr. 1964. *Swords into Plowshares: The Problems and Progress of International Organization,* 3d ed., rev. New York: Random House.

Cohen, M.; G. Sills; and A. I. Schwebel. 1977. Two-stage process for surveying community needs. *J. Community Dev. Soc.* 8 (1):54-61.

Collins, J. N., and B. T. Downes. 1976. The community developer and local problem solving: facilitating governmental responsiveness. *J. Community Dev. Soc.* 7 (1):28-40.

Community survey: Its use in development and action programs. 1964. Ames: Iowa State University, Coop. Ext. Serv.

Cotton, G. C., and W. W. Linder. 1977. Strategies for delivering educational programs to local government officials. *J. Community Dev. Soc.* 8 (2):19-29.

Council of State Community Affairs Agencies (COSCAA). 1978. State departments of community affairs: Assisting communities through mobilization of technical resources. Washington, D.C.

Department of Regional and Community Affairs. 1973. Directory of community development education and training programs throughout the world, 2d ed. Columbia: University of Missouri.

Dillman, D. 1977. Preference surveys and policy decisions: Our new tools need not be used in the same old way. *J. Community Dev. Soc.* 8 (1):30–43.

Domergue, M. 1968. *Technical Assistance: Theory, Practice, and Policies.* New York: Praeger.

Energy planning report, vol. 3, no. 6 (Dec. 18, 1978). Washington, D.C.: Resourc. News Serv.

Fisher, F., and R. Wolfe. 1977. Television for community problem solving in central Pennsylvania. In *Emerging Technology and Process in Community Development,* ed. by L. Gamm and D. Hyman, pp. 91–101. University Park: Pennsylvania State University.

Gamm, L., and F. Fisher. 1978. A cross national examination of emerging practices in local government management: A book review essay. *Gov. Publ. Rev.* 5 (4):493–97.

Gamm, L., and D. Hyman. 1973. Prolegomenon to action-oriented research in community development, Research and Development Priorities in Pennsylvania. University Park: Pennsylvania State University, Cent. Study Sci. Policy, Inst. Res. Human Resourc.

Goudy, W. J., and F. E. Wepprecht. 1977. Local, regional programs developed from residents' evaluations. *J. Community Dev. Soc.* 8 (1):44–52.

Higgs, L. D. 1975. Mapping the federal assistance effort: The pieces of a puzzle, but where's the picture? *Public Adm. Rev.* 35 (Spec. Issue): 743–48.

Hoos, Ida. 1973. Systems technique for managing society: A critique. *Public Adm. Rev.* 33 (2):160–67.

Janka, K. C. 1977. People, performance, results: A guide to increasing effectiveness of local government employees. Washington, D.C.: Natl. Train. Dev. Serv.

Jones, W. A., Jr., and C. B. Doss, Jr. 1978. Local officials' reaction to federal "capacity building." *Public Adm. Rev.* 38 (1):64–69.

Keep America Beautiful. 1976–1979. Clean community system: Organizing manual. New York: Keep America Beautiful, Inc.

LGMP (Local Government Management Project Team). 1977. The LGMP experience: Guidelines for organizational change in local government. Kingston, Ont.: Queen's University at Kinston, Sch. Bus.

Macaluso, A. C. 1975. Background and history of the study committee on policy management assistance. *Public Adm. Rev.* 35 (Spec. Issue): 695–700.

National Training and Development Service. 1974. Citizens view of the community—Its opportunities and problems (report to Park City, Utah). Washington, D.C.

————. 1977. Managing government (curriculum development project). Washington, D.C.

Nix, H. L.; G. S. Brooks; and B. C. Courtney. 1976. Comparative needs of large and small communities. *J. Community Dev. Soc.* 7 (2):97–105.

Parsons, T. 1960. *Structure and Process in Modern Societies.* Glencoe, Ill.: Free Press.

Poats, R. M. 1972. *Technology for Developing Nations.* Washington, D.C.: Brookings Inst.

Reeder, W. (n.d.) Determining the problems and needs of your community. Inf. Bull. 42. Ithaca, N.Y.: Cornell University, Ext. Publ.

Schmandt, H. J., and J. C. Goldbach. 1969. The urban paradox. In *The Quality of Urban Life,* H. J. Schmandt and W. Bloomberg, Jr., eds., pp. 473–98. Urban Affairs Annual Review Series, vol. 3. Beverly Hills, Calif.: Sage Publ.

Town meeting '76. 1975. Chicago: Inst. Cult. Aff.

Turk, H. 1977. *Organizations in Modern Life.* San Francisco; Jossey-Bass.

U.S. Agency for International Development. 1973. Selecting effective leaders of technical assistance teams. Washington, D.C.: Bur. Tech. Assist.

Van Meter, E. C. 1975. Citizen participation in the policy management process. *Public Adm. Rev.* 35 (Spec. Issue):804–12.

Wright, D. S. 1978. *Understanding Intergovernmental Relations.* North Scituate, Mass.: Duxbury.

CHAPTER 5

The Self-Help Approach

Donald W. Littrell

THE SELF-HELP CONCEPT

The concept of self-help, which is the notion or assumption that people can come together and work together to improve their situation, is a basic approach in both the theory and the practice of community development. Almost all descriptions or definitions of community development include references to the self-help approach (see Chapter 1). For example, community development has been defined as

the utilization under one single programme of approaches and techniques which rely upon local communities as units of action and which attempt to combine outside assistance with organized local self-determination and effort, and which correspondingly seek to stimulate local initiative and leadership as the primary instrument of change. [UN 1959, p. 291]

Likewise, a professional education group has stated:

Community development is the process of community education and action, democratically organized and carried through by the people themselves to reach goals they hold in common for the improvement and enrichment of the entire community. The college or University's role is one of actively assisting in this process through consultation with, and training of, individuals and groups concerned with solving problems community-wide in nature. The University makes available to the community its resources of knowledge and skills, but leaves decision-making in local affairs to the citizenry. [Lackey 1960, p. 2]

The self-help approach is generally defined as a process that assumes people can come together, examine their situations, design strategies to deal with various segments of their surroundings, and implement plans for improvement. The role of the CD worker and the sponsoring CD organization is to facilitate the process of self-help.

PHILOSOPHY AND HISTORICAL BACKGROUND

From the definitions and descriptions of the self-help approach, the philosophy is clear: People can help themselves, they should have the opportunity to do so, and it is the role of CD professionals to practice in such a manner that people become increasingly competent to guide their own destiny. Many people express this philosophy, but the notion of democratic self-help is easier to discuss than to practice. Democratic procedures may not make decision making easier—involving people often makes decisions more complex.

Community development as a profession has its roots in many different countries and in many institutions and agencies. Many early efforts were aimed at improving the quality of life and production capacity of underdeveloped rural areas both in the United States and in the developing nations of the world. This is evident through a review of the efforts reported by such organizations as the United Nations, the U.S. Agency for International Development, the Cooperative Extension Service, and others. Writers such as Biddle and Biddle (1965) and Batten (1957) have emphasized the work in community development in rural neighborhood settings.

The self-help concept and approach was formed in the local setting. In many areas where community development was initiated a strong sense of fatalism existed and the idea that ordinary people could intervene in shaping their own destiny was almost revolutionary. Early efforts often concentrated on assisting people to deal with local concerns, such as improved agricultural practices, health programs, roads, school buildings, wells, family economics, and literacy programs. These programs were usually carried out with the help of a CD worker assigned to the area by the sponsoring agency, such as a government, mission group, university, or other agency located outside the area. The worker often had access to or could help gain access to technical advice and simple tools and materials such as concrete, machines, shovels, plows, fertilizer, seed, roofing, and pipe. Access was often enhanced if the people's desires and the agency's goals matched, but the basic idea was that the local residents would plan and carry out improvement projects with limited help from outside resources. Little attention was given to the effect on surrounding areas unless cooperation was needed to carry out a project.

PRACTICING SELF-HELP

The programs and projects, goals, and objectives sponsored by various agencies ran the gamut of emphases and methods to achieve their purposes. The battleground of self-help community development was often based not in its philosophy but in its practice.

Role of the CD Worker

The CD worker's role in the self-help approach is stated in a 1975 task force report:

The primary objective of the community development professional is to help the community more clearly define and achieve its goals. [Task Force Report to ECOP 1975, p. 5]

This statement appears to be a simple, straightforward guide. However, it is in the application of the self-help approach that difficulties arise.

One obstacle may be that the goals of the worker and the goals of the people are different. The people's only goal (especially early in the process) may be the completion of a specific project or activity, while the worker wants the people to learn how to deal with a situation in an effective, demo- cratic manner and to transfer that knowledge to other situations so that they can become more independent. When the goals of the people and the goals of agencies do not match, what is viewed as a worthwhile project or a model of progress by a national government may be viewed as a curse by local citi- zens. This dilemma is succinctly described by Batten:

Community workers work for the betterment of people. But "betterment" is a very vague and general term which every person will interpret for himself according to his own ideas of what is good. Thus what the worker regards as betterment for the people with whom he works they may not regard as betterment for themselves. If this should happen, what then should the worker do? Should he try to direct, lead, guide, or persuade people to accept his judgment of what is good? If he does, how can he be sure that he is right? Or should he try to help them think out for them- selves what they want? If so, and if the people decide on something that conflicts with his own ideas of what is good, what then becomes of his purpose of promoting betterment for them? [Batten 1967, p. 3]

It is often stated that community development work should start where the people are. This statement is true, but starting where the people are does not mean agreeing with whatever people say they want to do. The people may desire a well or an industrial plant, but it is not the sole purpose of the CD worker to help them obtain the well or the industrial plant. Instead, the worker helps the people think through why they want what they want, the short- and long-run effects, and whether the thing they want will produce the intended results. Bennett points out that "community development edu- cation is not simply education for action, but education in action" (Bennett 1969, p. 10). Through its self-help approach, community development has extended the notion of grass roots, which means working with people to help them learn to deal effectively with their own community concerns, di- lemmas, and problems.

Companion Notions That Affect Practice

Community development practice has generated several companion notions that have a profound effect on the self-help approach to community development. Although none of these concepts are absolutely wrong or right they warrant careful consideration, for they can both hinder and help those who wish to utilize the self-help approach. These notions may be expressed as follows:

1. *Communities or groups of people have a basic autonomy.* The local community is an island and to a great degree can determine its own destiny and can formulate action programs with little regard for the larger society unless materials from outside sources are required.

2. *The self-help approach is a self-contained process.* For an activity to be considered a self-help process, the people who are affected must be involved in a physical sense in all its phases.

3. *Communities tend to be stable and homogeneous, with a common value base.* Communities have similar points of view regarding the common good. Geographic proximity tends to be equated with similar values and concerns.

4. *People know how to participate in the local setting.* If people are not involved, then it must be because they are apathetic or at best unconcerned with the problems or future of their area.

5. *The local setting is open for those who wish to participate.* Local leadership or power configurations are concerned with betterment of the community.

6. *When people come together to participate, somehow the decision-making process is easier.* Agreement will be reached with little conflict.

SELF-HELP TODAY AND TOMORROW

The self-help concept, which encompasses many strategies and techniques, has served and to a great extent still serves community development very well. What is to be the role of self-help in the future? Can this approach, originally formulated in simple settings concerned with primary needs, be functional in today's complex world concerned with complicated issues? The self-help approach is sound and workable, although in its present stage of development it has both strengths and weaknesses. The basic assumption of self-help is still viable; people in today's society can help themselves.

The remainder of this chapter focuses on the practice of self-help in community development in a changing world and examines the six notions listed earlier as they affect practice now and may affect it in the future. The aim of this section is to modify and restate these notions to give a better idea of how the theory of self-help can apply to the realities of CD practice.

1. The idea of community or group autonomy is sound, but it is a functional guideline for CD work only when considered in relationship to the autonomy of other intervening units of government or interests. Communities and groups of people do have a basic autonomy but they cannot

plot individual courses without regard to the well-being of the surroundings. A dilemma facing community development both in theory and practice arises from the basic autonomy of local groups and of larger units that
have conflicting needs and desires. Most CD case studies focus on one city,
neighborhood, or rural area, usually describing a community successfully
guiding its own destiny. What is the position of community development regarding imposed interventions in a local setting? What if a small group's autonomy is endangered for the good of a larger group of people? For example, let us assume the Corps of Engineers wants to build a dam in a site that
will inundate two or three small communities; let us further assume that the
dam will protect many more people than it will inundate. It would appear
that the community developer's role might be to help the differing parties
work out the best possible solution, realizing that perfect agreement is probably impossible. When considering larger units—a nation, or even a city or
county—an absolute common good concerning a proposed change seldom
exists.

2. The self-help model has often been presented as a self-contained
process; local people provide the resources and do the work. In today's
world this may or may not be the case. People are involved in many kinds of
projects, doing the work themselves; but increasingly people cause, or contract, the specific activity to be carried out. A group of people in the United
States who desire a water system or a medical clinic will probably contract
the actual implementation of the work; they may not lift a single shovel of
dirt unless a ceremonial groundbreaking occurs. This is still sound self-help
if the people helped to define the issue and to plan an approach to dealing
with the situation.

As our communities become more complex, many agencies or organizations have been delegated specific responsibilities in various aspects of
community life that citizens must recognize. Examples are educational commissions, health boards, labor councils, zoning boards, and other regulatory agencies. These groups, both public and private, are forces that must
be taken into account in local decision formation and project design. Thus a
group of citizens who cause a building to be constructed might have to con-
sult with a variety of organizations to bring the project to completion.
Sound CD practice brings local groups together with agencies of larger
scope to formulate decisions and carry them out.

Often the self-help process is described as one in which only local resources should be used. The implication is that outside assistance such as
monies, technical help, and specific supplies should seldom be used. It appears more logical in today's world that all potential resources be carefully
reviewed, especially in areas that have diverse levels of taxing authorities
and an interlocking private system; and the most appropriate resources
should be used.

The matter of control should be taken into account, for resources from
outside the local scene often have strings attached. Consumption of local re-

sources may limit what can be attempted in the future, especially if the project requires continuous maintenance either from fiscal or leadership resources.

3. The notion of a homogeneous community is increasingly fallacious. Communities are becoming more heterogeneous both from a socioeconomic point of view and in terms of interests. In modern society a contiguous geographic residence does not ensure similar interests, values, or beliefs.

People live in many communities of interest at the same time; these interests are often diverse and at times conflict. The decision-making process that affects local areas tends to be complicated, while governmental decision-making structures are fragmented. Semipublic bodies such as industrial development groups, environmental protection groups, and other interest groups affect what occurs in a host of settings. Increasingly, the private and public sectors formulate and implement decisions at some distance (both geographically and socially) from the people and communities affected.

As our population shifts and interests become diverse, structures that deal with various segments of life become more specialized. Interest rather than geography may be the real basis for many self-help projects.

4. Much CD literature assumes that people know how to participate in civic affairs. This literature has spawned strategies based on the assumption that if people are aware, they will participate in attempting to create some sort of improvement. The charge of apathy is often leveled at people because of their lack of involvement. It is important to recognize that people may be aware of situations needing attention but may have come to the conclusion that they cannot affect the situation. Hence they choose not to waste their time and effort.

In many cases a basic tenet—to start where the people are—may be applied to helping people see how they can make a difference. Practitioners need to develop methods and skills in such areas as analysis and action research through which people can visualize how they can take effective action. Close attention should be given to developing avenues for participation in ways viewed as safe or as having an acceptable risk factor. Many CD practitioners have worked with people who expressed interest or willingness to become involved but pled noninterest when asked to assume a leadership role. Lack of interest may have been given as an excuse to cover fear of failure based on lack of knowledge, skill, or confidence.

For the self-help approach to be effective, it may be necessary for CD workers to concentrate on helping people learn to participate in different arenas, using unfamiliar procedures and skills. Effective participation is necessary for self-help to occur, since it is the participation of people learning to do for themselves that distinguishes the self-help approach from others that assume people must be directed.

5. A basic value and belief of community development is that "people

have the right to participate in decisions which have an effect upon their well-being" (Littrell 1971, p. 4). Do not assume that all people share this value. Rather, some citizens may see as a threat the efforts of others formulating plans for their own betterment. Citizens making plans for others may sincerely feel that they know what is best, even while excluding the others from the planning process on the basis of sex, race, creed, age, class, level of income, or other equally invalid criteria. Littrell's ideal that "participation in public decision-making should be free and open to all interested persons" (1971, p. 9) is still not always met. Keeping a decision-making system open is not easy and people must perceive it to be open if it is in fact to be open. The CD worker's role is to raise questions about who will be affected, and how, in order to ensure that different points of view are included in the process. Workers will be opposed to situations and structures that limit or prevent citizen input. However, this opposition may engender conflict with existing structures.

6. Early self-help literature implied that by bringing people together to discuss their various concerns, agreement will be reached and plans of action will be made and implemented in relatively harmonious fashion. The philosophy of self-help includes the principle that people will support what they have helped create, but the opposite also tends to be true: If people have not had an opportunity to have a role in defining an issue, they will have a higher probability of nonsupport and may even oppose what has been developed.

Over the long run the self-help approach is greatly enhanced when carried out in a setting where all points of view can be expressed. Open discussions may seem to slow the process; but unless diverse points are considered, conflict can impede or prevent effective action. Too often the literature does not include details and negative aspects of self-help practice. The techniques and assumptions, the miscues, the settings and procedures, the theoretical guidelines are not reported. The length of time necessary to deal with a situation is not detailed. For the quality of community development practice to improve, more information is needed to consider and test these companion notions.

Policy Development as Self-Help

Self-help approaches have often been treated as activities to respond to specific needs. Policy formation, on the other hand, establishes the general direction a community will go. Thus, input into policy formation has great potential as part of the self-help approach for the future. Policy formation can place people in an initiating rather than a responding stance. Policy formation at the local, area, state, and national levels is not new, but the idea that people can learn to interact with various units of government to form policy at all levels is a somewhat new, exciting, and largely unexplored aspect of self-help.

Policy formation is often treated as a role of government agencies and large private firms rather than as a function of citizens interacting with various units of government or other organizations. What has been overlooked is that people can be influential in setting overall guidelines for various units of government to utilize in day-to-day functioning. Through the political process they can create policy and then monitor and enforce the policy's implementation. For example, many towns, rural areas, and cities are rethinking their growth policy. In many cases citizens' groups have played major roles in determining if the area will actively seek growth, no growth, or some point between. Likewise, in many urban areas school systems have been forced to change operational procedures and allocations as a result of organized citizen input. In some areas the court systems are being used by people to ensure their role in the formation of civic policy. In fact, many self-help strategies in recent years have used litigation as a basic tool.

CONCLUSION

The self-help approach to community development is actually a simple concept: People have the basic right and ability to come together and to form appropriate structures and procedures for the settings in which they must or choose to function. By working together they can create the conditions they consider to be desirable. Then "people can become meaningful participants in a developmental process and have considerable control over the process" (Littrell 1971, p. 3).

One of the basic tasks of community development is to help people learn how to operationalize the concept of self-help using democratic ideology and procedures. The people who are affected by or interested in an issue, a problem, a dilemma, or a concern should have an actual opportunity to participate in its resolution.

REFERENCES

Batten, T. R. 1957. *Communities and Their Development: An Introductory Study with Special Reference to the Tropics.* London: Oxford Univ. Press.

_____. 1967. *The Non-Directive Approach in Group and Community Work.* London: Oxford Univ. Press.

Bennett, Austin E. 1969. Reflections on community development education, Bull. 576. Orono: University of Maine, Northeast Reg. Ext. Public Aff. Comm.

Biddle, William, and Loureide Biddle. 1965. *The Community Development Process: The Rediscovery of Local Initiative.* New York: Holt, Rinehart & Winston.

Lackey, Katherine. 1960. Community development through university extension. Community Dev. Publ. 3. Carbondale: Southern Illinois University.

Littrell, Donald W. 1971. Theory and practice of community development, MP 184. Columbia: University of Missouri, Ext. Div. Publ.

Task Force Report to ECOP. 1975. Community development concepts, curriculums, and training needs, MP 424. Columbia: University of Missouri.

UN Document E/CN5/91. 1959. Programme of concerted practical action in the social field of the United Nations and specialized agencies. New York.

The Conflict Approach

Jerry W. Robinson, Jr.

INTRODUCTION

Why a chapter on the confrontation approach? While most community development work may be viewed as planned social change, it often involves or leads to conflict. Not all planned community change is led by self-help or technical assistance agents. Some professionals advocate the use of conflict as purposeful social intervention (Alinsky 1969, 1972*b*).

Conflict seems to be increasing in our modern world. It is international and inevitable (Hornstein et al. 1971). Countries that espouse free enterprise, freedom of the press, freedom of speech, freedom of assembly, and the right to dissent shall certainly continue to have conflict (Kriesberg 1973). Democracies are built on the foundation of an *adversary* system, and conflict is seen as having more good than evil (Coser 1971). Also, a widening economic gap between the developed and developing nations of the world and a scarcity of resources leads to conflict. A chapter on the conflict approach to community development seems most appropriate.

DEFINITION OF SOCIAL CONFLICT

Social conflict is a behavior threat by one party directed at the territory—rights, interests, or privileges—of another party. The threat is usually directed toward limiting or eliminating one party's access to some resource or goal (Robinson 1972). In conflict the goals of opposing parties are incompatible. Group and individual behavior in conflict situations is *threatening* because one party seeks to attain its goals or to achieve its interest with enough behavioral intensity to limit the goal attainment of the other party. It takes two or more parties to have a "good" fight.

Policies, goals, and values define rights, interests, and privileges in our society. All groups and individuals do not share commitments to common policies, goals, or values. One group may favor the development of a nuclear power plant and another may oppose it. One group may favor zoning, daylight saving time, strip-mining for coal, or organic farming, and another may oppose each. Because their goals and values are incompatible and feelings are strong, the respective groups are likely to encounter conflict.

While values are always important in conflict situations, the essence of a conflict is the *behavior threat*. Behavior threats are prompted by values and goals and directed toward policy change. Robin M. Williams (in Robinson and Clifford 1977, p. 220) writes that conflict can be studied as a "process of concrete events occurring in real time and space—not as a set of cultural patterns." Conflict does not become conflict *until* someone does something. This approach is highly operational in conflict management–resolution scenes. One cannot manage the feelings, frustrations, values, and goals of others; but one may be able to redirect or exert some control over behavior of others in conflict (Rubin and Brown 1975). If one is able to redirect behavior, one can begin to reshape the course of a conflict (see Fig. 6.1).

Conflict and Territory

Often conflict can be divided into tangible, concrete, specific parts. Then it can be analyzed and simplified in terms of behavior directed at territory. Almost everyone is familiar with traditional conflicts over land use, civil rights, and religious beliefs. How do these relate to territory? The explanation lies in viewing territory as more than physical or spatial. Humans have a need for space, but why do they define the space or place called home with such sentiment (Ardrey 1971)? One explanation can be found in a wider interpretation of territoriality.

Territory has a psychological dimension (Robinson and Clifford 1977). Psychological territory is based on personal values and beliefs, on individual privileges, or even on the myths that one believes. One's beliefs do not have to be "correct" in order to be real. Myths by definition are not true, but belief in them is real. People own their beliefs just as they own an idea, a city lot, or a piece of furniture. Examples of psychological territory are beliefs in the superiority of one nation or one race over another, that abortion is murder, or that one religion is better than another. Trying to change, destroy, or "take beliefs away" from some people can cause much conflict.

Conflict also occurs because of threats to social territory, i.e., society's role expectations and organization's job descriptions. If these "territories" are threatened, conflict develops. For example, certain places are just naturally reserved for "special" people at the dinner table, at church, in the parking lot, in the office, and even in the job market (although such discrimination in the job market is illegal). Since the ERA movement gained momentum many examples of social conflict have occurred in communities where women have moved into roles formerly occupied by men. To invade another person's space is regarded as socially inappropriate and it may be the precipitating event to a confrontation.

Psychological, social psychological, and physical territory are not mu-

Fig. 6.1.   An operational model of social conflict.

tually exclusive. Unique values, goals, and policies are related to how people view certain symbols in our society (Sherif et al. 1961). Territoriality is an example of how values, goals, and policies are intertwined in conflict situations and how conflict can be analyzed in terms of tangible behavior or intangible beliefs. If one analyzes a community conflict in terms of territoriality, one may be able to deal with it effectively. It facilitates an understanding of conflict in terms of emotional and rational issues and helps in understanding what the problem is and who is causing it. For example, the burning of biology textbooks at a local high school can be analyzed in terms of strong commitment to social and psychological territories, conflicts over roles of the family and the school, and who has the right to teach "certain" information to children. Sometimes the values, goals, and policies underlying a conflict are objective and highly rational; other times conflicts are charged with emotions and irrational behavior.

In brief, community conflict involves two or more parties with incompatible goals that relate to specific value attachments. The behavior of one party is threatening to the goals and territory of the other party, and the two parties compete with varying levels of interest and power. The relative power of the opposing parties is the key issue. The alternatives for resolution vary. Few resolutions please *all* persons associated with both sides of a conflict because of strong value attachments.

CONFLICT AND VALUES

The value orientation of supporters of a conflict strategy is quite contrary to the normative neutrality espoused by the professional using the self-help or nondirective CD approach. Normative principles are essential for advocates of social conflict. In many cases it is impossible to be neutral (Blizek and Cederblom 1973; Laue and Cormick 1978). Community conflict involves planned and unplanned strategies and awakes both emotional and rational responses (Alinsky 1972*b*). Persons causing or using conflict make no pretense at being value-free (Leas and Kittlaus 1973). The desired change is regarded as good as or better than the status quo. Advocates using a conflict strategy are goal directed as are agents of planned social change. They see conflict as good for the community or for themselves.

Functions of Conflict: Positive and Negative

Perhaps we can begin to understand conflict better by listing several of its functions. Coser (1971) in his classic work summarized six functions of conflict in society.

1. Conflict permits internal dissension and dissatisfaction to rise to the surface and enables a group to restructure itself or deal with dissatisfactions.

2. Conflict provides for the emergence of new norms of appropriate behavior by surfacing shortcomings.

3. Conflict provides means of ascertaining the strength of current power structures.

4. Conflict may work to strengthen boundaries between groups—distinctiveness of groups.

5. Conflict has the effect of creating bonds between loosely structured groups—unifying dissident and unrelated elements.

6. Conflict works as a stimulus to reduce stagnation. Conflict may alter society.

Conflict has positive and negative effects on organizational groups and individuals. A summary of these effects is seen in Fig. 6.2.

A conflict usually begins with the basic premise that there should be a different distribution of some type of benefits in society and that one group of individuals should have a more equitable opportunity to maximize their potential. Advocates of conflict believe that subjugation of people to the status quo is wrong. Conflict, contrary to some other movements in a community, usually involves the powerless versus the powerful. However, the powerless may not be deeply enough involved or skillful enough to proclaim their needs. They may not have the time, skill, or motivation to implement and maintain an effective program of conflict. One author writes that community development is often used as a pacifier in the hopes of avoiding conflict and disagreeable agitation and that most CD efforts avoid issues of the

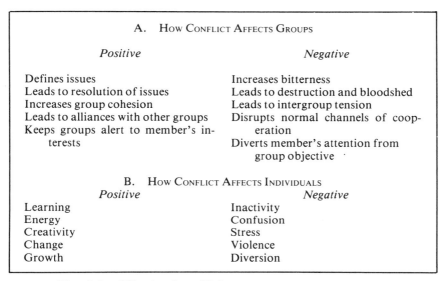

Fig. 6.2.   Effects of conflicts.

distribution of benefits (Erasmus 1968). Instead they work for the continued efficient functioning of the status quo.

While most community developers are familiar with the science of change and much is written about it, few write about the science of conflict as a planned process. Perhaps the emotional value orientation and action stance of conflict prohibit this involvement. Community developers might profit considerably by a more careful study of the work of political scientists in community disputes and political change. Careful study of the basic values of justice, freedom, and improvement might cause community developers to understand that conflicts are often justified, good, and even desirable before progress can occur.

TYPES OF CONFLICTS

Community confrontations come in all sorts, shapes, and sizes (Coleman 1957). Most conflicts are struggles for power and are related to justice and freedom. Some confrontations involve external forces against internal community forces. Such conflicts may be induced by court struggles or other efforts that attempt to force a community to comply with the values or changes in the society. Struggles over equal employment opportunity for minorities is a classic example of external versus internal community conflict.

Some conflicts arise from disputes within the community that are precipitated because of disagreement between local individuals in key power positions. Two leaders may disagree on an important issue. If their feelings are strong and concessions are not made soon, the conflict can quickly escalate into a community problem (Walton 1969). Issues such as the restoration or removal of a decaying building with a rich cultural heritage might be a problem. A powerful old-timer may wish to preserve the building while a newcomer, who is active in developing off-street parking in the downtown, may lead a coalition of opposition.

Personal conflicts often lead to conflicts between and within organizations and/or special interest groups. In the above example, it is easy to see how a chapter of a local historical society or the Daughters of the American Revolution might become an advocate for preserving the old building, while a committee of businesspersons with a mission to develop off-street parking would lead a campaign to get rid of the "old eyesore." However, not all organizational conflicts involve different organizations. Some involve actors within one organization; i.e., the business community may be divided on downtown renovation versus the development of a suburban shopping center.

CAUSES OF COMMUNITY CONFLICTS

Social and technological change in societies with a democratic form of government facilitates competition and promotes the adversary system. Change is inevitable and the conflicts preceding or following it are related to the reallocation of resources or the redistribution of power. However, other factors contribute to conflict, because some communities tend to have more conflicts than others. Why? What are the factors precipitating community conflicts?

Community diversity seems to be a contributing factor (Kriesberg 1973). Increased economic differentiation and changes in the population composition lead to heterogeneous values. These factors add to community diversity and increase the likelihood that disagreements will occur over territoriality.

Existing splits or cleavages in the community are another important cause of conflict (Miller and Preston 1973). Sometimes opposing power structures seem to be seeking out an issue over which to have a big fight. In some communities a residue of past experiences can be brought to the front on almost any issue. This may especially be the case in political struggles.

Coleman (1957) writes that significant and unique events are often the sources of conflicts. If an event such as the location of a new industry or retirement home touches an important aspect of the lives of enough people in a community and if it affects different power groups in the community in different ways, then conflict is likely to occur.

Another factor contributing to conflict is the presence of a leadership group with enough skill and feeling to gain support from local groups for its point of view (Leas and Kittlaus 1973). If it can develop a feeling of suspicion or fear, the conflict may be on the road to becoming a widespread community issue.

A final factor leading to disputes is a feeling of dissatisfaction among a group of constituents large enough to take some action (Alinsky 1972a). When the community's power structure ignores the interest of a minority, conflicts are likely to occur. Coleman (1957) writes that revolts against a power group tend to follow the following pattern:

1. The administration in power becomes the defendant.
2. A few activists become continual oppositionists and opportunists.
3. A large silent inactive group exists that does not necessarily support the administration.
4. An active group supports the administration.
5. The large, passive group (silent majority) becomes active.
6. The active oppositionists use the hostile atmosphere to promote their ideology and gain their ends.

In essence, through this process community conflicts are escalated, opponents become enemies, and disagreement leads to the development of antagonism. We shall now describe the escalation of conflicts in terms of a conflict cycle.

CONFLICT STAGES

Community conflicts usually follow predictable stages or steps (Kriesberg 1973). They begin with a threat, then progress to tension development, role dilemma, injustice collecting, confrontation and/or adjustment (Robinson 1978). Each of these stages is defined and illustrated (see Fig. 6.3).

The conflict process begins when one party feels strongly enough about an issue to make a *threat* directed at the territory—interest, rights, or privileges—of another party. If the threat is strong and the issues are clear, some community members may choose sides at this stage. Others may delay until additional information is available or pressure is applied. Sometimes threats are strong enough to cause community residents to experience fear or *tension development*. Peabody (1971) writes that *the fear caused by a threat is worse* than the actual conflict event itself.

Role dilemma follows tension development. Community residents and organizational leaders ask, What is expected? With whom should we agree? Shall we take sides? (Deutsch 1958). While asking such questions they seek out information and expectations regarding changes in policy, goals, and values (Leas and Kittlaus 1973). If the issues are clear, positions and roles are taken. If issues are unclear, the response may be withdrawal and/or testing behavior. The parties may seek to determine what actions they can take and how ''far they can go'' without being associated with either side in the

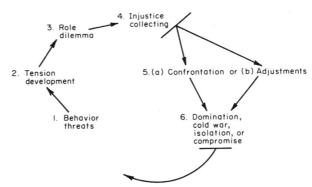

Fig. 6.3.   Steps in the conflict cycle.

conflict. Sides are usually taken by the time this stage ends. The community may become polarized and new organizations with partisan positions may appear. Often these new organizations lead to the emergence of new leaders. Conflict has a strange way of bringing out latent skills in some community residents.

Injustice collecting follows role dilemma and its arrival is easily identifiable. All conflicts do not progress at the same rate, so injustice collecting may occur soon after threats are made or it may take some time for the conflict to gain enough momentum for strong feelings to be expressed. During injustice collecting the adversaries become polarized further through a process of name-calling, innuendo, and taking public positions. Information and emotion are directed toward weakening the position of the opponent. This information is, or can be, emotional and rational or irrational; it may include accurate or inaccurate data. Some parties in a conflict seem to remember all previous negative experiences. They seek to weaken their adversary by itemizing or mentioning any previous injustices that come to mind, by name-calling, and sometimes by revenge. When feelings are strong they may be publicized in newspapers, on the radio, or on television.

Unfortunately, when one party seeks to use injustices, the other party tends to reciprocate. Coleman (1957) writes about the tendencies for injustice collecting to reinforce negative responses in community actors. This behavior leads to rigid polarization. In essence, injustice collecting intensifies a conflict, reinforces negative behavior, and encourages dysfunctional criticism in all parties. This led Sir Thomas Gresham to develop what he called the law of conflict:

The harmful and dangerous elements drive out those which would keep the conflict within bounds; reckless and unrestrained leaders head the attack; violent organizations arise to replace pre-existing or moderate organizations; derogatory and inflammatory charges replace discussions; solving the issue becomes secondary to winning, to putting down the opponent. [J. Coleman 1957, p. 14]

Some conflicts move from injustice collecting to *confrontation* (see Fig. 6.3). Others move to a stage of adjustment. When adversaries in a conflict see each other as enemies, they are likely to resolve the conflict through a face-to-face confrontation. People do not force conflicts to confrontation unless they have very strong feelings regarding the issue of the fight and feel they will win through a confrontation. Severe outcomes are possible from any confrontation where either party is extremely aggressive. Violent confrontations often lead to the destruction of property, to the usurpation of rights and interests of citizens of the community, and to permanent cleavages (Hornstein et al. 1971). Severe confrontations tend to reinforce the belief among some people that conflict is always bad.

The final stage is the *adjustment process*. Because all conflicts do not develop into violent confrontations, some conflicts may move quickly from the role dilemma stage to an adjustment stage. There are at least four adjustments to conflict: domination, cold war, withdrawal or isolation, and compromise (Robinson and Clifford 1977). While compromise may be regarded as a positive solution, domination, cold war, and isolation can have negative or positive effects depending on the opposing parties, the issue, and the feelings the parties have toward the particular adjustment.

Domination occurs as an adjustment when the party with the most power imposes a solution. Because of superior social, economic, or political strength, the weaker party is forced to "give in." Domination tends to be a temporary form of adjustment to many conflicts. Since the weak party has no alternative but to comply, the conflict may reappear as soon as strength is gained.

Cold war is another adjustment, especially when the "solution" is *not* acceptable to either party (Kriesberg 1973). Cold war is a temporary adjustment. The contending parties continue to weaken each other through innuendo and injustice collecting. Cold war occurs when: (1) the parties seem to be of equal power, (2) change would mean that they would have to surrender territory and power and lose face in the community, and (3) both parties see the change as a severe compromise. Parties in a cold war may find themselves in a hot war any minute.

Withdrawal or *isolation* occurs because some parties dislike disputes. Withdrawal is often a temporary adjustment of the weaker party to avoid losing face (psychological lynching). Isolation occurs when the "solution" to the conflict is intolerable to the weaker party—the stronger party is avoided because the "solution" imposed is more unbearable than isolation. Isolation is not permanent. It may end when the weaker party gains strength in numbers, in economic power, or in confidence (Miller and Preston 1973).

Compromise is generally regarded as the healthy, functional adaptation to community conflict if issues are negotiable (Kriesberg 1973). However, compromise is not managed easily, because compromise requires new definitions of territories. It redefines policies, goals, and sometimes even values. Compromise is achieved through persuasion—direct and indirect—or through an inducement and reward system that involves negotiation and bargaining (Rubin and Brown 1975). For a compromise to occur, both parties must be committed to a dialogue process (Deutsch et al. 1967). They must possess enough trust in that process and in themselves to communicate openly about aspects important to them in the negotiation process (Deutsch 1958). In some cases, much time is required. A third party may be necessary for the development of an acceptable compromise (Leas and Kittlaus 1973).

FACTORS AFFECTING CONFLICTS

Every conflict is unique. Community structure, leader skill, attitudes of community residents, the degree of discontent, the possibility for solution, requests for assistance, the presence of a mediator, and the problem itself are among the important factors that influence the conflict process (Coleman 1957; Deutsch 1973; Kriesberg 1973).

Community leaders shape controversies through their skills and attitudes. They may have the ability to remain calm in the midst of the developing turbulence and to carefully co-opt the leadership of the opposition in some situations. They may be skillful at using their authority to suppress or direct the opposition. When power brokers are able to translate a conflict into tangible and specific terms that are relevant and understandable by community residents, they enhance their control. When leaders manifest confidence and act with deliberate purpose they exhibit control that wins sentiment for their position.

The social structure of a community helps shape conflict (Warren 1974). The nature and strength of the predominant groups and the type of associational networks that exist help influence the nature and the outcome. The issue may not be important to the socioeconomic situation or it may be extremely important. If the conflict is seen as being initiated by outsiders (big government or big industry) who oppose grass roots leadership, the conflict is likely to have a strong local base. A local organizational structure is more likely to emerge to fight outsiders than to fight insiders.

When people are frustrated about something and discontent is high, conflicts escalate. The frustration may be caused by social or economic injustice and is closely tied to ideology (Hornstein et al. 1971). Participation in conflicts is intense when the controversy touches the important territories of a number of people in the community. Civil rights movements among blacks in the sixties is one example. When the ideology of equal opportunity led to attacks of discrimination in jobs, voting, and housing, the civil rights movement gained momentum and local protests emerged with force.

Specific issues help generate support; solutions must be realistic and achievable. Some conflicts occur where injustice is felt and no solution is perceived. Unless resources are available in the community to help people obtain jobs, housing, etc., the discontent is not likely to be channeled into planned action programs. When injustice is linked with realistic possibilities for change, success of a confrontation is enhanced.

Another factor affecting the course of a conflict is whether the leader of the conflict group that is advocating change comes from within the community, is invited to the community, or comes unsponsored as an outside agitator. If change is to have a long-term effect, the desire and major leadership for it must come from the community group seeking the change (Alinsky 1972b). If change comes through an outside agitator, it will disappear when the outsider leaves.

The presence of an intervenor or mediator also influences the nature and solution of a conflict. If the intervenor comes in at the request of both parties in the dispute, that person's actual presence in and of itself is a factor that generates pressure for dialogue and solution.

ETHICS AND STRATEGIES IN COMMUNITY CONFLICTS

A CD agent may be asked to assist a special interest group (businesspersons) who seek advice on the effect of mobile home locations on property values. Answers to this question may take time; zoning hearings may be involved. Mobile homes may be the *only* housing option for some low- income people in the community. Some landowners may oppose mobile homes, while others promote them. What should the agent's role be? What are the ethical considerations for the CD agent? Basic issues for the CD professional are raised by issues like this and some argue that neutrality in any form of development is a myth. The nondirective self-help approach appears to ignore many ethical issues, while the conflict approach uses ethical questions to formulate discontent and change (Alinsky 1969). In fact, a primary purpose of conflict may be to apply pressure on power centers to change the ideological position of those in power (Hornstein et al. 1971).

Ethical Issues

What ethical principles shall the change-conflict agent follow? Laue and Cormick (1978, pp. 217–18) suggest that the professional should ask:

Does the intervention contribute to the ability of relatively powerless individuals and groups in the situation to determine their own destinies to the greatest extent consistent with the common good?

They contend that humans are ends in themselves and ought to be treated as such. Involvement in community disputes is appropriate if it contributes to the achievement of three basic values:

1. *Empowerment:* a requisite condition for individuals and groups to achieve the desired end-state of society—justice.

2. *Justice:* a prerequisite to the maximum attainment of freedom by all individuals in the system.

3. *Freedom:* the condition that makes possible responsible choices from a number of options and the ability to live with the consequences of those decisions, thereby realizing the deepest form of meaning.

Freedom is essential for meaning. Justice is the ultimate social good, and empowerment for *all* is essential before groups and individuals can achieve freedom and justice (Laue and Cormick 1978, pp. 218–19). Laue and Cormick state that "empowerment, justice, and freedom are ends in themselves so long as all individuals and groups are equipped to advocate their interests to similar degrees."

Strategies

The strategy used in conflict situations is determined by one's value orientation toward conflict as a viable process for change. If conflict is seen as a functional social process, one is likely to be committed to it as a useful tool to achieve the change desired. If it is seen as a threat to the system or to the stability of the social and economic order, one is likely to oppose it and regard it as "bad" for the community. Thus, the basic strategies regarding conflict are to utilize it, to prevent it, and to manage or resolve it. Frameworks supporting the strategy for each orientation toward conflict are discussed.

Utilizing Conflict: Some Basic Rules of Thumb

Proponents of the conflict approach often desire to disrupt the social, economic, or political systems of a community. Advocates of conflict represent the disenfranchised elements—elements that lack economic or political power. Their position and "cause" represent that of a minority. Almost everyone who is involved in the political arena uses conflict. Conflict is seen as the only effective technique to change, so a strategy for agitation is planned.

One conflict approach that gained popularity during the fifties and sixties in the United States was associated with the leadership of Saul Alinsky and his Chicago-based "conflict school." This section draws heavily on his work (1969, 1972*b*) and on the works of Ross (1955), Kahn (1970), Coser (1971), Collins (1975), and Coleman (1957). While the discussion does not directly follow any one of these particular authors, it comes closest to representing the efforts of Alinsky.

Step 1. Appraise the local leadership. The first task of a conflict agent invited into a community is to appraise the indigenous leadership. Conflict leaders must have the ability of seeing the community as it is and have the vision to see what it could become. This vision must be both practical and communicable. Other characteristics desired of indigenous leaders are tact, courage, enthusiasm, and hard work.

The conflict agent must identify and involve individuals who can form an effective leadership team. Such effective power will not be found in one person but in a small group who can work together to effect change. One individual will probably be the spokesperson for the group and must manifest tact, enthusiasm, and courage in confronting the power structure. Other individuals will organize the daily details. Leaders must check that everything is done at the right time, in the right sequence, and with the necessary resources.

Step 2. Analyze the community power structure. The confrontation approach, to a greater extent than any other method of social action, focuses squarely on power. Power is the name of the game and is defined as the capacity to mobilize resources for the accomplishment of intended effects (Clark 1968). Other approaches work from the perspective of legitimization, that is, they get approval of proposed projects or objectives before initiating them. The conflict approach is concerned with the redistribution of benefits. It implies a confrontation between those who have and those who have not. Power structures of local communities and the decision-making process to be found therein manifest a wide range of variation; the pattern taken by the power structure in a particular community is a function of the kind of political life to be found in that community. The greater the number of elected positions and the greater the extent of public participation in the electoral process, the greater the dispersion of power among various groups.

Step 3. Analyze the situation and territoriality. Before suggesting tactics or approaches to change, a conflict agent must understand the types of people and groups within the community and their past grievances, conflicts, and areas of consensus. The complex territorialities that exist within the community, the social interaction of various community institutions, and the psychological ties that community members have to the entity called the community also must be comprehended. Essentially four components must be taken into account: (1) people, (2) geographical boundaries, (3) organizational interdependence, and (4) psychological ties. Such community analysis can help one understand where allies can be obtained, which issues could be brought into the subsequent confrontation, which groups need to be neutralized, and what types of actions would be most effective.

Step 4. Stimulate dissidents to voice grievances. A problem does not exist until people define it as such. Bringing people together to articulate their discontent creates motivation for action and helps individuals realize that their feelings of frustration are not isolated but shared by others. Such knowledge encourages them to realize shared consciousness in their plight. Power for the poor segment of society can be found only in numbers. As people get together to voice their discontent, the amplification of their frustration becomes an effective confrontation tool. The more people that share in the issue, the more likely results will occur. It is difficult for even a highly motivated small group to achieve change unless their sentiments and objectives are shared by a large segment of the community population.

Step 5. Define "a" problem. Social action, to be effective, most focus on a single issue. Such an issue may have many secondary implications, but all efforts focus on a *single* problem. It is particularly important at this time to hit at the heart of the problem, to focus on causes and not symptoms or solutions.

Step 6. Organize, organize, organize. Conflict agents usually work with clientele outside the power structure. They may work with poor people's organizations or low-income clientele. Thus, common organizational tactics have to be modified accordingly. Kahn (1970) comments that the key value in decision making within poor people's organizations is not efficiency but participation. He suggests that the time required to reach a decision is the amount of time it takes to educate all the members in the meaning of decision and to involve them in the decision-making process.

A major problem in managing a conflict is size. To be effective and to allow people to participate, the size of the working organizational structure must be relatively small. To accomplish this, it is often necessary to break down larger units into smaller localized subgroups. It is important to understand that low-income people tend to be skeptical of well-organized formal types of meetings and organizations. While *Robert's Rules of Order* may be helpful for some in promoting general participation in decision making, organizational meetings should be kept as informal and small as possible.

Step 7. Demonstrate the value of power. People outside the power structure are skeptical of their ability to move the power structure. They have neither power, money, property, nor influence. But as Alinsky notes, they do have numbers. They have the power of people. They must learn to perceive early in the planning process the value of a large number of people working together. It is equally important that the first demonstration of power should succeed. This will help the clientele realize the power they do have, the possibilities of using it, and the possibility of success in exercising their power in numbers. Alinsky (1972*b*, pp. 127–30) lists the following 13 power tactics for confrontation in his book, *Rules for Radicals:*

1. Power is not only what you have but what the enemy thinks you have.
2. Never go outside the experience of your people.
3. Whenever possible go outside the experience of the enemy.
4. Make the enemy live up to their own book of rules.
5. Ridicule is man's most potent weapon.
6. A good tactic is one your people enjoy.
7. A tactic that drags on too long becomes a drag.

8. Keep the pressure on.

9. A threat is usually more terrifying than the thing itself.

10. The major premise for tactics is the development of an operation that will maintain a constant pressure on the opposition.

11. If you push a negative hard and deep enough, it will break through into its counterside.

12. The price of a successful attack is a constructive alternative.

13. Pick your target, freeze it, personalize it, polarize it.

Step 8. Never confront the power structure directly. When people unite on a single issue they can present a rather impressive front of power. But it is by no means greater than the traditional exercise of power through money, property, and influence. In any battle, if a smaller army attacks a larger army head-on, inevitably the smaller army loses. In confrontation, as in military science, one tries to outflank the enemy. In the Back of the Yards of Chicago, Alinsky organized the meat-packing workers, not to confront directly the meat barons but to put pressure on the banks that made loans to the meat barons.

Step 9. Be realistic, compromise. It is very important that workers for change do not become stymied on minor issues or technicalities. The major issue must always be kept in perspective and the goal of people as ends within themselves must always be kept foremost in mind. Minor issues and the means of achieving these goals are a secondary consideration. Alinsky (1972*b,* pp. 24–25) listed eleven principles relevant to his means-ends controversy:

1. Only people from a distance moralize about means-ends.

2. Judgment about means-ends depends on the political position of those sitting in judgment.

3. In war—the end justifies any means.

4. Judgment must be made in reference to the time, not independent of it.

5. Concern with ethics increases with the number of means available and vice versa.

6. The relative importance of the end affects ethics in choosing means.

7. Possibility of success or failure greatly affects ethical choices.

8. Morality of means depends on whether the means is being employed at a time of imminent defeat or imminent victory.

9. Any effective means is automatically judged by the opposition as being unethical.

10. You do what you can with "what you have" and clothe it with moral garments.

11. Goals must be paraphrased in honorifics.

The credibility of these principles must be weighed against the basic values of justice, freedom, and empowerment discussed earlier.

Step 10. Develop permanent organizational structure. Various tactics are exercised to achieve the stated goal. Emphasis should be put on establishing an organization comprising all the various subgroups that can function effectively once the change agent leaves the community. This organization serves three purposes: (1) It allows one to avoid backlash from the power structure once the change has been achieved. (2) It helps one avoid Gresham's law of conflict in the breaking down of the change through radical unplanned efforts. (3) It provides for a group to carry on in the absence of the change agent.

Step 11. Begin again. Once the stated objective has been achieved the clientele need an evaluation to determine what other changes they could realistically attempt in order to better their life situation. At this stage, the conflict agent will help the indigenous leaders assess their situation, assess what they have achieved, and assess where they might go from here. The agent's intentions of leaving the community should be reaffirmed. It is probably best if the agent phases out of the community picture as quietly as possible, leaving the administration and the recognition to the indigenous leaders. The experiences derived from the exercise of planning change through conflict should provide local community organizations with the confidence and ability to carry on in the future.

Preventing Community Conflicts

Prevention strategies tend to be used primarily by the power structure, which has a vested interest in maintaining the status quo or in promoting a change in such a manner as to not disrupt the status quo. Some of the strategies used by the conflict agent may be used also by the preventer—organization, planning, etc. However, other tactics may be used by preventers who seek to work quietly and with great subtlety to keep an issue from becoming a conflict. This section presents some basic strategies that are used to prevent community conflicts. The reader must be cautioned about the success of prevention strategies. Community conflict is not easily stopped. It may be suppressed for a while or temporarily neutralized, but once a community conflict gains momentum it tends to run its course through the stages in the conflict cycle.

The basic problem with the prevention of conflict is timing. The sooner action is taken to prevent an issue from moving past the role dilemma stage of the conflict cycle, the better. Delaying action gives a dispute time to gain strength and support and provides opportunity for differing opinions to be solidified. Efforts at preventing conflicts are almost futile if an intervenor does not appear *before* the injustice phase of the conflict cycle arrives.

What are some tactics that can be used to prevent a conflict? Rosemary Caffarella (in Robinson 1978, pp. R-1–R-6) suggests the following: fragmentation, co-optation, outside expertise, education, and public relations.

Each of these tactics requires resources and skill and may have ethical problems. Each is operationalized in the following discussion.

Step 1. Fragment the conflict. Fragmentation involves reducing the proposed issue or project to a series of smaller components (Williams, in Robinson and Clifford 1977). These components may then be introduced to the community in an order of increasing significance. By ''piecemealing'' the relevant information, the nature of the total shock is reduced. The smaller components do not have the explosive effect that one big issue would have. For example, instead of introducing a plan for massive urban renewal with great economic and social expense, one might begin to talk about the problems of better housing for the poor, health hazards in the inner city, and how slums cost the city dollars in terms of tax revenue. In fragmentation, the big issue in a conflict is reduced to a small number of very tangible and manageable problems. The issue is reduced to rational, concrete terms and experiences that citizens can understand.

Step 2. Co-opt the leadership. Co-optation involves the redirection of the key leadership to another issue. Co-optation may have ethical connotations for the power structure that seeks to use it. When the power structure is using co-optation, it asks the key person or organization that is beginning to create a conflict in the community to serve on a study or planning committee to investigate the issue being debated and to report back to the established planning committee. Since this committee may be appointed by leaders in the power structure, the efforts of the opportunist can be redirected. When a report or suggestion for change occurs, it can be squelched or modified. It may seem that the establishment was the group that initiated the change, since they appointed the study committee.

Step 3. Employ outside experts who espouse established position. Experts who are critical consultants or national figures may be brought to a community to win over the opposition if they support your point of view and if the opposition holds the expert in high esteem. The power of the experts probably lies within the esteem held by the constituents rather than in their knowledge or information. Heroes, such as movie stars and professional athletes, are used frequently in advertising and political campaigns. They may be used in some community conflicts.

Step 4. Conduct an educational program. Education is a strategy often used by the establishment to prevent conflicts or to win over the opposition in a conflict. Educational programs are more effective when they are directed at specific issues or at individual and organizational policies and goals instead of values. Values change slowly. Policies and goals change before values change. Thus, educational programs are most effective when they are developed in pragmatic terms around a particular issue and/or project. However, education may not be as helpful as some believe. Power usually whips truth in conflict situations, especially in community controversy.

An educational program to be used in preventing conflict must be rational, unbiased, and directed at the individuals and organizations who question an issue. Effective educators in conflict situations are knowledgeable on the subject of interest, truthful, and fair. They must know the limitation of their information, be confident and tolerant in conflict situations, and be communicative.

Step 5. Implement a PR campaign. Another strategy that may be used to avoid a community conflict is a carefully devised public relations campaign. Some community conflicts begin when citizens read the headlines of their morning newspapers. The role of media and advertising in conflict (Coleman 1957) is important. Public relations involves the "selling" of a proposed project. It usually means the presentation of only the information that supports one side of an issue or project.

A good PR campaign uses all the prevention tactics. Outside experts may espouse the issue or project, educators may present programs on the benefits of the change, and any opposing leaders may be put to work (coopted) studying the impacts of the change. News releases and public meetings discuss the benefits of the proposed change in concrete, specific terms that are easily identifiable and within the realm of experience of the citizenry.

MANAGING COMMUNITY CONFLICTS: THIRD PARTY ROLE

Management of conflict is probably the most appropriate role for the CD professional. Since conflict is inevitable, coping with it creatively is essential. In recent years numerous agencies and organizations have been established to help community groups manage conflicts. Some of these are listed:

> Community Relations Service, U.S. Department of Justice
> Federal Mediation and Conciliation Service
> Institute of Mediation and Conflict Resolution, New York
> Community Disputes Services Division of the American Arbritration Association, New York
> Community Conflict Resolution Program, University of Missouri, St. Louis
> Center for Teaching and Research in Disputes Settlement, University of Wisconsin, Madison
> Department of Law, Justice, and Community Relations, United Methodist Church, Washington, D.C.
> Office of Environmental Mediation, University of Washington, Seattle

What criteria does one use to decide about becoming involved in a community dispute? The actions of the intervenor should contribute to the proportional empowerment of powerless groups for social change and promote the ability of the weaker parties to make their own best decisions. The rationale for an intervenor's decisions should be conscious, explicit, and public, without any claim to be neutral. Intervenors should not lend their skills to empowering groups who do not hold the values of empowerment, freedom, and justice for all peoples, regardless of race, sex, religion, or national origin. In fact, an intervenor should place a high value on working *against* such groups (see Laue and Cormick 1978, pp. 220–22).

Conflict intervenors are more effective when they can play third-party roles. As a third party, the mediator facilitates increased rationality in discussion, asking open-ended, nonjudging questions that require advocates to deal with their feelings and the issues in a conflict situation. Through this strategy the mediator facilitates the exploration of alternative adjustments and issues. The mediator assures that an open two-way system of communication exists; helps to regulate the psychological and social cost of a conflict; and helps to create an atmosphere whereby an individual or group can make a graceful retreat if desired, in order to change a position or withdraw. The mediator, at the earliest stage of a conflict management dialogue, helps the adversaries develop a set of ground rules of procedure and reinforces those norms. The mediator might help the adversaries secure additional resources (informative, economic, or physical) needed to manage a conflict.

Methods that can be used by a third party to manage conflict are coercion, contingent reward, and indirect persuasion. A third party using *coercion* must possess the power to enforce an adjustment to the conflict. A county zoning board member, who is impartial on a community issue about where to locate new low-income housing, may say to competing land developers and citizens. "If you people cannot agree on one location, *I will not* approve any request." The threat without power to implement it is meaningless.

The third party can use *contingent reward* in some situations, e.g., by giving approval to all efforts by both parties to accommodate. We are familiar with the use of bribes and incentives by adversaries in a conflict. Big business or big government may offer attractive awards to a community to squelch a conflict or gain a favor. Incentives can be used by third parties who are seeking to manage a community conflict.

Incentives may be extended to obtain accommodation from the adversaries. For example, an impartial county board member who is a third party may say, "If you will just stop fighting and get together on location about where to build the low-income housing, I will ask the county board to seek federal funds to provide low interest loans to the buyers of your houses." Incentives will appear to be bribes unless they are extended equally and fairly among all parties in a conflict.

Indirect Persuasion

The third party who uses coercion or contingent reward is likely to experience more difficulty in conflict management than the one who uses *indirect persuasion*. Rather than enforcing or buying an adjustment, the user of indirect persuasion facilitates the development of mutual accommodation and enforces agreed-upon rules of fair play. Instead of advocating a specific solution, the indirect persuader advocates dialogue and encourages the development and maintenance of a dialogue process. In essence, the user of indirect persuasion is an intervenor who is not an advocate for a particular party but for *both* parties, not an advocate for a particular outcome but for a process of discussion, negotiation, and adjustments. The goal of the indirect persuader is to mediate the conflict in such a way that both parties "win." A basic premise of indirect persuasion is that *community residents or adversaries are much more likely to support adjustments that they help to create.* Indirect persuasion facilitates the process of adversary involvement in solution building.

Third Party Qualifications

The mediator must understand the nature of conflict in order to help adversaries develop adjustments. The indirect persuader must be able to interpret conflict theoretically and operationally and have some understanding of group process and experience in working with groups. Mediators must be able to seek and accept feedback evaluation about the usefulness and effectiveness of their techniques and behavior on group action in the conflict situation. The ego of the third party must not be onstage in the outcome of conflict management dialogue. The role of the third party is regarded by some as similar to the role of a referee; the third party must be fair, alert, active, objective, skillful, decisive, insightful, and at times forceful.

Leas and Kittlaus espouse this position. In their insightful book, *Church Fights* (1973, pp. 65–67), they discuss the following as qualifications for an effective third party mediator (referee): (1) has a high degree of tolerance for ambiguity, ambivalence, and frustration; (2) is confident in conflict management and refereeing; (3) advocates process, sometimes firmly; (4) does not take sides on an issue; (5) does not take substantive conflict personally; (6) gives credit to all parties; and (7) is able to express and accept strong feelings.

Leas and Kittlaus (1973, pp. 67–72) list the following as third party assumptions: (1) conflict is inevitable and resolvable, (2) conformity is not required, (3) few situations are hopeless, (4) one party affects another, (5) each side has a piece of the truth, (6) there is some similarity between opponents, (7) present problems are the ones to solve, (8) the process is of great importance, and (9) there is no right answer.

SIX STEPS FOR MANAGING CONFLICT USING INDIRECT PERSUASION

Six steps or strategies (Robinson 1978) are used by a third party in indirect persuasion. These steps and appropriate substeps are outlined as follows:

   I. Initiate dialogue objectively.
      A. Introduce subject of process to all parties.
      B. Establish ground rules for everyone.
      C. Channel communication (use feedback—may have to dramatize it).
  II. Involve all parties.
      A. Question, stimulate.
      B. Listen actively.
      C. Accept credibility of feelings (avoid judging).
      D. Probe for causes of feelings.
 III. Assimilate feelings and information (use newsprint).
      A. Record, structure, and organize feelings.
      B. Record, structure, and organize facts.
      C. Record, structure, and organize agreements.
      D. Record, structure, and organize disagreements.
  IV. Reinforce agreements.
      A. Participants have right to agree or disagree.
      B. Feelings and expressions of them are real.
      C. Seek possible compromises.
      D. Suggest footnote solutions.
      E. Personalize alternative solutions in relation to benefits.
   V. Negotiate differences.
      A. Discover how each party feels about issues and why (see Step III A).
      B. Record, structure, and organize disagreement (see Step III D).
      C. Prioritize differences (get consensus) and begin with smallest problem.
      D. Seek adjustment on each issue.
         1. Seek alternatives from each party.
         2. Specify acceptable and unacceptable alternatives.
         3. Review and pursue adjustments.
      E. Process ground rules *for third party* at this step.
         1. Avoid solution giving.
         2. Remember to use feedback, timing, and reinforcement.
         3. Be sensitive to loss of face.
         4. Avoid threats.
  VI. Solidify agreements (adjustments).
      A. Review compromises suggested.
      B. Prepare contract summary.
      C. Check for accuracy of perceptions.
      D. Confirm areas of agreement and disagreement.
         1. Handshake or hug.
         2. Prepare and sign written contract.

Note that these steps are dependent, not mutually exclusive, and that adversaries cannot proceed to step V or VI until agreements are achieved on the first four steps.

These steps place the major responsibility for developing solutions on the adversary parties in conflict. Group consensus is more easily obtained through solution guiding than solution giving. Remember, people support adjustment they help create.

SUMMARY

This chapter presents an operational framework of the conflict approach to community development. Community conflict is given a behavioral definition; conflict usually involves a fight over social, psychological, and physical territory. Since conflict is not a value-free approach to community development, we discuss its uniqueness, the types of cooperation that may occur, its functions and causes, the conflict cycle, and factors affecting the outcome of a conflict. Three basic strategies for dealing with conflict are to (1) utilize it, (2) prevent it, or (3) manage it in a "how to do it" framework. The author leaves the selection of strategies to the readers and the situations that exist in their communities in their search for community development.

REFERENCES

Alinsky, Saul. 1969. *Reveille for Radicals*. New York: Random House, Vintage Books.
———. 1972*a*. Playboy interview. *Playboy* 19 (3):59.
———. 1972*b*. *Rules for Radicals*. New York: Random House, Vintage Books.
Ardrey, R. 1971. *The Territorial Imperative*. New York: Dell, pp. 3–4, 232–33.
Blizek, William L., and Jerry Cederblom. 1973. Community development and social justice. *Community Dev. Soc.* 4 (2):45–52.
Clark, Terry N. 1968. Community structure, decision-making, budget expenditures, and urban renewal in 51 American cities. *Am. Sociol. Rev.* 34:576–93.
Coleman, James S. 1957. *Community Conflict*. Glencoe, Ill.: Free Press.
Collins, Randall. 1975. *Conflict Sociology*. New York: Academic Press.
Coser, Lewis A. 1971. *The Functions of Social Conflict*. Glencoe, Ill.: Free Press.
Deutsch, Morton. 1958. Trust and suspicion. *J. Conflict Resolut.* 2:265–79.
———. 1973. *The Resolution of Conflict*. New Haven: Yale Univ. Press.
Deutsch, Morton; Y. Epstein; D. Canavan; and P. Gumpert. 1967. Strategies for inducing cooperation: An experimental study. *J. Conflict Resolut.* 11:345–60.
Erasmus, Charles. 1968. Community development and the encogido syndrome. *Hum. Organ.* 27 (1):65–74.
Hornstein, Harvey A.; Barbara Bunker; W. Warner Burke; Marion Gindes; and Ray J. Lewicki. 1971. *Social Intervention: A Behavioral Science Approach*. New York: Free Press.
Kahn, Si. 1970. *How People Get Power*. New York: McGraw-Hill.
Kriesberg, Louis. 1973. *The Sociology of Social Conflicts*. Englewood Cliffs, N.J.: Prentice-Hall.
Laue, James, and Gerald Cormick. 1978. The ethics of intervention in community disputes. In *The Ethics of Social Intervention,* Gordon Bermant, Herbert C. Kelman, and Donald Warwick, eds., pp. 205–32. New York: Wiley.

Leas, Speed, and Paul Kittlaus. 1973. *Church Fights: Managing Conflict in the Local Church.* Philadelphia: Westminster Press.

Likert, Rensis, and Jane Gibson Likert. 1976. *New Ways of Managing Conflict.* New York: McGraw-Hill.

Miller, Michael V., and James D. Preston. 1973. Vertical ties and the redistribution of power in Crystal City. *Social Sci. Q.* 53 (March):772–84.

Peabody, G. L. 1971. Power, Alinsky and other thoughts. In *Social Intervention: A Behavioral Science Approach,* Hornstein et al., eds., pp. 527–32. New York: Free Press.

Robinson, Jerry W., Jr. 1972. The management of conflict. *J. Community Dev. Soc.* 3 (2):100–105.

———. 1978. *A Conflict Management Training Program: A Leaders Guide for Extension Professionals.* Ithaca, N.Y.: Cornell University, Northeast Reg. Cent. Rural Dev.

Robinson, Jerry W., Jr., and Roy A. Clifford. 1977. Conflict management in community groups. Urbana: Univeristy of Illinois, Coop. Ext. Serv.

Ross, Murray G. 1955. *Community Organization: Theory and Principles.* New York: Harper & Brothers.

Rubin, Jeffrey Z., and Bert R. Brown. 1975. *The Social Psychology of Bargaining and Negotiations.* New York: Academic Press.

Sherif, O. J.; B. J. Harvey; W. R. Hood; and C. Sherif. 1961. Intergroup conflict and cooperation. Norman: Univ. Okla. Book Exch. pp. 151–86.

Walton, R. E. 1969. *Interpersonal Peacemaking: Confrontations and Third-Party Consultation.* Reading, Mass.: Addison-Wesley, pp. 1–7, 71–73.

Warren, Roland. 1974. *Community in America.* Chicago: Rand McNally.

Zurcher, Louis A., Jr., and Charles M. Bonjean, eds. 1970. *Planned Social Intervention.* Scranton, Pa.: Chandler.

Professional Roles

AN OVERVIEW / *Paul D. Warner*

If community development is the process whereby those in a community arrive at group decisions and take actions to improve their well-being, community developers are the professional workers who help these changes to come about. They are sometimes called change agents, planners, resource persons, educators, consultants, organizers, and various other titles. The roles of CD professionals are as varied as the groups they work with and the development strategies utilized.

This chapter presents an overall framework for understanding the role of the CD professional. Previous attempts to specify and categorize the different roles have usually centered on "what the person does" or on specific philosophies or strategies of development. In the first ten volumes of the *Journal of the Community Development Society,* at least six different classification schemes are presented. These typologies are helpful but they are limited in that most consider only a single criterion and often end in attempts to justify why one approach is superior to another.

It seems futile to attempt to refine the existing schemes without adding relevant criteria. Answering the question, What do CD professionals do? is not enough in itself. Other questions of importance include, What types of knowledge and skills do they possess? What organization or agency do they represent? Who is the clientele being served? The CD practitioner model presented here comprises the interrelationship of four elements: individual factors (I), organizational factors (O), task functions (T), and the nature of clientele being served (C).

$$\text{CD role} = f(I_{a,b,c,\ldots} \ O_{g,h,i,\ldots} \ T_{m,n,o,\ldots} \ C_{s,t,u,\ldots})$$

The CD professional's role thus is seen as a function of all four variables. Each of the four, in turn, represents a group of factors (*a, b, c,* . . .) that relates to the organization, the person, the task, and the clientele.

THE INDIVIDUAL

Each CD professional has a unique set of skills, experiences, and attitudes. These intellectual and personal characteristics are specific to the person and impact the role. It follows that a community organizer needs an educational and experience base in social organization and leadership, and a health planner needs to have technical knowledge of the field of health services and the planning process. These skills are obviously required for employment. In addition, the specialist also brings a style and philosophy of work, personality traits, physical appearance, initiative and imagination, motivation, sensitivity, established relationships and contacts, a status position and reputation in the community, and a capacity for making decisions. Mark Cohen concludes that the essential traits of a successful community developer are tolerance of ambiguity, common sense, perseverance, and humility (part F). The professional comes to the job with all the strengths and weaknesses of the human personality.

We might conclude that such characteristics as friendliness, enthusiasm, intelligence, decisiveness, persistence, and courage are desirable traits in successful professionals; however, as in trait-oriented research on leadership, rarely could we find two persons who would agree as to which are essential (Stogdill 1974). Individual factors are not unimportant; they are crucial in the understanding of the CD role. But a single set of traits that fits all situations is too simplistic. Rather, a multitude of personal characteristics need to be considered as important in defining the professional role.

The CD professional interacts within a work environment and is influenced by the structure and dynamics of the organization in which he or she works and by client groups served. At the same time, the professional is influencing these groups. And the relationship is constantly changing, adjusting, and adapting.

THE ORGANIZATION

The CD role is influenced to a considerable extent by the organizational context, which represents a whole set of conditions. Some of these characterize the organization's influence on the individual CD professional and others relate to the organization's relationship to its environment.

The organization possesses certain goals, purposes, and philosophy concerning development, which in turn are generally subscribed to by their employees. For example, Hamilton cites the definition and approach to community development that has been clearly specified by the Cooperative Extension Services' National Committee on Organization and Policy (part D). Organizations may espouse one of the three approaches to development as presented earlier: self-help, technical assistance, or conflict. The role expectations for the CD worker would vary accordingly. The goals of the organization may be specific or very general, short term or of long duration (for example, to build a new park or to improve the social and economic well-being of the people). Employees tend to pattern their roles according to the framework established by the organization.

To function effectively an organization requires some degree of shared beliefs and practices that unite the members, some agreement on important values. This *normative system* consists of the dos and don'ts that govern the actions and imply the sanctions and rewards for group members. An organization establishes patterns of interaction among its members and places them in various positions of authority in relationship to other members. Differing levels of responsibility and status are thus conferred by the organization. This status level, in turn, carries over into the community in the form of titles, prestige, etc. In addition to these relations between individuals within the organization, the status attributed to the organization itself is also important. It may be a new and struggling consulting firm of three members or a century-old university of 1,000 faculty.

Functional *specialization* within and among organizations has increased over the years. Developmental problems are generally complex in nature, requiring the input of many specialists. Most development efforts require, at a minimum, specialists in planning, financing, design, and organization. Increased specialization has made it necessary for the CD worker to interact across the boundaries of organizational subsystems and with other organizations and agencies. At the same time, large organizations have the capacity for possessing many specialists on call to address specific needs. One could conclude, therefore, that increased specialization has made the CD professional's role more complex but it also has the potential for providing the CD worker with more specialized support.

The *interorganizational climate* in a community can impact the CD professional role. Ecologists have generally distinguished between two basic types of relations: symbiosis and commensalism (Hawley 1950, p. 36–39). The former refers to relations of mutual dependence and advantage, while the latter describes competition for the same scarce resources. Because developmental problems often require the input of many organizations, cooperation among agencies and agency representatives is crucial (symbiosis). Formal and informal linkages between organizations, in turn, set the framework in which the professionals work. If the organizations are competing for the same resources (commensalism), recognition, or domain, joint efforts of the workers will be severely hampered.

TASK FUNCTIONS

In attempting to define the CD worker's role in terms of the task performed, one is struck by the wide range and diverse activities commonly identified with the role. Ross (1967, p. 40) suggests many of the task functions when he defines community organization as "a process by which a community identifies its needs or objectives, orders these needs or objectives, finds the resources to deal with these needs or objectives, takes action with respect to them, and in doing so extends and develops cooperative and collaborative attitudes and practices in the community.''

The most basic specialization of functional roles focuses on content versus process (Cebotarev and Brown 1972). Content refers to the provision of technical subject-matter information with a task orientation, whereas process deals with strategies for developing a capacity in individuals and groups for decision making and action (Mahan and Bollman 1968); the "what" versus the "how." These two concepts are often presented as if they represent a continuum.

More specific functions have been delineated in reference to identifiable professional roles. From the social perspective, Gallaher and Santopolo (1967) identified four roles that link the change agent to the client system: analyst, advisor, advocator, and innovator. From this point of view the CD worker is seen as a specialist in process skills and a generalist in technical subject matter. These functions approximate the tasks identified in Hamilton's study of community developers in the Cooperative Extension Service (part D).

From a city and regional planning perspective, Meyerson (1956) delineates the following five task functions: central intelligence, pulse-taking, policy clarification, detailed development plan, and feedback review. (These five functions are described in slightly different terms by Melvin in part G.) The central intelligence and pulse-taking functions serve to facilitate the orderly growth and development of the private and public sectors of the community. The policy clarification function is the statement and revision of community objectives. Preparing the technical plan is the function most widely identified with the planner role. In addition, the planner is expected to evaluate program consequences as a guide to future action (feedback review).

The Cooperative Extension Service has defined six functions as appropriate for the CD professional (ECOP 1966): (1) providing technical and analytical assistance, (2) helping identify community problems and development goals and objectives, (3) identifying consequences of development alternatives, (4) fostering liaison with outside individuals and groups, (5) stimulating community interaction, and (6) bringing together diverse groups.

Other efforts to define the role of the CD worker according to the task performed resemble the basic concepts in the change agent, planning, and extension roles. For example, Morris (1970) specifies four work roles: field agent, advisor or consultant, advocate, and planner. A more general level of approach is suggested in Cary's (1972) terms of enabler, activist, advocate, and community organizer.

In an attempt to synthesize the various listings of functions attributed to the CD role, Bennett (1973) developed a classification scheme based on five principal functions: process consultant, technical consultant, program advocate, organizer, and resource provider. The process consultant role focuses on the "hows" of problem solving, decision making, organizing, enabling, and implementing rather than on the particular group action outcomes; strategies for facilitating change are the process consultant's areas of expertise. The technical consultant, on the other hand, "provides information, know-how, and perspective to the community in relation to specific programs of change" (Bennett 1973, p. 64). Supplying accurate technical information to a community is a vital part of development; therefore information-giving and analysis concerning developmental alternatives are central to this role. The CD professional is seen as an expert in certain subject matter areas.

When CD workers propose a specific course of action, they are performing in the role of advocate. The professional analyzes the situation and decides what the best alternative is for the community. In this case the professional goes beyond presenting the alternatives to the community for their action and recommends a specific alternative as the best solution for the problem.

The organizational role is concerned with the formation and renewal of an organizational structure that can deal with community problems. With this approach, the CD worker helps a community organize for action. This role has often been utilized in neighborhood settings through the use of the Alinsky approach (part E). The organizer focuses on bringing individuals together in a group setting so they can have a voice in community affairs. The process consultant role is then involved in seeing that the organization continues to function.

The fifth role presented by Bennett is that of resource provider. He defines this function as the channeling of financial resources to the community. Ratchford (1970) and Ross (1967) also cited this role, though (contrary to Bennett) they did not limit the concept of resources to money, but rather focused on the role of the professional in the identification of a community need for outside help and how to go about securing it.

Though different categorical names are used by the various typologies, the Bennett scheme appears to include most of the important tasks generally attributed to CD professionals. A worker may perform one or more of the five tasks, all of which are important for community development.

CLIENTELE

Professionals work with a wide variety of clientele. The appropriate individual or group will be largely determined by what decisions are to be made, what actions are to be taken, and who will enter that process. The most general level of clientele involvement is the public-at-large. Some developmental goals impact most or all citizens; for example, programs of general education and awareness would come under this heading. However, most CD professionals tend to have regular, direct contact with a limited number of people. In this case, the client group is the segment of the public who is seen as the primary consumer of the services offered by the CD worker. The CD professional generally works through these individuals or groups for the ultimate benefit of the community residents.

Whether the approach to development be self-help, confrontation, or technical intervention, a basic assumption of the relationship between professionals and clients is that decisions are expected to be governed not by the professionals' own self-interests but by their judgment of what would serve their clients' interests best. Of concern is that professionals may fail to serve their clients' best interests because of a preoccupation with their own status or career or, on the other hand, become subservient to client interests at the expense of objective professional judgment.

The CD professional may work with individuals or groups. The nature of the professional assistance provided determines the setting, and the skills needed by the professional differ accordingly. For example, the worker may be responding to a very specific request of one person or helping a group through a decision-making process.

The clientele may be local *lay leaders*. Such persons are generally voluntary, unpaid individuals working for the good of the community. These persons possess a wide variety of preparation and skills, as well as time and effort that they contribute. They are from the local community and may be self-appointed, designated, or elected and may have a locally recognized status and following (Bilinski 1969). Working through voluntary lay leaders offers the professional an established linkage into the existing social structure of the community, though the volunteer leader may be limited in training and experience in CD efforts and lack sufficient time. In this case the professional needs to offer informal support, training, and information to these individuals within a very flexible time frame. In Hamilton's study of CD professionals in the Cooperative Extension Service, lay leaders proved to be the clientele group with which the most time was spent (part D).

Local officials make up another important client group. They are usually elected or appointed and are charged with the responsibility of caring for specific governmental functions. Some are unpaid but most receive some compensation, either on a part- or full-time basis. Like volunteer leaders, their knowledge, skills, and experience vary substantially. Also, their areas of responsibility and interests may be communitywide or very specialized. The success of the CD professional, to a great extent, lies in the professional's ability to support these officials without competing with them and thus threatening their power position in the community. The CD professional can provide such help as general awareness education and assistance in problem-solving and planning, as well as providing specific factual information. A prime example of professionals serving this client group is planners, who provide assistance to governmental officials in the areas of problem identification, data collection and analysis, plan formulation and implementation, and feedback (part G).

Civic and development organizations are often directly or indirectly involved in carrying out or encouraging development. Many lay leaders work through these organizations. The goals of these groups may or may not be limited to development and their involvement may be in a specific aspect of development (e.g., industry, health, education). The members are volunteer and their backgrounds and experiences are varied. Though sometimes the organizations' interests are very specific and the group process may be slow, they have had and will continue to have a great impact on the development of communities because of their ability to draw on a wide range of skills and experiences of their members and to exert influences to mobilize resources.

Many *developmental agencies and organizations* have paid professional staff in communities. These professionals are supported from outside the community and usually work with a local advisory board or group. They are professionally trained in specialized subject areas, and their status is derived principally from their professional position in the parent organization rather than from the community. Instances of this arrangement can readily be found in such federal agencies as the Economic Development Adminstration; Housing and Urban Development; Health, Education and Welfare; and the Farmers Home Administration.

Because of the independent nature of the many development organizations and individuals, the possibility for an uncoordinated, fragmented approach to development definitely exists.

Bilinski (1969, p. 162) describes the professional as possessing a feeling of "competition with other professionals trying to promote their segmental interests at the expense of the rest of the program of community development." The overall success of the developmental effort, as well as that of professionals, depends on a cooperative attitude of the professionals sharing information and working together while working toward the good of the community.

SUMMARY

This overview provides a framework for the discussion of seven different roles of CD professionals that follows. Each author speaks to the four elements outlined in the role model: individual factors, organizational factors, task functions, and clientele.

We do not include all the possible professional positions in community development but have selected roles that illustrate the diversity that exists. They provide a glimpse of who CD professionals are, the organizational setting in which they work, what they do, and for whom they do it.

Individual factors address such things as desirable training, experiences, and personal traits. Public versus private organizations, interorganizational climates, and profit and nonprofit organizations are considered. The broad range of functions performed by professionals are discussed at length, from process to content and advisor to advocate. Likewise, the recipients of the community developers' efforts are varied: volunteers and employees, individuals and groups, leaders and followers.

A. IN THE PRIVATE SECTOR / *Palmer E. McCoy*

In reviewing the literature; talking to community development professionals (public and private); and examining roles, task functions, training, linkages, and the overall thrust of this section, it becomes evident that, while the public sector is actively engaged in community development activities, there is little evidence that the private sector employs any number of CD professionals. Most professional community developers are found in government (at all levels) and in universities and colleges. The membership rolls of the Community Development Society of America reveal that few members come from the private sector. There are exceptions; they will be pointed out.

This section examines the role of CD professionals in the private sector, the relationships of the private and public sectors in community development, and the constraints that have acted as barriers to greater understanding and cooperation between the two sectors.

DIFFERENCES BETWEEN PUBLIC AND PRIVATE SECTORS

People in the private sector identify community development by a variety of titles and names other than community development, i.e., development department, planning department, public relations, foundation for . . . , public information department, community facilities, and so on.

Community development professionals come from a variety of disciplines—economic, social, and cultural—and have moved toward a common title with specialized subtitles or further identification, such as economic community development, community development specialist in housing, or community development specialist in health programs. As the term *community development* has become increasingly popular, governmental agencies at all levels are attaching the title to departments and individuals. Government has identified funding sources as community development block grants; this practice has further enhanced the term. Industry, business, and the private sector are also in the process of consolidating departments and titles into overall headings of community development with a breakdown into such subtitles as department of development and community development division. As in institutions, each segment in the private sector feels that its segment is primary in the CD function or process.

In the Great Society era of the sixties, it was generally concluded that money, matched with government expertise, could bring about the positive social and economic changes necessary for a better society and that the private sector would be caught up in the overall thrust; the nation and its communities would be molded into a pattern of positive social and economic change. Indeed, great strides were made and the CD process of citizen involvement and the importance of the individual were enhanced and rediscovered. The private sector was quick to respond to such things as citizen involvement, community involvement for a broader group of people, and the "dollar strings" attached to bring about these changes.

Today there is considerable confusion in the private sector as to what community development really is, what the CD process is, and whether it is important. Comments such as, "That's what we've been doing for years," are frequently heard. The professional is many times frustrated and feels that the private sector lacks sensitivity to overall community issues, allocates resources wrongly, and even works in opposite directions in resource allocation and priority setting within the community.

CONSTRAINTS OR BARRIERS

It is first necessary to understand the constraints or barriers that have been created. It is also important that readers identify and agree on some of the primary functions of the professional community developer as set forth in the preceding overview, i.e., technical and analysis assistance; identification of community problems, goals, and objectives; identification of alternatives; liaison between individuals and groups; community interactions; the bringing together of diverse groups; working as an advocate; and ultimately identifying and providing resources.

As these functions are reviewed, it becomes evident that much of the work or change accomplished in community development relates directly or indirectly to the private sector. To bring about close cooperation and greater understanding between the public and the private sectors, it is necessary to understand the following constraints and barriers.

The first constraint involves *goals*—the private sector is oriented toward economic growth. The public sector's concern for profit, growth, and expansion may or may not be a goal and is generally of a lower priority. The private sector must meet a payroll and produce a product or service that is salable; its goals may directly or indirectly be misaligned with the goals of CD professionals employed by the public. The goals of professionals employed by the private sector are generally aligned with the goals of the private corporation or company for which they work.

A second constraint centers around *process versus product*. The private sector generally is concerned with a fairly specific product or goal that is generally narrower than the overall community objective set by the public professional. Community needs may or may not relate to the specific product or change that the private sector identifies as a goal. The private developer is less concerned than the public developer with overall community effects and the weighing of one community priority against another. The private sector is concerned with doing rather than study, with facts rather than options, and with product rather than process. Interrelationships of community parts, resource allocation, and social implications may be looked on as stumbling blocks by the private sector. Consequently, the public-oriented community developer may view the process portion of study (process methods, group dynamics, citizen involvement, pulse taking, feedback, interaction, analysis assistance) as primary goals to the point that the public sector feels that process is more important than product or specific change.

Most CD professionals, public and private, have experienced such comments from community leaders or influentials as: "We don't want another study or survey; we're concerned with getting something done." "We know what needs to be done, let's get on with the project, get it done, and not spend a lot of time studying the situation; it's been needed for 20 years." "Don't study it to death."

Alluded to in the two previous constraints is *citizen involvement*. The private sector group may feel that if it previously accomplished a similar CD task in other communities, all that is needed is to repeat the task. Citizen involvement, surveys, etc., may be viewed as a waste of time and money, especially with the feeling that involvement may or may not reach the decision makers and it is quicker and easier to go directly to the power structure or community leaders, get their approval or sanction, and get on with the project. The feeling is that after all these leaders do represent the people and the community; otherwise they would not be in influential positions. To the dismay of new CD professionals, these thoughts and shortcuts many times do work. The professional feels that citizen involvement is a must—it is needed, it ensures input from all segments of the community, and the overall product will be superior and accepted to a greater extent. Depending on the variables and the community situation, this may or may not be the case. Yet the two divergent views are real and represent a constraint to public and private sector cooperation.

Language, semantics, titles all represent constraints in cooperation and understanding between the public and private sectors. Community development has acquired its own jargon, terminology, and language. In fact, these seem to be prerequisites to the identification of a profession. Professional community developers bring the professional language with them. While it is helpful to CD practitioners, it also sets up barriers.

The professional may talk or write about the holistic approach, group dynamics, power actors, interpersonal relationships, normative systems, cooperation and collaborative attitudes, activism, advocacy, community interaction, and development alternatives. The private sector may indeed wonder what it all means and how it relates to the new band shelter, hospital, or housing project. On the other hand, the private sector may be discussing P.E.R.T. charts, feasibility studies, marketability, and return on investment, much to the dismay of the community developer. In many cases the public is confused by both segments.

The *allocation of resources* such as people, dollars, material, and land and their importance also represent a conflict area. This area is of prime concern to the private sector. Community development projects or community changes have dollars connected to them. The private sector is concerned from the onset as to whether the project or change is economically feasible, whether it can be financed, and where the money will come from. The public community developer may view the process of community involvement, priority setting, facilitation, and community consensus as the prime concern.

This conflict area has caused the failure of many projects, ranging from housing to highways. The two concerns—resources and processes—must be intermeshed and understood and must become integral parts of any successful community development effort. Otherwise, "Everyone agreed it was needed and was great; but we never got it financed," or "The people didn't want or support it."

The *project scope* may represent another constraint. The private sector is generally concerned with a specific part of the overall community, such as a housing development, a downtown area, a civic center, an arena, a YMCA, or a library. Overall community problems, community priority setting, and broad citizen involvement are not the concern. The professional, on the other hand, may want to look at the trade-offs—the social and economic consequences to other parts of the community. The private sector feels that this is time consuming and wants to get on with the direct improvement of a manageable segment. Many times it is felt that total community concerns, proper resource allocation, and total involvement are an ideal only found in textbooks and academia.

While countless other constraints are found, the final one we will identify is the *profit motive;* it is a constant source of irritation between public and private sectors in the area of community change. Profit is of prime concern to the private sector; it is a must if the business corporation or company is to exist. The private sector looks to government as a facilitator or catalyst for private investment and development. The public sector sees government and government financing as a means of bringing about change in the areas of government functions, such as roads, public buildings, sewers, and water. It is also viewed as a means of wealth redistribution, accomplished through subsidies to certain areas of the community. The public community developer may view government and its related CD projects, such as low-cost housing or training for unskilled workers, as end products; the private sector looks at the same projects as building and jobs in the housing industry and job training for people.

The private sector may feel that any project it undertakes must render a profit; the public community developer may feel that any project undertaken needs federal, state, or local support and the needs represented within the community are more important than a profit. These conflicts often give the private sector the impression that the public community developer is a grants person with little or no concern for profit or economic feasibility.

POTENTIAL FOR COOPERATION

At this point the reader may be discouraged as to any possibility of the merging, the understanding, and the furthering of a joint effort of professional community development in the public and the private sectors. A number of private sector institutions, however, are not only active in the field of community development but have actually provided support and leadership for the profession. Depending on the literature one reviews, it is difficult to sort out "who did it." The private sector indicates that its input brought about some kind of physical change; the public professional says that the physical change the private sector takes credit for resulted from people and process. In most cases, both are right.

First it is necessary to understand that credit is infinitely divisible. Many corporations, companies, and industries of national, regional, and local scope have established foundations, divisions, and funds to bring about positive community change. Examples are the Kellogg, Mott, Rockefeller, and Ford foundations. Other large retailers, such as Sears Roebuck and Co. and J. C. Penney and Co., have established specific programs in community development. Some are concerned only with the communities in which they do business, while others disperse hundreds of thousands of dollars to branches and even to individual stores to improve their communities. In addition, most corporations, companies, and businesses encourage and even require their managers and employees to be involved in community betterment projects.

It may be worthwhile to examine selected literature that aids in looking at the importance of both the public and the private sectors in accomplishing community development.

In support of the public community developer and the involvement theory, Hunter (1953) indicated that legitimation and diffusion could be served more effectively by selecting program planning committee members as representatives of the hierarchy of influential persons in a community.

Price (1968) provides a framework for the methods of tapping influence and shows the importance of involvement of the power structure or influential. Moss (1970) provided further evidence that the private sector represents a high percentage of the influentials. Leadership within a community many times comes from the private sector, as indicated in a Columbia County, Wisconsin, leadership survey (1970); influentials are four times as likely to be in business as in other areas. Moss (1970) found that 60 percent of Columbia County, Wisconsin, influentials or community leaders were in business and banking.

Recognizing that the private sector represents the expertise in doing, financing, technology, and influence in bringing about community change, it is important to continue to seek methods to mesh the two sectors more closely.

The CD professional has traditionally relied on private enterprise for dollars, research, facility, and expertise in studying and bringing about change. The private sector looks and will continue to look to the public sector (government, universities, and colleges) to train and supply personnel in the area of community development. There is ample opportunity for cooperation. It must begin and continue with understanding the opposite segment. The public sector has much to offer in expertise, knowledge transfer, research, training, and CD process and technology. The private sector has much to offer in leadership, resources, employment, organizational expertise, and efficiency and productivity.

SUMMARY

It seems necessary to challenge both sectors to continue to explore ways in which greater cooperation and understanding can be achieved. Organizations such as the Community Development Society of America can serve as a bridge. Community development, as a profession, can easily become a narrow, homogeneous group that is overtly public process oriented with few ties to the public sector. This could result in a profession that centers around the academic community and government with little or no support from the private sector.

Conversely, the private sector can ignore the public professional and continue to feel the wrath of public resentment for lack of sensitivity and involvement in their CD efforts.

Neither is desirable. It is hoped that these words may stimulate further discussions and understandings relating to the constraints between the public and the private sectors of community development.

B. AS PRIVATE CONSULTANTS / *Robert C. Child*

The work of the private consultant in community development contributes substantially to the range of diversity that characterizes the practice. In a field in which role descriptions are multitudinous and often nebulous, the functions of the private consultant bring additional definitions into play. In an activity in which flexibility in approach is recognized as a prerequisite to success, the private practitioner must constantly maintain an operational balance between pragmatism and idealism. And in a profession that requires the sublimination of personal need for public recognition of accomplishments, private consultants must restrain themselves even further, secure in the knowledge that whatever successes they may have assisted their clients in achieving will ultimately result in other calls for consulting services.

This extension of the dimensions and definitions of the CD field, in its implications for both the client and the practitioner, constitutes an element of particular significance in the area of consulting roles (Lippitt and Lippitt 1975).

THE INDIVIDUAL

The individual practitioner can function as a private consultant in community development as the principal in a sole proprietorship, as a part of an informal grouping of professional associates, or as a staff member of a private company or corporation doing business in the field. While depth in particular areas of specialization is required in any of the foregoing capacities, generally the demands on professional preparation, training, and experience, and the overall understanding of business principles are most extensive in a sole proprietorship situation.

The nature and content of early formal academic training are not necessarily a determinant of proficiency in such a role. Some successful private practitioners had little formal training in their early career stages. The private consultant must have or quickly learn and develop the ability to determine relationships among people and institutions and to meld these relationships into the delivery of the services required. This skill is not easily learned in an academic setting. It can be learned through training and experience, and as is the case in all skill areas, some practitioners are more adept at it than others.

A necessary perspective is that the client's concerns are paramount, deserving of the consultant's loyalty, and subject to the best analysis and criticism of which the consultant is capable. This position must be maintained by the private consultant as long as the contract with the client holds. If the consultant cannot win the client over to a particular point of view, the consultant cannot be won over, and the consultant regards this as critical for whatever reason, the consultant should terminate the contractual relationship (Jones and Pfeiffer 1977).

The *contract* is a central feature of private practice. It is a formal agreement specifying the relationship of the involved parties. It has the expressed purpose of protecting the interests of both the client and the consultant. Clients have no vested interests in consultants such as those that sometimes exist between employer and employee. In most instances the consultant is viewed principally as a mercenary hired to do a particular piece of work, with none of the usual niceties of concerned paternalism that often are present in full-time regular employment situations. In these circumstances, the contract serves as a kind of "malpractice insurance" for the consultant. Its contents specify the specific responsibilities of client and consultant for the ultimate product of the consultation, and the negotiations that go into the development of the contract help both parties to understand better the kind of services to be rendered and the outcomes and delivery times to be expected (Ulschak 1978).

While the private consultants' expertise is what is sought by clients and this is the element that is touted, what consultants actually sell to clients is their *time*. To lose sight of the reality of the cost of time is to step on the pathway to ultimate failure. Persons engaged in public consultation generally have no idea of the actual costs of the services they render. Private consultants must know. They must anticipate all the work elements in a particular negotiation for services, have cost support figures at hand, and apply these costs during the writing of the contract. At a minium, they must be aware of the suporting costs required for labor, travel, subsistence, telephone, shipping and postage, overhead, general and administrative activities, reserves, and profit.

But while private consultants base their total dollar figure on the time and support that will be necessary to meet the requirements of a contract, they must avoid relating the total dollar figure to time during contract negotiations. The consultant is offering to deliver a package of services to accomplish a given task for a client, and if negotiations for the client are carried out by experienced administrators this will generally be understood. If it is not, the consultant must attempt to keep the negotiations at the level of services to be performed and therefore avoid problems generated by client parsimony triggered by simple division of estimated time requirements into the total dollar figure.

ORGANIZATIONAL SETTING

Four distinctions can be made between private and public consultants in community development work. The first concerns the source of financial support. The public consultant is tied directly to a money supply generated from some form of public taxation, from corporate income, or from grants. The public consultant is a direct employee of an institution or organization that maintains its operations by creating such public income. The private consultant is engaged in a business that, while sometimes generating income from public sources in the form of pass-through money for services rendered, relies on a variety of sources of income for maintenance purposes.

A second distinction is the range of choice in the operations or programs as activities relating to income generation. A public consultant can commit resources to development activities that not only do not produce income but also produce a drain on resources. This choice is open to the private consultant only as far as income or reserves are sufficient to support it. Some deserving or demonstrational CD activities that are nonincome producing can be initiated or supported by the private practitioner only so far as current discretionary cash balances permit and always as weighed against long-range anticipated income.

The third distinction between private and public consultants is the nature of each one's clientele. Public consultants almost always work directly with people or the organizations that represent people. Private consultants, however, are generally a third party to the CD activity, being retained by institutions or agencies that themselves have a one-to-one relationship with their communities. That triangular relationship carries with it a need for private consultants to continuously and directly inform and involve the organizations that have retained their services.

The final dimension rests in the existence of a mandate. Mandates are developed to define territory and justify action, and public consultants usually have as a matter of course a statement of purpose and direction in advance of initiating work. Private consultants have no mandate except that of profit, and it is rare when such motivation can be publicized to good effect.

TASK FUNCTIONS

Private consultants in community development must have or must quickly develop a capacity for sustaining themselves financially and emotionally (Mitchell 1977). A statement of purpose is an essential part of that sustaining process. Such a statement is a maintenance tool and as such is not static but is consciously modified from time to time as circumstances may warrant. The statement becomes basic to the delimitation of professional tasks that are undertaken. The elements that define purpose for private consultants consist of answers to four questions:

Who are we? What are our skills, our competencies, our weak points? What have we done? What can we do? What do we like and not like? What gives us the greatest satisfaction?

What do we want? What are our short-range goals, our long-range goals? What level of quality do we seek? How much money do we need? How long do we want to be involved? How large do we want to become?

What will we do? What services will we offer, or not offer, and to whom? What kinds of service linkages will we establish? How will we deliver services? What is needed that we do not now have?

With whom will we work? Will we work with urban people, rural people, or both; public or private organizations; agencies; institutions; neighborhoods; cities; self-help advocacy groups; federal, state, local governments?

A thorough self-examination on the preceding four questions contributes substantially to a statement of purpose for the private consultant.

The defined purpose also determines policy, which in turn provides direction for administration of the operation. Most important, a benchmark is established that can be examined and reviewed as the program develops or when outright changes are regarded as necessary (Steele 1975; Jones and Pfeiffer 1977).

The national success rate for businesses, measured by the capacity to stay in business, is obviously considerably less than the number of private ventures that are launched. Businesses that maintain themselves over a long period have several things going for them, namely, a quality product, a constant market, satisfied customers, reasonable profits, good management, and flexibility. Because private consultation in community development is a business, those who move into it must be concerned with the same considerations that make for the survival of any other business. Survival for the CD professional who is working as a private consultant either singly (with a loosely knit group of associates) or as a member of a corporate structure depends directly on the quality of services delivered, their effect on the success of the client, and the client's resulting satisfaction.

A detailed definition of the product and territory developed by the private consultant aids the client in determining the specific nature and quality of assistance that is being offered to assist the client in attaining immediate goals and fulfilling long-range strategy (Ulschak 1978).

A specification of the tasks to be performed and the products to be delivered to constitute task fulfillment will provide the client with an understanding of the limitations of the work of the consultant, the functions that the consultant and the client will each perform, and a monitoring procedure that can be used by both in evaluating progress.

A specified pricing structure realistically based on recognized cost principles will enable both client and consultant to have the information required for whatever negotiations may be necessary to fulfill a contract. Most important, an adequate pricing structure will support the consultant in delivering a quality product on time.

Tasks performed by the private consultant are similar in many respects to those undertaken by the public consultant. They include (in addition to the overall maintenance function) initiation functions such as recruitment, research, conceptualization and design; operations functions such as organization, logistics, and event presentation; and closure functions such as final evaluations and data storage.

Examples of specific activities include decision-making procedures, such as workshops for the identification and prioritization of goals or issues; public involvement procedures, such as areawide citizen participation in a water quality program or local recreational planning; training procedures, such as training for urban outreach workers, area and CD procedures training for staff members of agencies with field programs, community organization process component training for graduate students in fields of specialization utilizing community resources, and training in relationships and roles for staff and board members of regional agencies; organizing and conducting formal public involvement and hearing processes for agencies with that mandate; services and program integration procedures for organizations with integration as a focus; community organization support development for agencies with a substantive program requiring involvement of other community organizations; and in-service training in CD processes and procedures for staff members of agencies engaged in field programming.

CLIENTELE

Clients of the private consultant have a number of specific requirements of which they may or may not be aware. These include an understanding of exactly what they are contracting with the consultant to accomplish, an understanding of how the consultant will perform that function and the responsibilities for it, an understanding of the client's responsibilities and how the client is expected to perform, a series of benchmarks or deadlines to be used for monitoring progress, the dollar amounts required for consultation and the times and manner in which these costs become payable, and a definition or description of the final product. While the needs listed above are the minimum that a client should reasonably expect, they are the absolute minimum that the consultant must demand. If a client is unaware of these requirements, the consultant must educate the client to their importance. In brief, the requirements constitute responses to the following checklist of questions:

What is to be done?
How is the task to be accomplished?
What are the consultant's role and responsibilities?
What are the client's role and responsibilities?
How will the consultant and client know that the task accomplishment is on schedule?
How much will the consultation cost and what is the manner of payment?
What product will constitute evidence that the task has been accomplished?

These elements must be reduced to written form and the resulting document (contract) agreed to by both client and consultant. Work in CD activity is imprecise and subject to the vagaries that can result from human involvement. When difficulties occur it is possible to negotiate changes in the work program between client and consultant if the above elements have been adequately addressed during the initial negotiation and contract development stage (Lippitt and Lippitt 1975).

Examples of clients served by private consultants can be found in any listing of clients prepared by public consultants. They include health systems agencies, city governments, special taxing districts (such as water and sewer and recreation), university and college academic departments and service units, private health and welfare organizations (such as the Young Men's Christian Association and the Girl Scouts of America), regional planning and development agencies, chambers of commerce, community action agencies, regional crafts organizations, federal and state agencies and bureaus, and national organizations.

IMPLICATIONS

The number of persons engaged in private consultation is a question without more than a qualified response at this time. Is anyone personally aware of more than one or two? Are we aware of many current members of the national professional organization who are working in the private field? Not many persons have been private consultants for more than a few years.

Why is this so? At least part of the answer is the manner in which employment expectations of persons are developed. University- and college-trained people—who make up by far the largest number of community developers—learn in their socialization process to think of their employment opportunities in terms of corporations, institutions, large businesses, and the like; one advantage is the degree of personal comfort that is possible in a large organization. Persons who are career-oriented toward community development are generally not exposed to the entrepreneurial possibilities in the field. Also, most CD jobs are in the public consultation category.

Most private practitioners have become so by seizing opportunities that suddenly materialized, such as the availability of a sweetheart contract; that were incrementally created, for example a gradual build-up of moonlighting activities; or that were thrust on them, as in the case of loss of employment. These circumstances are all sufficient in themselves to support the move toward private practice. Getting there is one matter. Staying there is another, more complex issue. Market identification, product sales, flexibility, product modification in response to market changes, growth, and financing issues all enter into the maintenance equation. And staying there is not always easy, especially because institutions and agencies and large organizations continue to beckon for experience and talent.

The impact of private consultation on the overall field of community development, while important from the standpoint of an essentially different operating model, is not particularly noticeable. It may even be minimal in its influence. But it does have an established role. And it is a dynamic and exciting activity. It is too early to tell how the country will ultimately respond to the current reduced resource level. But life continues to grow more complex and relationships reflect this. Community developers, both public and private, will respond to the needs created by shifts in client-community relationships or even sometimes attempt to bring those shifts about on their own.

As the reduction in resource levels affects institutions of higher education, government agencies, and many large businesses, it will probably also mean a leveling out in programs reflecting CD interests. In turn, the opportunities for private consultation may increase. But it will be largely incumbent on the private consultation group to bring this possibility to fruition. It is also incumbent on the private sector to give all support possible to maintaining programs in the public consultation area, where the bulk of important CD work will continue to occur and the majority of persons who will ultimately enter private consultation will first be employed.

C. IN GOVERNMENT / *John M. Huie and*
Ronald T. Crouch

We live in a complex society where governing the nation and its political subdivisions is a difficult task. Governments provide the formal framework for making the decisions a dynamic society requires if it is to respond adequately to changes affecting the integrity of that society, be they demographic, technological, or other. Durkheim (1964) wrote of the changes inherent in society nearly a century ago as it became more and more complex and required that government play an increasingly important role in maintenance. In the past quarter-century we have seen major changes in the role of governments at all levels as the responsibilities and functions mandating them have greatly increased.

As CD professionals branch out into various sectors of society they can greatly expand their impact. Working in government (whether local, state, or federal) does have frustrations; however, it also presents an opportunity to help shape public policies that affect every one of us. At the local level it may mean developing a community or county land use plan; at the state level it could mean helping to develop legislation or regulations or helping to plan a statewide emergency ambulance service program to serve all communities; and at the federal level it could be legislation, regulations, or a national community health service program. The issues affecting communities are impacted at the local, state, and federal government levels and the CD professional can lend expertise of impartial and systematic analysis to identify and clarify alternative solutions to be considered.

THE INDIVIDUAL

Each CD professional has a set of abilities, attitudes, traits, training, past experience, etc., that condition professional thinking and actions. These attributes are unique to each person and independent of the organization, the community setting, and the role performed. Certain traits, such as an even temper, a willingness to listen, and a knowledge of the art of negotiating and compromise, will serve the CD professional well in government.

Community development professionals come to their work associated with an organization that has certain historical attitudes and current perceptions pertaining to the role they should play in community development; these factors influence their expectations.

Professionals must understand that in government they will address the governmental officials they serve rather than the public. At the same time they can seek to influence the framework of social analysis and raise the democratic sensitivity within which officials must function (Marris and Rein 1969). In doing this, individuals must be sensitive to political concerns and the political consequences of programs. This does not mean that professionals must become political—only that they are functioning in a political setting and must be aware of that fact. They must address issues in terms understandable to those they serve and must avoid academic discussions and over intellectualization (Marris and Rein 1969). In short, professionals must understand the political realities under which they work.

ORGANIZATIONAL ENVIRONMENT

Community development professionals who choose to work in government must be aware that they are part of a bureaucracy. They may be able to avoid developing bureaucratic traits but they will be working with others who have developed bureaucratic insensitivity and an unwillingness to change policies. March and Simon (Pugh 1971) in discussing the development of bureaucracies list three consequences. First, the bureaucracy is a set of relationships between offices or roles and individuals are reacted to not as individuals but as representatives of positions with specified rights and duties. Second, rules designed to achieve organizational goals assume a positive value that becomes independent of changing goals. And third, an increase in the use of categorization as a decision-making technique leads to decreases in any search for alternatives. Community development professionals in government need to be aware of these consequences and try to ameliorate their effect on policy decisions. Having a sense of purpose developed from the profession and understanding the government setting within which they work provide tools necessary to be effective. Whether they work in the executive or legislative branches of government, professionals will be working in and with bureaucracies. For example, two years ago Kentucky changed its emphasis in treating mentally retarded individuals from large institutions to small, community-based homes and facilities. At first the state agency that oversees treatment of the mentally retarded greatly resisted changing policies and developing alternatives. Individuals within the agency said change was needed but official policy did not reflect this attitude. The mentally retarded and their treatment had been categorized. The issue came before the state legislature, and professionals on the legislative staff were able to gather information on the issue and show that alternatives were successful elsewhere and were cheaper and better than institutionalization. Citizens' groups also were provided a forum to speak on the issue. The results were that the needed changes came about and the professionals with their information were, in large part, responsible for the change.

In looking at the formal power and limitations that affect all governments one must be aware of the consitutional provisions, statutes, administrative regulations, and judicial interpretations that define the roles of federal, state, and local governments. Each level and unit of government is unique in characteristics that condition the decisions it makes within the framework established by external forces. Anderson (1975) has stated that policy actions are generated in the environment and transmitted to the political system, while at the same time the environment places limits and constraints on what can be done by policymakers. Areas of concern are available resources, demographic variables, political culture, social structure, and economc conditions. As these differ from one setting to another, policy actions and solutions to problems vary.

The officials who are elected or appointed to make public decisions are sensitive to the conditions in their environment or they would not have been elected or appointed. Their primary role is to develop policies and manage programs to carry out those policies. As they act out these roles, their performance and that of the government they serve are under constant evaluation. The constituency evaluating performance may be composed of diverse and conflicting groups. Some constituents are concerned only with specific issues that occasionally arise, while others may continually monitor policies (Anderson 1975). These groups have special interests and may compose only a small segment of those affected by the policy. Most policies go unnoticed by the majority of constituents, with the implication that at any point relatively few people are involved in affecting the decision-making process.

Because society is complex, elected and appointed officials cannot be experts in every field in which they must make decisions. They require assistants with detailed knowledge in specialized fields, such as road construction and maintenance, waste disposal, fire and police protection, health and public welfare, public finance. However, few if any of their assistants are qualified to analyze a broad range of problems not related to their specialties. A host of organizations and persons seek to influence public decisions in favor of their special interests and willingly supply public officials with selective information and arguments to promote their particular ends. For these and other reasons, most units of government have a compelling need for access to information and advice from sources having no axe to grind other than a professional interest in serving the public. Community development professionals, through their broader orientation and expertise in looking at whole systems, can play an important role. When the power to influence the decisions of government are tightly held by a few people operating through a variety of formal and informal arrangements (Hunter 1953, pp. 248–59; Olsen 1970; Anderson 1975), the professional may through training and expertise be able to help open up the process to assure that all sides are considered in the decision making and that decisions are made with all the best available information.

TASK FUNCTIONS

A critical need to improve the governmental decision-making process is present. It is our purpose to emphasize this point and to outline the role most likely to maximize the long-term impact of professionals on the decision-making process. The role of providing information is crucial. By the term *information* we mean data that help government officials to make more-informed decisions. Such information helps to determine who pays for and who benefits from alternative courses of action, which organizational structures are likely to be most efficient in accomplishing stated objectives, and whether the role of individuals in the decision-making process should be changed. Such information is part of the context of the decision-making process. The framework within which the information is presented is equally important. To be most helpful, information must relate to a perceived problem and should be presented in such a way that it will assist government officials to choose among the alternatives.

Professionals assume responsibility for influencing the decisions that are made. The moment they begin to interact with officials they have an opportunity to influence decisions. Their impact in the long run depends on the degree to which they help the system attain goals supported by the public. This is especially true in government, as officials are dependent on public support for actions. Thus, the professional must understand community needs and goals and any significant barriers to the attainment of these needs or goals.

In presenting information, the professional can help officials to meet policy goals by: (1) identifying and clarifying problems, (2) developing alternative solutions, (3) analyzing the consequences of those solutions, and (4) designing effective programs to implement the alternative selected. There is a constant need to identify and clarify policy issues. Some issues are not assigned a high priority by public officials simply because they have not yet been perceived as issues by the public. Alert CD professionals in government will assist officials to identify potential problems so that they can be solved before they become public issues. Often, however, major public issues must reach a high level of community concern before a public official can take the necessary action.

Once officials have placed a problem on their agenda, they are receptive to alternative courses of action. At this point CD professionals have an opportunity to be innovative and creative and to use skills and present solutions for new ways of solving a problem. It is also an opportunity to share knowledge of the manner in which other communities or governmental units have dealt with a particular problem. The better understanding that professionals have of the issue and the setting and the more experience they have, the better they are prepared to offer alternatives that are realistic and useful.

Each alternative has consequences that must be evaluated. While economic consequences are not the only ones, in government they are often of primary concern because of limited tax dollars. It is essential to know who pays for changes in the status quo and who benefits from them. It is also necessary to provide the political and social costs and benefits. In analyzing any issue, the professional must understand what sets of consequences are most critical to the selection of a solution. Information should relate to these critical concerns and should be presented as concisely as possible.

The nature of most community problems requires a multidisciplinary analysis of consequences. The professional's job is to synthesize the relevant material provided by the various disciplines. For instance, in looking at emergency medical services and development of a comprehensive system, a number of areas are of concern: the transportation network, the availability of emergency vehicles, the proximity of medical facilities, the best scale for development (county or regional), the economic cost of various systems, and the social costs and benefits of various systems in lives saved. These all must be considered and drawn together in a manner that facilitates selection of the appropriate alternative by public official(s).

In considering consequences, professionals should be as unbiased as possible in their analysis. The use of such words as *good, bad, advantage, disadvantage,* etc., should be carefully omitted since they reflect value judgments. What is considered to be an advantage to one group may be a disadvantage to another. It should be the responsibility of the official to place values on each consequence. By remaining neutral, the professional is able to work effectively with all groups; being an advocate for any alternative will make the professional's role less effective.

Once it has been decided that a problem deserves priority consideration, the consequences have been analyzed, and an alternative has been selected, it is important that a plan for implementation be developed and carried out. Such a plan is often not given adequate consideration and may result in failure. Officials need expert assistance to develop a strategy for implementation and to outline specific steps to accomplish desired objectives. Responsibility must be assigned and a time-frame set to ensure that decisions are transferred into actions.

The tasks outlined here are not easy. However, in our opinion, until enough people are identified as CD professionals who can perform such roles competently, the profession will continue to struggle for recognition.

In this discussion it may seem that professionals are expected to be all-knowing experts in all areas. This is not the case. They are expected to be professional problem-solvers who can bring to light whatever knowledge exists that will help government officials solve perceived problems.

To be most effective, professionals must interact with officials in a manner that will inspire the full trust and respect of those officials. Only after this trust and respect is earned will the professional become an integral part of the decision-making process within government. Repeated successes in helping officials perform their tasks more effectively is the most certain way to establish CD professionals in government.

SUMMARY

There is a critical need for professional community developers' input into governmental decisions; their role in government is unique. They (1) provide meaningful input for public policy decisions; (2) help assure access to and input of all groups affected; (3) provide an unbiased problem-solving approach with factual information and an overview of alternative courses of action; and (4) if serving in a staff role, provide staff continuity as officials leave and arrive in government.

Community development professionals must communicate in a manner that allows governmental officials and others to understand the issue. Individuals within the profession who learn how to perform the role outlined here will be highly successful because there is a strong demand for such service. They need to be able to clarify problems, develop alternatives, analyze the major consequences of each alternative, and assist in the development of an implementation plan. These individuals will ultimately be the professionals on whom government officials will depend for their expertise and knowledge.

D. IN COOPERATIVE EXTENSION SERVICE /
Vance E. Hamilton

The role of the CD professional in the Cooperative Extension Service (CES) is highly influenced by the philosophy of the organization, which places emphasis on providing educational programs based on the needs of the clientele and is exemplified by the variety of approaches employed. From an overall perspective, the CES program includes efforts to inform local citizens of issues, opportunities, and barriers associate with developing community resources; to assist them in organizing effective structures or groups to study community needs and resources; and to guide them in establishing goals and implementing programs (McCord 1979, p. 3).

Several typologies have been developed to describe the approaches utilized by CES. While each typology provides some insights and advantages not found in others, none appear to fully describe the diversity of approaches. The typology developed by Cosgriffe (1968) provides one meaningful way to view these approaches. It utilizes five categories that are summarized below.

Managerial development: The professional undertakes the educating of community influentials about theory, content, processes, and problems of economic and social development and the use of scientific inquiry to effect desired community change.

Sensitivity development: The professional provides information to concerned citizens and public officials on issues, community growth potentials, policies, and special interests in an effort to build community relations and loyalties, ease tension, and gain support for community programs, etc.

Environmental development: The professional seeks to complement the work of official agency personnel and voluntary development groups, thereby spreading the expertise of the university to multiply CD efforts.

Project development: The professional works with relevant groups to systematically determine problem(s) and seeks to involve existing organizations in projects to reach a desired solution to problem(s) identified.

Organizational development: The professional attempts to establish new citizen organizations in an effort to enhance the economic well-being and quality of living of the community; the primary focus is on organizational development and maintenance.

To secure current information for this chapter a survey of CES community development state leaders was conducted by the author in 1978. Forty-seven states, Guam, and the District of Columbia responded. The survey focused on three objectives: (1) to ascertain the number of state and area CES community development positions and the training of the individuals occupying these positions, (2) to determine the roles performed by CES community development professionals and the relative importance of the roles as viewed by the state leader, and (3) to identify the clientele served.

This overview provides some insights into the role of CES professionals in community development. This role is discussed in more detail in the remainder of this chapter.

INDIVIDUALS

Community development professionals are employed by the Cooperative Extension Service as administrators, specialists, and agents with staffing normally provided at the state, area, and local levels. Individuals employed for state and area positions (nationally approximately 500 professionals) are generally trained in disciplines related to community development. Individuals occupying these positions function as process specialists or as specialists in subject-matter disciplines related to the state's extension CD program thrust.

"Process-oriented" professionals usually view programs from the perspective of people rather than product. They possess skills that enable them to work effectively with groups and individuals without assuming an authoritative leadership role. These CES personnel must be able to help community leaders identify problems, set goals, and determine solutions. This role requires an understanding of the social and economic forces impacting on communities and the ability to impart this knowledge so that it can be understood and utilized by community leaders.

Individuals technically trained in subject-matter disciplines also provide an important contribution to the extension CD program. These subject-matter disciplines are economics and agricultural economics, forestry, recreation, planning, engineering and agricultural engineering, and agronomy. Table 7.1 gives information about training of state and area CES CD professionals in the content and process areas. Forty-six percent received their training in content departments, while 42 percent have educational backgrounds in the process areas of education, sociology, or one of the other social sciences (excepting economics). From these data it is evident that the majority of state level professionals have Ph.D. degrees, while persons with master's degrees are more prevalent at the area level.

In addition to agents formally assigned to community development, much community development is being done by agents assigned to home economics, agriculture, and 4-H. Several recent extension publications discuss the importance of the contribution being made by these agents (Dyer and McMurtry 1972; ECOP Report 1974). This involvement is most likely associated with the increased number of community problems that are surfacing through CES programming and the success experienced in the CD process. When agents have multiprogram responsibilities, their formal training is usually not directly related to community development. In such

TABLE 7.1.   Educational Background of CES State and Area Staff Members

Field of Study	State		Area			Total
	Ph.D.	MS	Ph.D.	MS	AB/BS	
Economics (includ. agric.)	83	27	4	22	1	137
Sociology (includ. rural)	31	11	2	13	1	58
Other social sciences	15	9	8	18	. . .	50
Adult educ.	11	3	. . .	11	1	26
Ext., contin. educ.	7	7	. . .	13	. . .	27
Other education	6	8	1	16	5	36
Agric., related	16	8	1	14	3	42
Planning	9	. . .	. . .	8	1	18
Recreation	4	3	. . .	8	. . .	15
Admin., manage.	6	12	. . .	5	. . .	23
Miscellaneous	5	12	1	14	1	33
Total	193	100	17	142	13	465

Source: CES Community Development State Leader Survey (Hamilton 1978).

cases in-service training is the primary means of preparing these individuals to function as community developers. A large body of training material has been developed for in-service training by state extension staffs and subcommittees of the Extension Committee on Organization and Policy (ECOP). Most states provide extensive in-service training on a regular basis for local staff members. Local CES professionals account for the majority of the total CD staff and they are a vital force in program delivery.

The data in Table 7.2 indicate that the roles performed by CES professionals are closely associated with the educational mission of CES. More time is utilized in helping community leaders delineate problems, set goals, and determine courses of action than in any other single function. It is closely associated with problem-solving, decision-making education that occurs as leaders participate in a "learning by doing" situation. Professionals also spend considerable time in organizing and maintaining organizations that serve as educational vehicles for CD programs.

ORGANIZATIONAL SETTING

The Cooperative Extension Service represents a joint effort of the USDA, the land-grant institutions, and local governments. As the educational arm of USDA and under the supervision of the Science and Education Administration, CES conducts programs in agriculture, home economics, 4-H, and community development. The organization can be viewed as being vertically integrated for such purposes as funding, broad program direction, and staff resources. However, CES stresses the need to base programs on local needs and emphasizes the involvement of local citizens.

Most states have local units that work directly with the clientele. In addition, multicounty and state units provide backup resources for field staff and clientele audiences. The state units are normally housed on land-grant university campuses and staff members function as faculty members. A variety of arrangements are found among states for housing, staffing, and

TABLE 7.2.   Roles Performed by CES Community Development Professionals

Roles	*Weighted Score
Helps communities identify problems, goals, and courses of action	371
Provides information and educational assistance on technical subjects	291
Assists in organizing and maintaining community organizations	278
Interprets research and analyzes data for community use	228
Provides information about and referrals to other agencies and groups	224
Provides leadership training	110

Source: CES Community Development State Leader Survey (Hamilton 1978).
*Weighted score, based on relative importance of roles, was established by assigning the highest number to the role perceived as being most important in each state, second most important role received 1 less, etc.

administering CD programs. These arrangements are not discussed, but note that they influence the roles of CD professionals, the administrative procedures employed, and the approaches used in developing and implementing programs.

The federal unit of Cooperative Extension Service is housed within the Science and Education Administration of the USDA. The relatively small federal staff provides many vital functions, including inputs into the federal policy and budget processes, promoting program formulation, serving as resources to state personnel, and providing linkage to federal agencies and organizations.

The philosophy of CES and the land-grant universities has a significant influence on CD programs. Land-grant universities were established in 1862 and 1890 to provide practical training for the masses in preparation for useful employment (Ferguson 1964). In 1914 the Cooperative Extension Service was established to extend the knowledge generated and accumulated through these institutions to local people to help them improve their level of living. While many organizational factors influence the role of the CD professional, this philosophy has the greatest impact.

TASK FUNCTIONS

The main function of the Cooperative Extension Service in community development is to provide educational experiences, factual information, and data to help the people of a community make decisions that will result in achieving their goals (Watkins 1970). To accomplish this function, county and area CES CD staff members live in the community and work directly with local people. They serve as educators, organizers, motivators, and facilitators in their role as change agents. According to an ECOP Report (1975):

The county and area workers are the most important members of Extension's community development team. Among their many roles, they occupy the very important roles of creating awareness of situations, stimulating action, educating the general public and expediting and facilitating the use of human, financial, and physical resources. They help the citizens to be better able to make community decisions, but they do not attempt to make the decisions for them nor to promote their own favored solutions to the problems.

A National Task Force Report (1978, p. 1) found that in 1975 as much as 450 staff years of professional time were devoted to community organization and leadership development. This represented more than one-fourth of the total extension time devoted to CES CD programs for that year.

A more detailed listing of tasks performed by CES professionals was reported in the ECOP Report (1975, p. 6). This list included eighteen tasks that were listed according to the competency expressed by the professionals performing the tasks (see Table 7.3). Surely more time was spent on tasks in which professionals felt a high degree of competence than those in which they felt less competent.

While some of the task functions in Table 7.3 apply to specialists on the state extension staff, they more directly describe the role of county and area professionals. State CD specialists serve as a resource to field staff and their role is somewhat more narrowly delineated.

The primary task of the "community development" specialist on the State Extension staff is that of developing a milieu for effective community development education. As an educator, his chief responsibility is to provide training and program support for county and area personnel. As a facilitator, he helps develop access to other resources—university, public and private—needed by field staff and communities. [ECOP 1975, p. 6]

Emphasis is placed on professionals at the various levels functioning as a team to develop and implement programs based on the needs of local communities. In this sense, specialization of functions does occur, but overlapping of roles is frequent and desirable.

CLIENTELE

The clientele of the CES is traditionally considered to be rural residents. In most states, rural communities and small towns are still the

TABLE 7.3. Tasks Performed by CES Community Development Professionals

Tasks	Percent Expressing Competence
Consult with organizational leaders to service their needs	89
Help leaders understand concept of community development	86
Teach leaders and citizens in face-to-face groups	82
Establish communication among development groups	79
Locate needed resources	78
Organize development groups	76
Design educational programs	72
Lead discussions on public issues	70
Involve citizens in determining goals and priorities	69
Guide resource inventories and analyses	67
Interpret relevant research	65
Design and map plans for projects	59
Promote plans and projects	59
Work in applied research	55
Prepare written materials on controversial issues	54
Organize and conduct educational tours	42
Prepare applications for financal and technical assistance	40
Participate in educational TV programs	34

Source: USDA, 1975, Community development concepts, curriculum, training needs. Data is from a CES study conducted in 1968 that included 229 CES professionals throughout the United States.

primary targets of CD programs. However, the programs and information generated by the CES are usually applicable and often used by urban communities, with some states devoting considerable resources to urban clientele.

The CES philosophy places considerable emphasis on serving all segments of the population. While small farmers, lagging communities, and other clientele outside the mainstream of society have always received educational assistance, funding has often been considered insufficient to provide in-depth programs for these audiences. In 1972 and subsequent years, federal funding was provided traditionally black land-grant universities to develop programs for new audiences including the hard to reach, the unreached, and citizens with special needs. Community development programs conducted by such institutions include improving housing, employment training, and counseling (Thaxton 1976).

Clientele served by CES community development professionals varies to some degree from state to state. However, a pattern emerges when clientele served by all states is viewed collectively as in Table 7.4. The three groups receiving the largest proportion of time are government officials, community leaders, and government agencies. Community leaders and organizations are represented in a number of the audiences listed and would collectively represent the clientele with which the most time is spent.

Earlier reference was made to the relationship that exists between CES CD programs and the other program areas of agriculture, 4-H, and home economics. The data in Table 7.4 confirm that these audiences are included as clientele. While home economics clientele are not specifically identified, they are included in several of the groups listed. Youth audiences represent an emerging clientele for community development. In addition, the pace of CD programs in agriculture and home economics has accelerated in recent years.

TABLE 7.4. Clientele Served by CES Community Development Professionals

Clientele	*Weighted Score
Government officials	356
Community leaders	221
Government agencies	209
Planning and development groups	96
Committees and groups	89
Community development organizations	84
Civic, business, and service organizations	71
Youth and youth groups	60
Farmers and farm groups	60
Special interest groups	60
General public	56

Source: CES Community Development State Leader Survey (Hamilton 1978).

*Weighted score based on time spent was established by assigning the highest number to the clientele receiving the most time in each state, clientele receiving the second most time received 1 less, etc.

SUMMARY

Community development has been a significant Cooperative Extension Service program for the last twenty years (Sargent 1973); however, when compared to other extension programs, it is still relatively new and in the developmental stage.

Nationally, CES CD program approaches range from those that are mostly process oriented to those that are mainly task oriented. It is unlikely that any state limits its program to a single approach, but some emphasize one approach more than others. This in turn influences the role of the professional staff.

While it is not possible to predict the exact nature of future CES CD programs, some trends that will influence the role of the professional include:

1. No significant changes in staffing procedures and roles are likely to occur at the county level. Staff members with CD responsibilities will likely have additional program responsibilities in agriculture, 4-H, or home economics. The CD aspect of their roles will focus on process skills but will include providing technical information for which the staff member has been trained.

2. If additional funds become available, multicounty staffing is likely to be expanded. Staff members will have full-time responsibility and will likely perform process roles—that is, develop leaders through community problem-solving activities. Staff members in these positions will require training in the social sciences.

3. Expansion at the state level will probably be kept to a minimum. New staff will likely be employed to provide a technical subject-matter base and existing staff members may move toward specialization. State staff members will be expected to provide program materials and resources to county and area staff who serve process roles, thus creating more of a system approach within a limited range of subject-matter areas.

4. Some change appears to be occurring with regard to the clientele being served by the Cooperative Extension Service. Community development professionals in a large number of states are presently spending more time with government agencies and officials than with any other single group. The roles performed with this clientele are different from those performed with local community organizations and citizens at large.

5. Community development involvement with other CES program areas—agriculture, 4-H, and home economics—is likely to expand in the future and will account for any significant increases in the total staff time devoted to CD programs.

It is likely that CES community development programs will continue to be refined in the future. The roles of local staff will be of a process nature, while the state specialist staff will become more technically oriented. This will result in a more coordinated approach to program delivery and could result in the shifting of emphasis to a narrower range of subject matter. Some expansion in staff is likely with most of it occurring at the multi-county level.

E. WITH NEIGHBORHOOD ORGANIZATIONS /
Ian Harris

Community development implies a group of people at a local level meeting together to achieve a common goal or collective purpose. To facilitate this, the CD professional must pay attention to the product and process tasks that the groups sets for itself. To facilitate process tasks, professionals have to be skilled in organizing community people into groups with clear priorities, a sense of cohesion, a decision-making process, and power to win support for whatever projects they undertake. While the group is trying to achieve certain products in terms of a specific CD project, the professional must pay close attention to process so that the group can realize its potential as an organization that will give those working for it a sense of accomplishment and well-being.

For a neighborhood organization to be able to achieve solutions to locally defined goals, CD professionals must constantly strive to ensure widespread participation and involvement. Maintaining a high level of citizen participation will enable a project to become an exercise in democratic self-management where neighbors get together at the grass roots level to work on economic and social projects that will enrich their lives.

The professional working with neighborhood organizations has to work hard "to keep the democracy alive." As Alinsky has stated (1969, p. 53):

If we persist in our inquiry as to what is meant by a people's program, raising a series of questions—"Who thought of the program?" "Where did it come from?" "Who worked in its creation?" and other simple queries—we rapidly discover that too often the program is not a people's program at all but the product of one person, five persons, a church, a labor union, a business group, a social agency, or a political club—in short, a program that can be traced to one or two persons or institutions, but not to the people themselves.

Community development professionals working with neighborhood groups can be staff of city, state, or county planning and development agencies; university professors; extension specialists; or paid staff of neighborhood organizations that have received sufficient funding to hire full-time directors. Professionals' roles with neighborhood groups will vary, depending on whether they are positioned outside or work within the organization. One working outside an organization serves more as a traditional consultant, although not always for pay. From inside the professional is more a partner, serving on a board over an extended period of time, or an activist, working with members of a particular neighborhood organization to achieve mutually agreed-upon goals.

AS CONSULTANT

It is important that a group in fact requests assistance before a CD professional attempts to work with it in the capacity of a more traditional consultant. The history of community organizing and development is littered with struggles between community groups and professionals. Many grass roots organizations do not want professionals "messing with their business" and are fiercely territorial. It is crucial to respect local traditions and turf considerations.

One way to clarify the relationship between a neighborhood group and a professional is for the community group to work out a contract requesting specific services. As Cottrell (1977, p. 555) pointed out, community groups need to learn

how to use experts and specialists without being controlled by them. One important device is to structure the situation so that the experts are clearly subordinate to a broadly representative, tough-minded citizens' group which can be trusted to see that the technical issues are translated into terms the community can understand.

A formal contract can define expectations for the professional and can give a neighborhood group control over the relationship. Though the use of a contract is desirable, in reality most relationships between CD professionals and neighborhood groups are seldom that formal (Peattie 1968; Grosser 1973).

AS PARTNER

From time to time neighborhood organizations will ask professionals to serve on their boards or work with them over an extended period of time. In this capacity they work within the organization as supportive consultants, giving expertise to the groups. Such organizations are groups whose goals the professionals support, and it is usually in the interest of the professionals to see that the groups succeed. For example, a practitioner may serve on the board of a local child advocacy group because improved programs also enhance his or her reputation.

AS ACTIVIST

Sometimes a CD specialist becomes very closely involved with a group of people as an activist working hard to achieve the goals of the group. This role can be distinguished from the partnership role in that it requires practically a full-time commitment. When working as an activist, the professional serves as a peer with other members of the organization, and it is in the professional's self-interest to see that the organization succeeds. In this capacity professionals put their organizing skills to work helping to lobby for the organization, developing resources, setting realizable goals, establishing strategies for accomplishing those goals, and mobilizing citizens to build a mass base of support for the group.

FUNCTIONS PERFORMED

To develop priorities with a group of citizens, CD professionals need to be goal setters and researchers. They help groups set goals for themselves that include the needs and desires of a wide assortment of people. An organization where leaders or a select few people set goals is not democratic, so CD professionals spend time finding out what people want and incorporating those wants into specific projects that will be realizable, will have a time line, and will reflect the level of skills of the individuals in the group. As a researcher, the professional must gather information about funding sources, problems to be surmounted, potential allies and enemies, and possible plans of action. The results of this research can help a group of citizens set practical goals that can be translated into successful projects.

A group of neighbors who undertake a CD project must become a collective that can work well together. To develop a sense of cohesion within a group, professionals need to be skilled group practitioners. A professional who is a working member of a group must become part of the collective and subsume personal wishes and desires to those of the group. Professionals who relate to groups as consultants should be familiar with the different roles that people play in group settings, have to be able to give groups feedback about how different individuals are acting within the group, and have to be able to help the group get through the inevitable moments of frustration and interpersonal crises that will develop as it matures and assumes its own identity.

In addition, professionals have to know the formal and informal structures that will help facilitate decision making within an organization. They need to know how an executive committee or steering committee operates, how to hold public hearings, how to run a meeting, how to establish a chain of command, how to facilitate good communication between different committees and subcommittees, how to elect or choose officers who can assume leadership, and how leadership is to be exercised. With these skills, professionals can help a group of neighbors set up a structure that will allow for a great variety of participation and will create a smooth-working organization that has the potential to realize its goals (Davidoff 1965).

People who get together in neighborhoods to work on CD projects often have very few resources. A key task for professionals is to act as resource developers. In this capacity they must be able to develop a volunteer corps of people who believe in the project and are willing to work on it, raise money to pay for expenses, locate physical resources (such as offices and desks) so the group will have facilities for working, and enlist the aid of other professionals (lawyers, accountants, social workers, educators, etc.) who can offer technical assistance to the project. Without these resources no CD projects will ever succeed no matter how enthusiastic and motivated the participants may be.

Once such a group of residents has been formed into an organization with clear goals, a sense of cohesion, and resources, it will have to build a power base to achieve its objectives. To do this community developers will have to help the group organize within the public and the private sectors and the business community.

The private sector includes all people who live in the neighborhood. Professionals must sell the idea of the project in a way that will motivate people to work on it and reduce whatever hostility neighborhood residents may be feeling toward the project. Community developers need to organize within the neighborhood to build broad citizen organizations with hundreds if not thousands of members. These members, by paying dues, can contribute to the financial demands of the project and will supply the political base to give the project esteem and recognition in the eyes of influential people, business leaders, and politicians who have the power and resources to make the project a reality.

Simultaneously, professionals will have to approach businesspeople within the community and win their support for the project. No community development project will ever be successful unless it has the support of at least a few influential business leaders in a neighborhood. In this capacity the professionals must act as public relations experts, constantly selling people on the benefits of a particular project and training people involved in the project in good public relations so that strong ties can be built with business leaders.

Finally, professionals will have to help people develop positive ties with representatives from the public sector, such as city council members, county supervisors, and state representatives, as well as bureaucrats who have access to the funds that will make CD projects a reality. These people will have to be lobbied and supported in their elections. Community organizations may find, when they are faced with hostile government officials, that they have to enter the electoral arena and run opposing candidates who are willing to support their goals. In this capacity professionals have to know the political and economic dynamics that affect a given neighborhood and guide community residents through the intricacies of those dynamics.

In their capacity as community organizers, professionals working with a community group have to be familiar with the tactics of community organizing. These tactics will mobilize citizens and neighbors to attend hearings, write letters, talk to influential people, and in general build a mass base of support. By including a wide variety of citizens in CD projects, the professional utilizes democratic procedures in setting up and maintaining organizations. As Alinsky said (1969, p. 55),

After all, the real democratic program is a democratically minded people—a healthy, active, participating, interested, self-confident people who, through their participation and interest, become informed, educated, and above all develop faith in themselves, their fellow men, and the future.

Professionals can assure this democracy by using community organizing techniques to involve continually a broad spectrum of people in CD projects.

IMPLICATIONS

Working in a professional capacity with neighborhood groups can be fraught with difficulties. One of the problems concerns the issue of acceptance. Many people are resentful of professionals who make more money than they, who do not have to put up with the day-to-day headaches of a struggling organization, and whose training and background is often so theoretical that it has little or no practical applications for their work. Thus a distinction is needed between working within and outside neighborhood organizations. In the role of a partner or an activist, CD professionals are usually accepted by the members of a neighborhood group and credibility becomes established over a period of time. As a traditional consultant, though, the professional stands outside an organization and has to deal with the suspicions of the people.

Community development professionals working with community groups always face the dilemma of being experts and having other people rely on their expertise. One solution to this dilemma is for professionals to constantly be aware of their role as educators and strive to share skills with people in community groups so the people can carry out the work on their own. Neighborhood groups must strive not to become too reliant on professionals and to ensure participation from a wide variety of people to fulfill the program's promise as democratic. They need to set yearly goals for themselves and sponsor regular public events, such as festivals and fairs, that will help build their reputation. Neighborhood groups need to work out recruitment programs that will draw new people into the organization.

Further difficulties for professionals concern crisis resolution. Any organization will go through internal crises—arguments over power, personality conflicts, and differences over goals. On occasion, a CD professional is asked to help resolve a situation where the group has been unable to work out personal differences. It is important that the professional not get drawn into resolving such conflicts and thus alienating elements of the group.

In working with neighborhood organizations the most important and difficult task will continue to be maintaining democratic involvement. Many CD projects start out with an eager group of citizens who coalesce into a working group of from 5 to 20 people. As soon as this group raises enough money to hire staff and no longer maintains a high level of activity itself, it loses the dynamic citizen involvement that is at the core of successful community development. To counteract these tendencies towards centralization and reliance on a few leaders, professionals need to constantly be aware of how people are feeling about the project, why people drop out or sign up, and how to recruit new members. They must help arrange transportation for members who do not have cars, provide day care for young parents, schedule social events for people who are alienated from the neighborhood and its activities, counsel people who are having problems, and in general cater to people's needs for human interaction and a sense of belonging. These process tasks, the ones that will make people feel comfortable in an organization and will motivate them to continue within it, are perhaps the most creative and emotionally demanding. When these tasks are realized they will involve people in a revitalization process in their neighborhoods that will give meaning to their lives by allowing them to exercise their power and acquire a sense of importance through participating in the community development process.

F. AS A COMMUNITY PSYCHOLOGIST /
Mark W. Cohen

When I think over my past eight years of involvement with community development, three scenes repeatedly flash through my mind. The first is an interdisciplinary group of faculty and graduate students meeting for the fifteenth time to determine how best to become involved in community affairs. As usual, intellectual discussion prevailed over action; rather than make a decision on which direction to take, a consensus was reached that the group would not commit itself until it was sure that it had fully resolved the issue of defining what the term *community* really meant. The second memory is a vivid recollection of what was to be the first meeting of interested neighborhood residents to plan a community self-study project. Parenthetically, the project and the process by which it was to be accomplished was to be my dissertation topic. After weeks of publicity and assurances from community leaders that the project was needed and would be widely supported, I found myself on a dreary winter's evening in a church basement meeting room with only two other people, one of whom was a reporter from the neighborhood paper who was present to document the event. With a sinking feeling in the pit of my stomach, I wondered how this could have happened to me and why this situation had never come up in our seminar discussions. The third memory is more pleasant—a potluck dinner held by a senior citizens group in a small South Dakota town. My wife and I had been invited to attend and meet the local citizenry. The evening was delightful and led to a close and long partnership culminating in the purchase and renovation of a building that became a permanent senior citizens center.

Three conclusions can be drawn from these experiences. First, serious planning is essential before committing oneself to a course of action, but when taken to an extreme, the process of critically analyzing events becomes an end in itself. Such activity keeps one busy but can prevent meaningful change from occurring. Second, in community development work Murphy's law prevails! One who cannot be flexible and tolerate uncertainty should be in another field. Rarely do events unfold as planned, a fact that should be of no surprise to most people working in applied social sciences. Third, one who uses common sense, keeps pressing on, and does not give up more than likely will be pleasantly rewarded.

For me the key terms for success in this field are flexibility, tolerance of ambiguity, common sense, perseverance, and most important, a basic belief in the notion that people are capable of making competent decisions about programming that will directly affect their lives. My formula for effective intervention in community affairs was developed through working largely by trial and error, never being really sure whether I was correct in my judgment, and constantly being forced to address one overriding issue: What is my role as a psychologist in helping to create a climate conducive to producing community change? This feeling of groping in the dark and searching for an identity is still with me after years of involvement in CD work. The uncertainty is often frustrating and sometimes depressing; however, I am quite convinced that a state of continued questioning and mild confusion is the essential personal ingredient for maintaining a relationship of trust and integrity with a community.

The ability to accept uncertainty in one's professional role and ambiguity within the work setting is crucial to the psychologist actively involved in community development. At the present the position of the community psychologist as part of the community of service providers is unclear. This basic confusion stems from a fuzzy definition of the place that community psychology, a relative newcomer to the discipline, holds within psychology itself; the water is muddied even further by the issue of whether social scientists should become involved in activities that deal with variables too numerous to control and too loose to measure (Silverman 1971). These problems are directly related to the process by which community psychology developed and to its current dependence on the university for nurture.

Briefly, community psychology developed in the mid-1960s (Rosenblum 1975), partly as a reaction to the community mental health center movement's failure to address adequately the issue of primary prevention—the attempt to prevent new cases of emotional disease by modifying the environment as well as strengthening people's ability to affect their situation (Caplan and Grunebaum 1967). Questions were raised about the value of concentrating on larger social issues as opposed to treatment of individuals apart from their environment. A fear had arisen that over the years we had lost sight of the forest for treating the trees, with some evidence that even the trees were not faring too well as a result. If emotional distress can be viewed as largely a factor of environmental stress and a breakdown of community support systems, one must question whether the most appropriate action is to focus primarily on changing people to adapt more successfully to a poor environment or to concentrate more on changing the environment so that it is healthier for people. However, the demands of helping people with already existing emotional difficulties, coupled with a public funding policy aimed primarily at the area of direct treatment, have given little impetus to work in prevention.

Since public agencies have been somewhat reluctant to commit funds to primary prevention efforts, which often are slow to bear fruit and whose outcomes are quite difficult to measure, the growth of community psychology has been dependent largely on university-based support.

In an era when relevance of the university to the community has been questioned vociferously by state legislators sitting on budget committees, academia has welcomed people who could demonstrate in concrete terms its immediate usefulness to society. Thus the community psychologist, who spends considerable time and effort in the community helping people improve the quality of their lives, has found a home in institutions of higher learning.

However, being dependent on the university places the community psychologist in a bind. In the first place, while community psychologists are supposed to be "relevant," they are also expected to uphold scientific excellence. Being a scientific purist in a community setting where very little can be controlled is a difficult task indeed. Second, although methods for training community psychologists have been suggested (Kelley 1970) and many psychology graduate training programs have incorporated community psychology curricula (Isco and Spielberger 1970), most courses in the field are offered in traditionally oriented clinical psychology training programs where primary emphasis is still direct treatment of emotional casualties. Thus, students are taught the principles of community change in programs that prepare them ultimately to provide psychotherapeutic treatment. Since direct treatment is emphasized and since most jobs for psychologists outside of academia exist in agencies whose major reason for being rests on a foundation of psychotherapeutic services, one can easily see the difficulty of inspiring students seriously to consider community psychology as anything more than a minor interest area.

The individual who learns to live with confusion and becomes a community psychologist is a hybrid with multiple allegiances. Being part clinician, part community change agent, part educator, and part social scientist does pose problems; however, such a person can effectively "carve a niche in the community as a perceptive, caring, value-aware person with sharply honed observational abilities and an amply stuffed bag of strategies for understanding and augmenting decisions related to community needs" (Nottingham 1973, p. 427).

The variety of training experiences received (clinical work, research design, community theory) plus the demand for analytic thinking imposed by both the educational and employment setting present the community psychologist with a variety of potential services to offer the community. In the past eight years my activities have included evaluating community mental health center programs and educational programs for schools for native Americans, working with a local youth services center to develop a program for lowering the high school dropout rate, helping a community develop and conduct a household survey to determine what new volunteer programs to initiate, helping a community develop a community information center, working with a multicounty mental health planning agency to determine what services could best be provided in outlying rural areas, and working with an area planning agency for aging in conjunction with local church groups in rural communities to provide neighborhood support systems aimed at preventing or delaying institutionalization of the elderly. In all but the first instance, my involvement occurred while I was employed by a university to provide a community psychology training experience primarily to graduate students in clinical psychology. Working out of a university does allow one the advantage of working with a large variety of people while owing allegiance to none in particular. My own clientele has ranged from governmental units, to existing community groups, to organized interest groups. The development of a community information service resulted from requests by three disparate individuals.

My conception of a successful community psychologist is a person free from disciplinary dogma who is able to listen to people and provide them with the assistance they want. My own involvements have been varied in an attempt to be sensitive to actual community needs and not to impose my own belief on others. The ability to work with diverse people on a variety of projects has come from being continually forced to question who I am and to accept the notion that, while I possess skills that can be used for problem-solving, I have no answers.

In essence, the ambiguousness of the term *community psychologist* is valuable in that the practitioner is forced to accept some degree of humility. One can conclude that the role of CD workers is undefinable; all one can say is that they help people create change. This fact is true no matter what discipline the worker represents. In the future, areas of involvement and methodology will continue to expand. At the present there is a movement within community psychology to base educational programs in the community itself (e.g., Rappaport et al. 1975). While such changes bring with them additional problems, they offer much hope. One sees the potential for keeping the freedom offered by university affiliation while at the same time decreasing inter- and intradisciplinary conflict. The danger posed is the potential for institutionalization of community psychology. When clarity of purpose is attained and consensus of what we should be doing is achieved, we may lose the flexibility that has proven so helpful in the past.

G. AS PLANNERS / *Ernest E. Melvin*

Some community developers consider professional planners as a breed completely apart from themselves (Parsons 1978). Parsons notes that ''planners, welfarists and other 'do-it-for-them' practitioners must derive their initiatives largely from books and superior wisdom.'' Professional planners frequently regard community developers as software types who do not deal with the realities of community life.

There are scores of definitions of both *community development* and *community planning,* so one is comparatively free to choose or derive one that seems to serve best. One authority in the field defines community development as ''a continuity of complex action episodes in which the selection, planning and achieving of goals are deliberate and oriented to the collective good of an entire place-oriented society (Sutton 1970). Community planning was perceived by Friedmann (1966) as charting courses of action into the future—a process that leads to the definition of organizational goals and their reduction to specific programs and courses of action. On the basis of these two definitions, community development and community planning as professions are philosophically closely related; indeed, the two fields parallel.

Today's well-informed planner is expected to have an intimate knowledge of the community (comprehensive) planning process. The planning function includes five steps:

1. problem identification and goal definition
2. data collection and analysis
3. plan formulation and project development
4. implementation and action
5. feedback and plan modification

The planning function also includes six general substantive elements:

1. land use and the physical environment
2. transportation systems
3. human resources
4. economic functions
5. community facilities
6. government and finance

PREPARATION AND FUNCTION OF PLANNERS

Although there are recognized planning programs at the undergraduate level, most professional planning preparation occurs at the graduate level. There is a general opinion that a young person entering the planning field at the undergraduate level has a less adequate background than would be possible for the person entering from a graduate program with the master's degree. In 1975, 81 American and Canadian universities offered the master's degree and 20 American and Canadian universities offered the doctorate (Brooks 1976). The central themes of graduate programs in planning range from planning administration and social action to physical planning and urban design; concentrations of geographic emphasis are city and/or regional.

The professional planner must be technically qualified but should also have an ideological stance (Friedmann 1966); that is, the planner should be willing to help achieve a measure of self-direction in the evolution of a social system. The technical planner may be very mechanistic in approach, but the people-oriented planner must have an ideological or moral commitment as an understanding of the comprehensive planning process and the social system wherein it works (Melvin 1974). A detailed list of planning functions is cited (Melvin 1974):

1. identifying problems and indicating their magnitudes
2. assisting in goal-setting
3. disseminating factual and technical information
4. providing technical assistance
5. assisting in establishing priorities
6. developing projects aimed at problem-solving and attaining goals
7. assisting in developing comprehensive plans for systematic implementation
8. coordinating various activities for balanced programming and ultimately more successful implementation
9. evaluating progress at all stages in the planning process
10. reviewing results to determine whether goals have been attained and the client is satisfied
11. educating in a broad sense (not the primary job of a planner but clearly one that must be done through the cycle of the planning project or program)

ORGANIZATIONAL SETTINGS

Community planning serves three principal sectors of the community: the public, the private, and the institutional sectors.

In the public sector the planning function makes important contributions to the legislative, executive, and judicial bodies; to the planning commission; and to the understanding of the general public—in effect, it serves the public interest through the allocation of resources. In the private sector the planning function can be most effective in helping to serve economic development organizations, chambers of commerce, residential builders, shopping center developers, and other private interests with investment aims. Within the last quarter of a century religious denominations, hospitals and medical complexes, institutions of higher education, and similar groups have made use of the skills and knowledge the planning profession has to offer.

Although planners work as advisors to, and often as advocates for, specific entities within each of the three sectors, they are more often involved in a complex of horizontal interorganizational structures, working especially in community and regional settings with combinations from all three sectors. Perhaps the most significant vertical interorganizational environment is the intergovernmental scene in which local, multicounty, state, and federal levels of government are likely to be involved in comparatively simple projects on the one hand and complex, comprehensive planning and development efforts on the other.

SERVICE FOR SECTOR CLIENTS

The principal service of the planning function in community development is the derivation of strategy, which may be defined as "a process of analysis and action leading to a determination of deliberate intervention that constitutes the planning and ultimately transforms the problem into the solution" (Cartwright 1973). In this context, planning has also been defined as the "application of scientific-technical intelligence in societal action" (Friedmann 1969). Planners must consider the goals of society and the framework within which goals can be pursued (Altshuler 1965). Their service is characterized by time-frame, continuous process, and flexibility. The planning process must include social, economic, administrative, and fiscal as well as physical matters (Black 1968).

For the public sector, the professional planner serves through communication; conveyance of advice; education; providing the basis for implementation of programs; assisting in giving direction to research and development activities; and providing a basis for public understanding of community, government, legislative, and city planning activities.

For the private sector, the planning profession provides advice and counsel on the allocation of resources of all sorts, guidelines for the location of economic activity (site selection, residential development), technical assistance in matters of energy and environmental conditions, and information relative to planning and policy in the public sector. Essentially the same services are provided to the institutional sector; in addition, providing data of a specialized nature in demography, social conditions, quality of life, and neighborhood assessment may be of special value.

As a matter of fact, many of the planning services provided for each sector as indicated above may be provided for all sectors, depending on the nature of the problem at hand.

IMPLICATIONS FOR PROFESSIONAL PLANNERS

In the planning–community development milieu, it is not surprising that both the professional community developer and the professional community planner experience frustration generally because of the traditional backgrounds of education and experience that each brings to bear. Traditional CD professionals, often coming from a psychosocial background with a set of values that directs them to serve as change agents in social action processes, are more likely to be process oriented. Traditional planners, often coming from education and experience that are task oriented and bureaucratic, are more inclined to be project oriented. The philosophy of the former American Institute of Planners (now amalgamated with the American Society of Planning Officials to form the American Planning Association) conceives of the community planner as being involved in the comprehensive planning process. The challenge is for each professional group to move practice and philosophy closer together so that an effective community development–planning function can indeed be adequately performed. Having had conversations with many planners over a ten-year period as a member of the Examining Board of the American Institute of Planners, it is the opinion of the author that this challenge is easily met. It has been met by many professionals of both sorts through an appreciation and practice of the skills and knowledge that each profession has to offer.

Since the mid-1960s, there has been an ever increasing requirement for community involvement in the comprehensive planning process. Because of the more formalistic, task-oriented planning tradition, many planning professionals, especially those engaged in socioeconomic efforts, have had to learn much from the professional community developer. Requirements for community involvement (citizen participation) became the name of the game for those active in model cities programs in the late 1960s and then again more recently in revenue sharing and community block grant planning. Citizen participation and participatory planning involving the professional planner require ideological or moral commitment and have the potential for a much less mechanistic and a generally more satisfying experience for the professional planner.

In defining the role of the professional planner, a point of considerable discussion has been whether the professional planner should be purely advisory, actively advocate, or administrative. The advisory role is the traditional and safe road, but the professional planner also has an equally legitimate advocate role. Planners are, in fact, advocates for their clients in every case. The degree of advocacy may range from a purely advisory nature to that of a militant proponent for a particular plan or design. Ultimately the community planner and/or community developer may move into implementation or administrative responsibilities. The professional of either type must suffer certain frustrations in the shift from one of these three positions to another, but none of the three may be evaluated as *bad* in terms of what a professional in the community service field should be doing.

Dynamic forces and issues in today's society indicate ever more involvement of the community through citizen participation processes in the solution of these concerns. This is completely consistent with the nature of American democracy. Some of the forces and issues that clearly call for community involvement are public policies emanating from the federal level, an overall societal desire to enhance the quality of life, costs of energy and resource development, constraints of environmental regulation, socioeconomic justice for disadvantaged and disenfranchised citizens and groups (minorities, low-income segments of the population, the handicapped, etc.), a political objective for more autonomy in local affairs, and security needs to maintain a position of strength in a politically unstable world situation.

In summary, the role of a community planner is not as separate from community development as many of our professional colleagues might believe. Each profession has much to offer, and as the aforementioned and perhaps other unidentified forces and issues require resolution, the two professions in concert and separately have much to offer.

REFERENCES

Alinsky, Saul D. 1969. *Reveille for Radicals*. New York: Random House, Vintage Books.

Altshuler, Alan A. 1965. *The City Planning Process: A Political Analysis*. Cornell Univ. Press.

Anderson, James E. 1975. *Public Policy-Making*. New York, Praeger, pp. 18–25.

Bennett, Austin. 1973. Professional staff members' contributions to community development. *J. Community Dev. Soc.* 4 (Spring):58–68.

Bilinski, Russell. 1969. A description and assessment of community development. In *Selected Perspectives for Community Resource Development,* Luther T. Wallace, Daryl Hobbs, and Raymond D. Vlasin, eds., pp. 143–80. Raleigh: North Carolina State University, Agric. Policy Inst.

Black, Alan. 1968. The comprehensive plan. In *Principles and Practice of Urban Planning*. Washington: Int. City Manage. Assoc.

Brooks, Michael P., ed. 1976. *Guide to Graduate Education in Urban and Regional Planning,* 2d ed. Chicago: Assoc. Coll. Sch. Plann. and Am. Soc. Plann. Offic.

Cary, Lee J. 1972. Roles of the professional community developer. *J. Community Dev. Soc.* 3 (Fall):36–41.

Caplan, Gerald, and H. Grunebaum. 1967. Perspectives on primary prevention. *Arch. Gen. Psychiatry* 17(9):331–46.

Cartwright, Timothy J. 1973. Problems, solutions, and strategies: A solution to the theory and practice of planning. *J. Am. Inst. Plann.* 39 (2):179–87.

Cebotarev, E. A., and E. J. Brown. 1972. Community resource development: An analytic view of work strategies. *J. Community Dev. Soc.* 3 (Spring):40-55.

Columbia County leadership survey: A report to the leaders. 1970. Mimeographed. University of Wisconsin, Dep. Agric. Ext. Educ., Coll. Agric. Life Sci.

Cosgriffe, Harry A. 1968. Five approaches to community development. *J. Coop. Ext.* 6 (Summer):85-92.

Cottrell, Leonard S. 1977. The competent community. In *New Perspectives on the American Community,* Roland L. Warren, ed. Chicago: Rand McNally.

Davidoff, Paul. 1965. Advocacy and pluralism in planning. *J. Am. Inst. Plann.* 31 (6):331-38.

Durkheim, Emile. 1964. *The Division of Labor in Society.* New York: Free Press, pp. 221-22.

Dyer, Del, and Gene McMurtry. 1972. 4-H/CRD: Youth in action improving their community. Blacksburg: Virginia Polytechnic Institute and State University.

ECOP Report. 1966. Community resource development. USDA, Coop. Ext. Serv.

ECOP Report. 1975. Community development: Concepts, curriculum, training needs. USDA, Coop. Ext. Serv.

ECOP Task Force Report. 1974. Focus II: Extension home economics. USDA, Coop. Ext. Serv.

Ferguson, Clarence M. 1964. Reflections of an extension executive. Madison: University of Wisconsin, Coop. Ext. Serv., pp. 45-66.

Friedmann, John. 1966. Planning as a vocation, part 1. *Planning* 9:100-101.

_____. 1969. Notes on societal action. *J. Am. Inst. Plann.* 35 (3):311-18.

Gallaher, Art, Jr., and Frank A. Santopolo. 1967. Perspectives on agent roles. *J. Coop. Ext.* 5 (Winter):223-30.

Grosser, Charles F. 1973. *New Directions in Community Organization.* New York: Praeger.

Hamilton, Vance E. 1978. Survey of state CES community development leaders. Raleigh: North Carolina State University.

Hawley, Amos H. 1950. *Human Ecology.* New York: Ronald Press, pp. 36-39.

Hunter, Floyd. 1953. *Community Power Structure: A Study of Decision Makers.* Chapel Hill: Univ. North Carolina Press.

Isco, Ira, and C. Spielberger. 1970. *Community Psychology: Perspectives in Training and Research.* New York: Nailburg.

Jones, John E., and J. William Pfeiffer. 1977. Ethical considerations in consulting. In *Annual Handbook for Group Facilitators,* pp. 217-24. La Jolla, Calif: Univ. Assoc.

Kelly, James. 1970. Antidotes for arrogance: Training for community psychologists. *Am. Psychol.* 25 (4):524-31.

Lippitt, Gordon L., and Ronald Lippitt. 1975. Consulting process in action. *Train. Dev. J.,* May, pp. 48-54; June, pp. 38-41.

McCord, R. Warren. 1979. Community resource development in the South: How extension helps. In *Community Development Southern Style.* Starkville, Miss.: South. Rural Dev. Cent.

Mahan, Russ A., and Stephan R. Bollman. 1968. Education on information giving. *J. Coop. Ext.* 6 (Summer):100-108.

Marris, Peter, and Martin Rein. 1969. *Dilemmas of Social Reform: Poverty and Community Action in the United States.* New York: Atherton, p. 31.

Melvin, Ernest E. 1974. The planner and citizen participation. *J. Community Dev. Soc.* 5 (1):40-48.

Meyerson, Martin. 1956. Building the middle-range bridge for comprehensive planning. *J. Am. Inst. Plann.* 22:58-64.

Mitchell, Michael D. 1977. Consultant burnout. In *Annual Handbook for Group Facilitators*, pp. 143–46. La Jolla, Calif.: Univ. Assoc.

Morris, Robert. 1970. The role of the agent in the community development process. In *Community Development as a Process*, Lee J. Cary, ed. Columbia: Univ. Missouri Press.

Moss, Gwenna Mary. 1970. Analysis of community leaders: Orientations toward adult education. Ph.D. dissertation, University of Wisconsin.

National Task Force Report. 1978. An evaluation of community organization and leadership development in Cooperative Extension's community development program. Mississippi State University. Coop. Ext. Serv.

Nottingham, Jack. 1973. Can community psychology afford to be only scientific? *Prof. Psychol.* 4 (11):421–28.

Olsen, Marvin, ed. 1970. *Power in Societies.* New York: Macmillan.

Parsons, Tom. 1978. Professional certification for practitioners of C.D. *J. Community Dev. Soc.* 9 (1):4–10.

Peattie, Lisa. 1968. Reflections on advocacy planning. *J. Am. Inst. Plann.* 34 (2):80–88.

Price, James L. 1968. *Organizational Effectiveness: An Inventory of Propositions.* Homewood, Ill.: Richard D. Irwin.

Pugh, D. S., ed. 1971. *Organization Theory.* Baltimore: Penguin.

Rappaport, Julian; William Davidson; Melvin Wilson; and A. Mitchell. 1975. Alternatives to blaming the victim or the environment. *Am. Psychol.* 30 (4):525–28.

Ratchford, C. B. 1970. The CD profession in today's society. *J. Community Dev. Soc.* 1 (Spring):5–13.

Rosenblum, Gershen. 1975. Community psychology and mental health administration: From the frying pan into the fire. In *Current and Future Trends in Community Psychology*, Stuart Golan, ed., pp. 41–82. New York: Human Sci. Press.

Ross, Murray G. 1967. *Community Organization: Theory, Principles, and Practice*, 2d ed. New York: Harper & Row.

Sargent, Charles A. 1973. The educator and community development. *J. Ext.* 4 (Winter):28–34.

Silverman, Irwin. 1971. Crisis in social psychology: The relevance of relevance. *Am. Psychol.* 26 (6):583–84.

Steele, Fritz. *Consulting for Organizational Change.* 1975. Amherst: Univ. Massachusetts Press.

Stogdill, Ralph. 1974. *Handbook of Leadership: A Survey of Theory and Research.* New York: Free Press.

Sutton, Willis A., Jr. 1970. The sociological implication of the community development process. In *Community Development as a Process*, Lee J. Cary, ed. Columbia: Univ. Missouri Press.

Thaxton, Louis C. 1976. Cooperative Extension Service: The 1890 land grant colleges and Tuskegee Institute in the evolution of universal education, an American dream in education. Ph.D. dissertation, Ohio State University.

Ulschak, Francis L. 1978. Contracting: A process and a tool. In *Annual Handbook for Group Facilitators*, pp. 138–42. La Jolla, Calif.: Univ. Assoc.

Watkins, M. O. 1970. Role of extension in community and area development. In *Strategy for Community and Area Development*, Gene McMurtry, ed., pp. 161–68. Raleigh: North Carolina State University, Agric. Policy Inst.

Teaching Community Development

Lee J. Cary

TEACHING is one-half the teaching-learning equation and the emphasis here is on the part of the enterprise concerned with making information available and providing experience designed to facilitate learning. The focus will be on the teaching of community development in terms of: (1) the institutional base for education and training in community development, (2) the nature of what is taught in these programs, and (3) the content of the teaching effort. While it is realized that much teaching takes place informally through on-the-job, apprenticeship experiences, the discussion that follows is based on the more formal, organized efforts to teach community development.

A HISTORY OF TEACHING COMMUNITY DEVELOPMENT

Teaching community development grew, in part, out of the earlier teaching in community organization in social work and Rural sociology and the early training of extension workers. Dwight Sanderson, professor of rural sociology, Cornell University, presented a paper titled "Community Organization for Extension Workers" at the First National Country Life Conference in 1919. Jesse Steiner in 1925 published *Community Organization: A Study of its Theory and Current Practice,* which developed out of Steiner's course in community organization at the School of Public Welfare, University of North Carolina, and the Graduate School of Social Service Administration, University of Chicago. In 1939 Sanderson and Robert A. Polson published *Rural Community Organization,* which was based in large part on material used in a course on rural community organization they had taught for several years at Cornell.

The teaching of community organization in social work focused on a coordinating function among the established social welfare services and was overshadowed by the clinical emphasis in social work, thus giving too little attention to the need for broader training in helping communities act in their own behalf. The teaching of community organization in rural sociology placed its emphasis on the small rural community and, with some notable exceptions, focused on the study of community organization rather than the practice of it.

Community development's debt to community organization in social work and rural sociology is recognized as is the early teaching efforts in these two fields. However, because community development saw itself as different, the need to teach people how to carry out community development in practice called for a different approach. To be sure, the earliest community developers received their training in fields other than community development and had to learn on their own, using common sense and good judgment and drawing on their earlier training and whatever related experience they might have gained.

Although the focus here is on the more formal approaches to teaching community development and space limitations do not allow for a full discussion of the less formal types of such training, some attention needs to be given to the earlier programs that added to our understanding of community development and to the training efforts that take place outside the formal programs offered by the institutions of higher education. For example, the work of UNRRA, the Marshall Plan, and other foreign aid programs that grew out of the experiences in relief, rehabilitation, and reconstruction efforts after World War II, contributed to the conceptualization and development of theories and methods of community development. The United Nations technical agencies and the U.S. Agency for International Development have added to this body of knowledge and have developed training materials and training programs for use here and abroad.

Thousands of Peace Corps volunteers have received short workshop training in community development prior to assignment overseas. The Economic Opportunity Act of 1964 led to the development of informal short-term training, which included far more trainees than were involved in Peace Corps training. Private organizations, such as the American Friends Service Committee, carry out training in community development in this country and abroad. On the local scene, the Community Development Division of the National University Extension Association has offered its services for many years to various national organizations in training their members for local development work. One example is the cooperative effort with the Community Improvement Program of the General Federation of Women's Clubs, which began in 1955. These examples are just a few of the less formal approaches to teaching community development.

Because of space limitations, very little attention can be given to the many who have contributed to the teaching of community development. In addition to the few names already mentioned one thinks of the pioneering work of P. Ruopp, Peter Du Sautoy, and T. R. Batten. In this country and Canada a number of names come to mind. With no attempt to list them in order of importance and realizing that many equally important names have been left out, the list would include Baker Brownell, Father M. M. Coady, Curtis and Dorothy Mial, Irwin T. Saunders, Howard Y. McClusky, Richard Franilin, Otto Hoiberg, Richard Poston, Sevryn Bruyn, Willis Sutton, Jack Mezirow, and Roland Warren. These people are closely identified with many of the training programs and much of the writing in community development.

It is difficult to establish when the formal, organized teaching of community development began. One of the earliest such efforts was the Program of Community Studies and Dynamics that began at Earlham College, Richmond, Indiana, in the fall of 1947 under William W. Biddle. The first annual report of the program stated that its primary purpose was "to provide a better all-around education for students. More specifically, it seeks to develop socially aware, concerned citizens who have learned some skills in solving the problems of the communities in which they live." A seminar in community problems was open to juniors and seniors; it was not a standard academic course. As the first report pointed out, "The activities of the Seminar consisted of going out into a number of communities to confer with citizens, to help them form councils, to help them make surveys of need, to cooperate with them in solving problems."

By the second year there were three or four part-time graduate assistants working for master's degrees in community dynamics. The eleventh annual report of the program (Community Dynamics 1958) stressed the importance of training. It acknowledged that "trained people are sought for overseas operations and for local domestic activities of many kinds. The call is for professionals in the newly emerging field of community development." It went on to state that "no educational institution has yet accepted the training responsibility on a serious scale." In June 1960, the Program of Community Dynamics was officially terminated when this new field of training became the responsibility of the social science division of Earlham College.

Antigonish, Nova Scotia, is the location of Saint Francis Xavier University and is the name of an internationally known early program in cooperative and adult education known as the Antigonish Movement. In the late 1920s, M. M. Coady helped to organize a cooperative, the United Maritime Fishermen. In 1929 the Extension Department of Saint Francis Xavier University was established with Coady as the first director. This extension program, the Antigonish Movement, was built on the simple premise that by learning and working together people could achieve meaningful goals. In 1959, the Coady International Institute, which drew on the experience of the Antigonish Movement and made training available to students from developing countries, was founded at the university.

In 1957, the Center for Community Studies was established as a joint undertaking of the University of Saskatchewan and the government of Saskatchewan. The center grew out of the recommendations of a five-year study by the Saskatchewan Royal Commission on Agriculture and Rural

Life. "Its purpose was to carry out research, training and consultation on techniques and processes of community development and planned change." The training emphasis of the center was on "helping leaders become more competent in helping their communities" (Solomon 1959). Because of the limited amount of material available for training, the center made extensive use of case studies.

The earlier experiences at Earlham College, Saint Francis Xavier University, and the Center for Community Studies raised several of the key issues that are still not fully resolved. What is the nature and content of training needed for community development? Who is to be trained? In answer to the first question, most of the early training programs relied heavily on the experience gained in working in communities as the basic teaching technique. The communities provided the setting in which, working with local community leaders, the process of decision making and action by the community was carried out. Not only was this community-based approach beneficial to the communities but it helped train those who were involved in the process. The content of these programs focused on observing, recording, and learning from human reactions to actual community problems. At Earlham, particularly, the emphasis was on integrating this experience with the rest of the college curriculum.

The second question, who is to be trained, was not clearly established at that time. The Program of Community Dynamics at Earlham originally had as its purpose the providing of a better all-around education for students, training them "in developing greater democratic initiative." As early as the second year, however, several graduate assistants were working for master's degrees in community dynamics. The concept of training for a career in this work was introduced. In contrast, the center in Saskatchewan focused its training efforts on local community leaders rather than on college students seeking experience in community development or graduate students seeking careers in this new field.

Arthur Dunham (1960), in preparing a paper for the 1958 National Conference on Social Welfare on "The Outlook for Community Development," asked a number of leaders in the field to comment on a draft outline of the paper. One question asked if a new profession focused on general community improvement was likely to emerge and would this be desirable or not. Dunham saw the need for a considerable number of persons "who are consciously trained to give leadership in general community development." His views were not shared by most of those responding—some questioned the need for and desirability of community developers.

However, two Midwest universities were about to establish master's degree programs in community development. Beginning in the 1950s, the University of Missouri, Columbia, and Southern Illinois University, Carbondale, offered consultation services and informal training in community development. In 1962 both universities established graduate professional education programs offering a master of science in community development. The programs included core courses, field experience, research, and electives. Programs with particular emphasis on CD training for work in urban areas developed somewhat later. The University of Louisville established a master's degree in community development in 1968. Hunter College, City University of New York, through its Department of Urban Affairs, offered a master's program in urban processes in 1971. A number of other urban universities, while not offering a degree in community development, do include the teaching of community development in their departments, centers, and institutes that focus on urban affairs and urban development.

DIRECTORIES

In 1969 and again in 1973 the Department of Regional and Community Affairs (Community Development) at the University of Missouri, Columbia, published directories of CD education and training programs.

The first directory (Benson and Cary 1969) listed programs leading to (1) a graduate degree in community development, (2) a diploma or certificate in community development, (3) a graduate degree in other fields with a major emphasis in community development, (4) a diploma or certificate in other fields with an emphasis in community development, and (5) an undergraduate degree with a major in community development. The information for this first directory was gathered in 1967–1968 and reflects the range of academic approaches to the teaching of community development. The directory listed 17 institutions in the United States and Canada offering at least some courses in community development. Four institutions offered master's degrees in the field, including (in addition to Missouri and Southern Illinois) the University of Alberta and North Carolina State University at Raleigh.

The second directory (Department of Regional and Community Affairs 1973) listed 48 institutions and organizations offering 55 different programs including both a degree and special training in community development. The directory entries were divided into five categories that were different from those in the earlier directory. The first category included 11 programs leading to an undergraduate degree with an emphasis in community development. The second and largest category contained information on 24 programs leading to an advanced degree. The third category included 5 programs offering an associate degree, diploma, or certificate with an emphasis in community development. In the fourth category were listed 12 short-term training programs offered on a regular basis (at least once a year). The fifth and final category included 3 proposed programs in community development education and training. Seven of the programs were offered by institutions in Canada. Note that all education and training programs were listed as offering ''an emphasis in community development'' rather than some more specific designation such as ''a degree in community development." The designation seemed both appropriate and necessary, since a number of programs did not offer specific degrees or certificates in community development, yet were clearly involved in the teaching of community development.

The most recent directory, the 1976 edition, was published by the Community Development Society (Cary 1976b). It lists 48 institutions and organizations offering 52 undergraduate, graduate, associate degree, diploma, or certificate programs and 8 short-term training programs. A paper comparing the data obtained for the 1973 and 1976 directories was presented at the Eighth Annual Conference of the Community Development Society at Boise, Idaho (Cary 1976a); the author pointed out that the number of undergraduate programs had increased over 20 percent and the number of students enrolled was up 60 percent. The number of graduate programs had increased, but this was offset in part by three programs that were listed in 1973 but by the time of the 1976 directory did not offer sufficient emphasis in community development to warrant inclusion. Associate degree and certificate programs remained about the same in number but showed substantial growth in enrollment (up one-third). Short-term training underwent the greatest change, with a drop in the number of such programs, according to the information available.

TYPES OF COURSES

With this background we are in a position to look at the types of courses offered. In 1974 the late Harry Naylor attempted to identify the major components in community development curricula. The six types of courses found most frequently were: (1) introductory courses; (2) theoretical perspectives, including the examination of social science theory as it applies to the change process; (3) CD process and program development; (4) group dynamics and group processes; (5) research and analysis of data; and (6) field experience or internship (Naylor n.d.).

Information supplied for the 1976 directory included additional data about courses and related activities for 22 of the programs offering advanced degrees with an emphasis in community development. Although respondents were not asked about the six categories established by Naylor, they did furnish information that tended to lend support to the six types of courses identified earlier. All but one of these 22 programs offered and frequently required community development "core courses," usually covering such topics as introduction to the field, theory and practice, and program development. Sixteen required field experience or internships and 15 required research and/or a research project. Respondents for nearly two-thirds of these programs (14 of 22) indicated that their programs also allowed for electives or optional courses. No information received related to one of Naylor's six categories, group dynamics and group processes (Cary 1976a).

Response to another item in this survey may be of interest. Respondents were asked to identify whether a development, planning, or action emphasis most nearly described the CD approach of their staff. Definitions for these three approaches were offered in the questionnaire to aid respondents and were similar to the definitions used by Rothman (1970) in his material on the three practice models of community organization. Respondents for 8 of the 22 programs indicated a development emphasis and 3 a planning emphasis. Four other respondents felt they emphasized all three approaches, 2 emphasized development and planning, 1 indicated a development and action emphasis, and 4 gave no indication of program emphasis.

One final research report seems important at this point. A study of CD master's degree programs in the United States and Canada was completed by the writer with the aid of two graduate assistants (Cary, Azar, and Turley 1977). Five universities in this country and one in Canada award master's degrees in community development. They are: University of Missouri, Columbia; Southern Illinois University, Carbondale; University of Louisville; University of Alberta; University of Maine at Orono; and University of California, Davis. Again, using the Naylor framework, all six institutions include courses in process and program development and research and analysis of data. Five of the six have a field experience or internship requirement and offer course work in the theoretical perspectives of community development. Three of the six have introductory courses in community development and courses in group dynamics and group processes.

The 1977 study goes on to present catalog descriptions, course outlines, and a list of bibliographic material (when this information was provided by the institutions). The programs at Missouri, Illinois, and Alberta have quite similar offerings and degree requirements. The programs in Maine and California are relatively new and as yet have not had sufficient time or enough students to develop fully. The program in Kentucky is different from the other five in several ways: It does not have required or core courses; almost all the students hold full-time positions and attend the University of Louisville on a part-time basis; and all the instructors, other than the director, are part-time with the program and engaged to teach a particular course.

Space does not permit a thorough discussion of all the other information contained in the 1977 study, but we will look at the content of courses, as reported by the respondents of these six programs, in Naylor's six categories. Introductory courses try to provide a general understanding of community development through a study of its historical and philosophical perspectives. Concepts, values, and principles are examined as an introduction to theory and practice. Courses on the theoretical perspectives are designed to draw on relevant social science theory as it applies to deliberate efforts to affect human, social, economic, and political development. Major interpretations of change, as found in the various disciplines, are reviewed to create a conceptual understanding of the mechanics of planned change at the community level. Courses in process and program development are planned to engage the student in a study of the application of CD theory in specific situations through the establishment and operation of the process in programs and projects.

Courses in group dynamics and group processes combine theory and laboratory experience with an emphasis on interpersonal competence, understanding and working in small group situations, and the use of group techniques. Research and the analysis of data provide an introduction to social science research methods and techniques, including the basic tools and procedures for conducting research relevant to CD situations. It is believed the course also helps to meet the needs of students planning individual research projects. Finally, the field training or internship provides practice in a professional setting where the student can test and develop skills under a qualified field instructor. Together these courses help to prepare the student for professional practice by combining theory and practice and by contributing to the student's knowledge, skills, and experience in community development.

MAJOR CONCEPTS

Another way of viewing course content is to identify the major concepts that are central to community development and are interwoven in the array of courses offered in most CD curricula. While the concepts listed may not embrace all that others feel are most important, these will be recognized as central. They include (1) human groupings; (2) communication, power, and leadership; (3) social change; and (4) human relations. Each is discussed briefly.

Human groupings is an umbrella term that covers a number of other concepts important to teaching community development. Included is the classification of groups into what Charles Horton Cooley called "primary groups" and larger and more formal clusters of peole that others have referred to as "secondary groups." Community development takes place in both types of groups, but the positions and roles of individuals and the relationships between individuals in primary and in secondary groups are quite different and need to be fully understood. Important too are the intensity, duration, and frequency of interaction in human groupings and the relationships among various groups.

Interaction between groups may follow several patterns including cooperation, competition, and conflict. Warren (1978) has referred to these as situations of issue consensus, issue difference, and issue dissensus, calling for, respectively, a collaborative, a campaign, and a contest strategy.

Interaction between groups also has impact on interaction within the group. Over time, repeated contact between groups can lead to adjustments and accommodations and even assimilation of the groups into one.

The concept of human groups raises questions concerning what brings individuals into groups and what holds groups together. A comprehensive response to these two inquiries is beyond the limits of this discussion, but several important factors can be cited. Geography is a factor to the extent that physical proximity increases the opportunity for interaction, while distance decreases such possibilities. Sutton (1970) points out that the important point is not what is "local to" but what is "collective for" a particular population, placing the emphasis more on common needs and interests rather than common terrain. Other factors bringing individuals together and holding them together is identification with the purpose or goal of the group and, after joining, the experience and satisfaction in working together. Finally, boundary maintenance is important in keeping a group together. Through a variety of techniques, the unity of the group is maintained and individuals are less apt to leave to join other groups because of these efforts to achieve boundary maintenance.

The second broad concept, including communication, power, and leadership, focuses on a system of social relationships and the instruments that help to coordinate and harmonize these relationships. From this point of view, communication, power, and leadership are closely related and are difficult to consider alone. However, for our purposes we will consider each separately. Communication is essential to any group activity and basic to any human interaction. The structure of communication is a central concern as is an understanding of the potential blocks to effective communication. Power, the ability to exercise control, is an important instrument of coordination. The larger the group, the more essential is the coordinating function and the more complex the power relationships. Power is frequently granted or allocated by a group to those who can help to fulfill the group's needs and expectations. Individuals accorded sufficient power and prestige are identified as leaders and may be called on to perform a variety of leadership roles. As the roles become established, they may rotate among members of a group as the members assume specific roles. Leadership training helps individuals learn how to perform roles essential to a group's task accomplishment and maintenance.

The third concept is social change, which is a very complex and continuous process occurring everywhere and constantly altering social relationships. One part of social change is concerned with changes that are planned, and some portion of these planned changes are carried out through a process identified as community development. In teaching community development it is important to identify the major practice variables that apply specifically to this process and how they differ from those associated with other processes of planned change. The concept of social change poses a number of difficult questions. What constitutes progress or desirable change? Who decides what planned changes to undertake and how are they carried out? Change carried out through an open and democratic process involves certain value assumptions about the way in which it is brought about. Most basic is the orientation that people should participate fully in the decisions that affect their lives and all those who are affected should have open access to the process. Whether we have yet developed adequate mechanisms for putting this principle into practice is open to question.

The fourth concept is human relations. The theory and practice of human relations is primarily concerned with the most effective ways of helping people organize to accomplish specific objectives. The behavior and attitudes of individuals change, in part because of changes in the relationships among individuals. Cooperation develops from joint activity and from an individual's attitudes toward others in an organization and toward the organization itself. The individual's behavior is conditioned by the social systems within which the individual functions. Each social system, each organization is made up of two interrelated systems, one formal and the other informal. The formal system focuses on the rational relationships among the parts and appears on the organization's chart. The informal system results from informal ties within the organization and is created by members. In understanding and working with these relationships within an organizational structure it is important to recognize the vital role played by effective two-way communication. Involvement, common experiences, and shared symbols that signify one belongs are equally important to the development of positive feelings and cooperative attitudes among individuals in an organization.

While these four concepts are quite broad and their presentation here is somewhat simplistic and generalized, understanding them is basic to an understanding of how individuals alone and in groups carry out a CD process in the context of their immediate community and the larger society. A task force of the National Association of State Universities and Land-Grant Colleges published a report in 1975 that listed over 30 concepts considered central to community development (Task Force Report 1975). What we have presented here embraces a number of the more basic concepts in the Task Force Report and focuses attention on the importance of social science theory as a basis for CD teaching and practice.

In summary, the teaching of community development is a function of institutions of higher education. Although there are no agreed-upon minimum standards for professional education in community development, many programs share a number of similar courses and similar degree requirements. Most of those teaching in these programs also share a concern for maintaining a relationship and balance between theory and practice, between the classroom and experience in the community. The primary objective of these programs is to prepare students for beginning professional practice in community development. The success of these teaching efforts can be measured, in part, by the ability of graduates of these programs to perform satisfactorily in community settings as CD professional practitioners.

REFERENCES

Benson, A. E., and Lee J. Cary. 1969. *Community development: A directory of academic curriculums throughout the world,* 1st ed. Columbia: University of Missouri, Dep. Reg. Community Aff.

Cary, Lee J. 1976*a*. Community development education: An overview of programs throughout the world. *J. Community Dev. Soc.* 7 (2):115–21.

_____., ed. 1976*b*. *Directory: Community development education and training programs throughout the world.* Columbia, Mo.: Community Dev. Soc.

Cary, Lee J.; Sheryl Azer; and Richard Turley. 1977. Master's degree programs in community development in the United States and Canada: A status report. Mimeographed.

Community Dynamics, 11th annu. rep. 1958. Richmond, Ind.: Program Community Dyn.

Community Studies and Dynamics, 1st annu. rep. 1948. Richmond, Ind.: Program Community Stud. Dyn.

Department of Regional and Community Affairs. 1973. Directory of community development education and training programs throughout the world, 2d ed. Columbia: University of Missouri.

Dunham, Arthur. 1960. The outlook for community development: An international symposium. *Int. Rev. Community Dev.* 5:33–55.

ECOP Report. 1975. Community development: Concepts, curriculum, training needs. Columbia: University of Missouri, USDA, Coop. Ext. Serv.

Naylor, Harry L. (n.d.) Working paper on core curricula in community development. Mimeographed.

Rothman, Jack. 1970. Three models of community organization practice. In *Strategies of Community Organization: A Book of Readings,* pp. 20–36. Itasca, Ill.: Peacock.

Sanderson, Dwight. 1919. Community organization for extension service. In *Proceedings of First National Country Life Conference,* pp. 208–22. Ithaca, N.Y.: Cornell Univ. Press.

Sanderson, Dwight, and Robert A. Polson. 1939. *Rural Community Organization.* New York: Wiley.

Solomon, Darwin. 1959. An approach to training for community development. *Int. Rev. Community Dev.* 3:26.

Steiner, Jesse F. 1925. *Community Organization: A Study of Its Theory and Current Practice.* New York and London: Century.

Sutton, Willis A., Jr. 1970. The sociological implications of the community development process. In *Community Development As a Process,* Lee J. Cary, ed., pp. 57–83. Columbia: Univ. Missouri Press.

Warren, Roland L. 1978. *Community In America, 3d ed.* Chicago: Rand McNally, chap. 12.

CHAPTER 9

Research on Selected Issues in Community Development

Lorraine Garkovich and Jerome M. Stam

INTRODUCTION

Community development conjures up different images in the minds of listeners, reflecting the diversity of its practitioners. This variation in meaning and practice makes difficult the process of identifying and classifying research on community development. If one adopts a broad definition of development, much of the research in the social sciences could have relevance for CD practitioners. But, like the sorcerer's apprentice who summoned up too much assistance, a review of all research relevant to community development would flood the authors and the readers. What is important to remember is that there are no universal answers for community development specialists. The answers to development issues depend on the problems addressed, the situational context, and the methodologies adopted.

Hence, this chapter will review research relevant to three areas of activity: (1) needs assessment, (2) community services, and (3) economic analysis focused on the impacts of industrialization and population change. These areas of emphasis reflect development issues confronting specialists in all types of communities and illustrate the diversity of methodologies and solutions utilized by researchers. Each section highlights some of the major research problems, perspectives, and findings related to the particular development issue and so can provide a convenient summary of research resources available to the CD specialist. This chapter permits practitioners to sample a vast array of research literature to select those items most suited to their needs.

NEEDS ASSESSMENT

Needs assessment research has proliferated in the last decade so that at any one time several communities, regions, or states must be undergoing the

---

The authors wish to acknowledge Paul Gessaman, University of Nebraska, for his critical evaluation and suggestions for improving this chapter.

experience. However, as Vintner and Tropman (1974) point out, needs assessment research does not always seem to fulfill its promise because the concept of needs assessment encompasses a diversity of purposes and techniques. A review of the literature suggests four questions that differentiate the approaches utilized. All four emphasize the primary theme of this review: One must know the ultimate goal or purpose of the needs assessment to devise an adequate mechanism for achieving that goal (Table 9.1).

What Needs Will Be Assessed?

The needs assessed by various authors (Dillman 1971; Nix and Seerley 1972; Christenson 1973, 1975, 1975–1976; Hagood, Rankos, and Dillman 1974; Alternatives for Washington State-Wide Task Force 1975; Miller, Dressel, and Nix 1976; Warner et al. 1976; Garkovich 1979) encompass a wide variety of subjects. In some cases the needs are *action preferences* (Blake, Kalb, and Ryan 1977) assessing the types of action that should be taken in specific areas of services and/or programs. This research focuses on preferences for government actions—specific or general—designed to achieve some end—specific or general. There are major differences in the specificity of (1) the action assessed (spend more money as compared to mandatory installation of heavy insulation in existing homes) and (2) the ultimate goal or purpose of the action (fire protection as compared to providing the elderly transportation to local hospitals, clinics, and doctors' offices). The basic tenets for the action-preferences approach are: The respondents have informed preferences on the range of possible solutions, some decisions on the priority of issues facing the community have already been made, and the action preferences offered have some correlates in the decision-making framework of the local community. The latter issue is influenced by the specificity of the actions posed. Simply determining that 75 percent of the respondents support spending more money on education does not provide any information as to how the funds should be disbursed (programs versus facilities). In addition, since most communities have limited funds, increased spending in one area would lead to reduced spending in others. A general assessment of action preferences is not often couched in terms of "if we spend more money on X, what other program or service do we prefer to have reduced?" This question is not asked because assessments of specific action and goal preferences require a tailoring of the research instrument to the special conditions in each community, placing constraints on the scope of the research.

In other cases, the needs assessed focus on the respondents' concerns and their perceptions of the issues confronting the community. These needs assessments are of two types: quality of life and quality of services or programs. Research on the first issue attempts to assess what factors combine to produce a community with an acceptable or desirable *quality of life*. These assessments involve considerations such as the social climate of the community (friendliness) and opportunities for participation in a variety of

TABLE 9.1. Issues and Approaches to Needs Assessment

What Needs Will Be Assessed?	Who Will Do the Assessment?	How Will the Assessment Occur?	How Will Assessments Be Utilized?
Action Preferences Type of action general specific Type of goal general specific	Policymakers Community organizations Citizens Extralocal agencies	*Primary Analysis* Type of sampling random purposive Method of data collection mailed questionnaire personal interviews	*Focus of Data Analysis* Descriptive general specific Goal setting general specific Action recommendations general specific
Concerns and Issues Quality of life concerns actual community ideal community Quality of services and program issues actual community ideal community *Availability and Utilization of Services and Programs*		*Secondary Analysis* Census data State and local government Private organizations	*Recipients of Data Analysis* Policymakers Community organizations Citizens

activities or organizations. The quality of life is evaluated from the perspective of factors that compose the ideal community or are actually present in the community, making it a desirable place to live.

Issues dealing with the *quality of services or programs* focus on the respondents' assessment of current services or programs or their feelings that the delivery of a particular service or program would contribute to the development of the ideal community. A review of the research reveals that most of these assessments involve inventories of all possible services or programs from mental health care facilities to day care centers. The evaluation of a service or a program takes many forms, ranging from satisfaction with it to perception of the size of problem it represents within community life.

Frequently both quality-of-life concerns and quality of services or programs issues are evaluated in a single research effort to assess overall quality of community life. This inventory approach assumes (1) the respondents are familiar with each of the services or programs listed and (2) there is some relationship between their perceptions of the quality of life and the actual quality of services or programs. In addition, an interpretation of the results must be couched in generalities, since stating that 70 percent of the respondents feel it highly important to improve police protection provides no guidelines on how to improve the service or its importance vis-à-vis other services or programs. However, within a comparative context, such information can be valuable. For example, if we know that 75 percent of the respondents in county *A* state that lack of police protection is a serious community problem, while only 10 percent of the respondents in adjacent county *B* agree to this statement, some implication can be drawn concerning the quality of police services in county *A* and the relative attention given to police services in counties *A* and *B*.

A final type of needs assessment concerns the *availability-utilization* of services or programs. This focus is more specific, since the respondents note if the service or program is available and if they have used it prior to evaluating whether (1) it is convenient to use and (2) they are satisfied with it. This approach makes more specific the respondents' evaluations (Christenson 1979).

Each of the three approaches to needs assessment offers potential advantages and pitfalls. All three provide an inventory and ranking of perceived needs but from differing perspectives. The action preferences approach produces an ordering of services or programs in terms of priorities for action. The concerns and issues approach creates a hierarchy of the problems confronting the respondents. The availability-utilization approach ranks concerns with services and programs but permits the researcher to determine partially if the concerns are based on problems of availability, utilization, or knowledge. Information on the respondents' ordering of *problems* does not necessarily suggest this will be the ranking of *action preferences* or vice versa. Likewise, that a service may not be available in a community does not necessarily imply that it should be or that its absence is a cause of respondent concern or dissatisfaction with the quality of life. Hence drawing inferences from dissatisfaction with a community condition to the need for action directed at the condition is a most difficult process.

Finally, all three approaches face a continuous problem of lack of specificity. While action preferences have been expressed in terms specific to the community under study and to the decision process within that community, such studies are an exception.[1] More frequently, respondents comment on a range of general issues, services, or programs that represent what may be called "a market basket approach" to community assessment. The problem resides not in the nature of the question posed but the inferences drawn or policy decisions derived from these general catalogs. A general approach to needs assessment can have utility in highlighting areas of concern (Schwebel et al. 1978) but cannot identify a specific mechanism of change that will necessarily meet public approval at a later time (Dillman 1977). This is not necessarily an indictment of needs assessment, but a cautionary note: A clear vision of the ultimate use of the assessment is necessary in deciding what needs should be assessed.

Who Will Do the Assessment?

A variety of individuals or organizations within a community have served as respondents (Blake, Kalb, and Ryan 1977). The selection of an appropriate sample of respondents for a needs assessment should be based on the purpose of the assessment. If the purpose is to identify general problem areas confronting the community or to identify prevailing conceptions of the quality of life, a sample of community residents is appropriate (Cocherhan and Blevins 1977; Goudy and Wepprecht 1977; Schwebel et al. 1978). Or as Cohen, Sills, and Schwebel (1977) comment: "If you want to know about a community's needs, ask them." Citizen preference surveys have been employed as a mechanism of needs assessment on both state and local levels utilizing each or combinations of the described approaches. All these surveys provide citizens with an opportunity to express their action preferences or comment on concerns and issues.

Alternatively, one can assume that community organizations or their representatives can provide more relevant feedback to the decision-making process, since they may influence (formally or informally) the decision on policy alternatives (Basson 1970). Or effective leaders (policymakers) in a community can perform a needs assessment within the decision alternatives available to the community (Nix and Seerley 1973; Nix, Brooks, and Courtenay 1976). This approach assumes that the purpose of the needs assessment is to identify action preferences or the concerns and issues of a community's leadership or organizations that may influence critical deci-

---

1. An example of this approach is, "In the solution to the traffic problem in downtown Nicholasville, which of the following would you favor? 1. By-pass on east side of Nicholasville. 2. By-pass on west side of Nicholasville. 3. Improve downtown route. 4. Other (please specify).

sions. It blunts a frequent criticism that needs assessments represent simple "wish books" with no base within the framework of community alternatives. Needs assessment by formal or informal community leaders offers a more informed analysis of community needs. In some cases (Nix and Seerley 1973), the needs assessment may compare and contrast the evaluations of both citizens and leaders, illustrating the points of convergence and divergence in views on community life by persons in different status positions.

A final approach utilizes extralocal agencies or experts to evaluate the quality, availability, or utilization of services or programs. These agencies employ standardized criteria, such as physicians or hospital beds per capita (Cordes 1977), to assess, on a more objective basis than citizen perceptions, service needs in the community. The evaluation is based on how the community's services or programs compare with those available and/or operating in other places and is restricted to an assessment of services or programs.

The first three respondent options (citizens, policymakers, community organizations) assume those persons who live in the community are most appropriate for defining its needs. The use of extralocal agencies or specialists presupposes that evaluations of service or program needs should be performed by those not influenced by partisan preferences.

How Will the Assessment Occur?

The needs assessment can occur through primary or secondary analysis. Obviously if the assessment is to be performed by citizens, policymakers, or organizations in the community, some type of sampling (random or purposive) must be utilized to obtain the necessary data. A primary analysis will require decisions as to the type of sampling and the method of data collection (questionnaires or personal interviews). Several needs assessments have employed combinations of these methods. For example, Cohen, Sills, and Schwebel (1977) utilized open-ended interviews with citizens to define areas of community concern and followed this with an areawide survey. The second phase employed a closed-ended questionnaire to measure the severity and frequency of the problem as defined by a sampling of citizens. While questionnaires permit a wider sampling of either citizens or leaders, personal interviews provide a more intensive examination of issues and concerns.

Much literature has developed on different methods of data collection. Dillman's (1978) "total design method" outlines procedures for mail and telephone surveys based on previous research efforts. Dillman details a step-by-step approach to mail and telephone surveys of the general public or special populations and also includes an extensive reference bibliography. Gordon (1969), Johnson (1976), and Rogers (1976) provide general information on the problems and advantages of personal interviews.

A needs assessment may also be derived from a secondary analysis.

State and local governments, census information, or private organizations may offer data on programs and services provided, problems, equipment, clients served, characteristics of population, etc. This information base may be utilized in combination with primary data to provide a holistic view of community conditions (according to some objective criteria) and how citizens or other respondents perceive the community's conditions (Christenson 1976a; Dillman 1977; Garkovich 1979). Secondary data can be utilized to define issue areas, which may then be further clarified as to what extent community members experience the situation as a deprivation or a problem. For example, secondary analysis may show that the number of physicians per 100,000 population in a nonmetropolitan area is below some national standard indicating an unmet need; yet residents may not perceive this shortage as a problem or major community concern, since commuting to a metropolitan area may satisfy their demand for medical services.[2]

The choice of primary or secondary methods of needs assessment is in part restrained by who will do the assessment, or vice versa. But the ultimate purpose of the assessment should always be the guiding concern.

How Will the Assessment Be Utilized?

One of the most common critiques of needs assessments is that they frequently are "wish books" of preferences; while many people may want more police protection, for example, most would not be willing to vote for increased taxes to achieve this preference. This criticism applies only to general action preferences or recommendations.

Data analysis must be focused on one of three major goals. One goal is a *description* of general concerns, issues, or action preferences or of specific concerns, issues, or action preferences centered on some aspect of community life (i.e., recreation, land use planning). Needs assessments may also be used for a *definition of goals* for the community. These goals may be general (to improve the availability of housing in the community) or specific (to provide 100 units of low-income housing over the next five years). Finally, needs assessments may produce *action recommendations* for local decision makers. Again the action preference may be general (there is a desire for public access to scenic rivers; landowners and river users are currently disputing how to achieve access and most people want government action on this issue) or specific (the majority of property owners along the river prefer a term lease to a state agency assuring public access for a specified rent).

The goal of the assessment determines its nature—from what needs will be assessed to the method of assessment. The goal of the assessment also in-

---

2. A "need" for medical services is the quantity of medical services an individual or community should have regardless of economic considerations to attain some desirable state of "optimum" health. A "demand" for medical services is an economic concept that refers to the quantity of medical services an individual or community is able and willing to purchase (Cordes 1977, p. 231).

fluences how the analysis will be presented (press releases, formal reports) and to whom (citizens, policymakers, special interest groups). Needs assessments must be carefully designed to achieve a specified goal through a series of research steps that produce an integrated analysis.

Dillman (1977) illustrates this process through the Alternatives for Washington survey, which was designed to set goals that would "guide the state government's program planning and provide criteria for making budget decisions" (p. 270). The preference survey, in this case, represented only one phase of a policy setting process that was conducted after "policy issues and alternatives have been clearly defined by the relevant decision-makers" (Dillman 1977, p. 264). This approach is illustrated in Fig. 9.1.

In the Alternatives for Washington goal-setting process, four preference surveys of different populations were conducted "so that each might complement the others, and contribute something the others would not." The questions ranged from general concerns and issues to specific goal preferences. The results of these surveys then served as the basis of further policy discussions on "how those goals might be achieved, and the costs of doing so" (Dillman 1977, p. 272). Another survey presenting specific action preferences followed to determine citizen preferences among these choices.

The Alternatives for Washington project offers an excellent illustration of a coordinated approach to needs assessment. In this case, the needs assessment is conceptualized as one phase of a larger goal setting and action recommendation process (Christenson 1976*b;* Garkovich 1979). Also, the needs assessment may serve to describe concerns and issues or the availability and utilization of services and programs that could serve to initiate policy discussions. In either case, it is important to note that an understanding of where we are going—the purpose of the needs assessment—structures how we get there—the approach to the needs assessment.

In summary, the CD specialist has available a variety of tools and approaches for assessing community needs. The tools selected must be appropriate to the design, requiring careful consideration of the purpose and use of the needs assessment to avoid the "bitter frustration" of unanswered citizen preferences or policy recommendations rejected at the polls. A

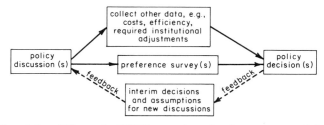

Fig. 9.1.   Dillman's (1977) synchronized survey model of needs assessment.

review of needs assessment literature has shown that at each step the researcher must select an appropriate option for action. The selection should be based on the primary questions: What is the purpose of the needs assessment? How will the information be utilized within the framework of community development efforts? If used appropriately, needs assessments can meet Koneya's (1978) challenge to transform citizen participation into effective community development.

COMMUNITY SERVICES

A major focus of needs assessment research has been the quality and delivery of community services. This section reviews research of the community services delivery system. (For a more detailed discussion of the concepts of public goods, government goods, and community services, see Samuelson 1954; Eckstein 1967; Cordes 1977.) A framework that highlights the major aspects of this system provides a means for integrating the research findings of the social sciences. The term *community services* refers to any work or activity of immediate economic value to another or to the provision of some facility by either the governmental or the private sector (Sloan and Zurcher 1970). Hence, the community services delivery system includes capital or labor, output, and providers offering tangible goods or commodities to the residents of a locality.

Delivery System Components

The basic framework, outlined in Fig. 9.2, shows resources being organized to produce both direct and indirect community service outcomes. This framework shows that certain community service outcomes are demanded by the public and they must be met via certain organizational and

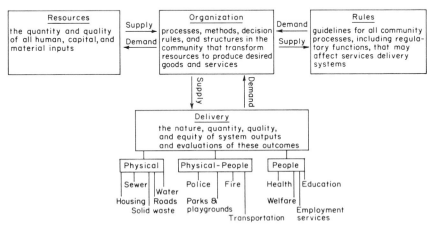

Fig. 9.2. A diagrammatic sketch of the community services delivery system.

resource requirements (Stam 1977, pp. 13–17). While this framework outlines the general major components of the services delivery system, the nature and functioning of the system among communities vary widely. Each block in Fig. 9.2 is considered briefly.

Resources, historically, have been interpreted as primarily financial inputs derived through taxation, fees, or transfer payments. Recently, more consideration has been given to nonfiscal inputs such as human capital or information.

Organization refers to the process by which resources are utilized and transformed into desired community goods and services. This facet of the system includes processes, methods, and structures employed in the production of services. Research has focused on production and cost theories; the relationship of formal structures; and the processes of government, interorganizational networks or linkages, and the role of various community actors in the decision-making process.

Delivery of community services has been analyzed by various criteria. Hitzhusen and Napier (1978, p. 132) note 12 service policy criteria; (1) output measurability, (2) capital or labor intensity, (3) relative cost, (4) size or scale economies, (5) externalities or spillovers, (6) growth versus maintenance emphasis, (7) number and complexity of technical alternatives, (8) income redistribution, (9) merit-good attributes, (10) ease of excluding users, (11) political proximity, and (12) unanticipated social consequences. These can be subsumed into three general standards—quantity, quality, and equity. Delivery also concerns the actual output of the system and how this output is perceived or defined by the users.

A number of services are arrayed in Fig. 9.2 according to their delivery—*physical* (services that influence, alter, and determine the physical and biological environment) *physical-people* (services that influence both the physical-biological environment and the behavior patterns of individuals, i.e., joint physical and social services affecting the environment), and *people* (services that directly affect the individual in a nonphysical sense and therefore affect the social environment of the community members) (McCalla, Cauchois, and Hackett 1970; Northeast Regional Center for Rural Development 1976).

Note that community services may be either a final or an intermediate output. They perform a variety of functions, including enhancement of the stock of human capital, serving as an economic base, and attracting industry to nonmetropolitan areas. Thus, they are not only a simple final output but also part of a complex community system.

Research indicates the relationship between the organization and delivery areas may be complex, simple, or nonexistent. For example, a technical engineering size-economies study for sewage treatment plants in a county may have negligible impact on most organizational concerns. The decision to build one large versus two small plants in the given service area obviously would not, for instance, affect the county's form of government. Similarly, one can envision a needs assessment study of a given service in different areas that finds all organizational concerns nearly identical and not a problem but different funding levels in need of change.

The relationship between the organization and delivery areas is not simple. The difficulty is that organization covers such a wide scope of issues and activities—ranging (for example) from multicounty governments, townships, and special districts to more micro concerns regarding the number, size, and location of elementary, intermediate, and secondary schools and from local production of services to performance contracting. Alternative organizational patterns can be expected to have different impacts on the output of the system in terms of such items as quantity, quality, costs, and citizen satisfaction.

Rules represent the formal and informal guidelines that structure the operation of the entire system. They include not only the formal regulatory functions of the system (land use, utility regulations), but also the informal norms that affect the process of decision making. Rules may be seen as an input to or an output of the services delivery system and as such have a major affect on the scope and manner in which the services are delivered.

Some major research issues related to the different facets of this delivery system are presented. In determining specific items to be included, one must evaluate priorities among and within each box in Fig. 9.2. A balance of criteria must be employed, including relevance, significance of the problem area, resource availability, and current status of research. Utilizing these criteria, space limitations and the desire to deal with tangible or direct service outputs result in the exclusion of the rules area (box *D*).

Resources and the Delivery System
The study of system inputs has traditionally focused on the fiscal resources available to the community, but many nonpecuniary inputs—such as volunteers—also contribute to the production of goods and services.

Public finance deals with the financial operations of all levels of government, including such operations as budgeting, taxing, appropriating, purchasing, borrowing, lending, disbursing funds, and regulating the currency. As such it is one of the oldest areas of inquiry in the field of economics. In the modern setting it also is concerned with adapting economic principles to areas of both economic and social concern, such as economic growth, countercyclical measures, income redistribution, and unemployment. With the development of modern computer technology, public finance economists were able to construct predictive models of macroeconomic behavior. However, these quite powerful analytical tools and an extensive public finance literature have tended to focus primarily on national problems almost to the exclusion of microeconomic issues. (Articles on public finance appear in journals such as the *National Tax Review, American Economic Review,* and *Journal of Economic Literature.*)

Today the literature on subnational finance continues to be in the minority, since current research issues reflect the field's close linkages to the policy arena (Peterson, Spain, and Laffey 1978). The passage of the State and Local Fiscal Assistance Act of 1972 (P.L. 92–512) induced a spate of publications on the topic of revenue sharing (Nathan and Adams 1977). The fiscal crisis in New York and other communities has renewed research on municipal bonds and the problems of the bond market (Twentieth Century Fund 1974, 1976).

A management-oriented approach to the financing of local governments has also stimulated interest in public employment issues (Aronson and Schwartz 1975; Moak and Hillhouse 1975; Jump 1978). Thus, the bulk of public finance and related literature is relevant here, yet utilization of this field depends on the economic training, skills, and particular concerns of the CD worker.

But the resources area is not all public finance; in recent years there has been a growing interest in nonpecuniary inputs to the services delivery system. Information is important to any system, especially when institutional regulations require the processing of enormous quantities of data to secure funds or operate a program.

There also has been a growing interest in voluntarism and human resources in the public sector. The entire field of voluntarism has expanded rapidly and covers a wide spectrum of interests, including the problem of local government inputs. (The *Journal of Voluntary Action Research* illustrates the variety of issues in this area.) Stam and Stinson (1976) and Hitzhusen (1977) have shown how important voluntarism is in the CD process and the implications it holds for local governments, which utilize a comparatively large volunteer labor input (Stinson and Stam 1976). For example, these governments may suffer from systematic negative biases relative to any revenue sharing or other funds passed down from higher levels of government where the distribution formulas are based wholly or in part on tax efforts of the local governments.

While an impressive theoretical system internal to the finance area has developed, more attention must be paid to other resource issues, such as linkages between who pays and who uses services. In the future, more research will be required on the distributional and redistributional effects of various community services and how these vary with the types of financing and taxation used. Also, innovations in telecommunications will provide more and better information to facilitate the planning process. It is important to determine the effect of more complete data on community conditions, needs, and demands on the decision-making process. Alternatively, as local communities come to rely more on federal transfer funds for local programs, regulatory requirements produce heavy information-processing demands on local administrators. These reporting obligations have already led some communities to drop particular services or programs because administrative costs have seemed prohibitive. Research on the resources segment of the community services delivery system, then, must consider not only the kinds, sources, and quantity of inputs, but also the capacity of the system to utilize these inputs.

Organizational Nature of Delivery Systems

Organization is a complex subject involving such elements as the form of government, functions performed, and specific powers. It includes how citizen inputs are registered and the combining of production factors to produce public goods and services. Traditionally, research on organization has been viewed narrowly as involving only basic questions of form, yet obviously the area is much broader in content and involves such research concerns as predictions of cost, quality, quantity, and equity as a function of alternative structures. Also involved are the complex areas of intergovernmental relations and consolidation, including questions relating to intergovernmental service agreements, transfer of functions, annexation, consolidation, and federation. Research in the area is further complicated by the fact that community services range on a continuum from public to private goods.

Economic theory provides criteria by which private goods can be efficiently allocated in a private, competitive market. Prices at which sales are made reflect production costs, the marginal value of resources in the product, and the marginal value of the product to the consumer. Price movements signal producers to increase or decrease their production or to divert resources from one good to another. However, the market situation is not the usual mode of operation in governmental sectors. Governmental or public goods and services do not lend themselves to direct money price determination because of joint consumption problems, externalities, exclusion costs, and distributional or welfare considerations.

The most restricted approach to the organization areas is by economists who have addressed issues such as intergovernmental fiscal relations or fiscal federalism (Oates 1972; Musgrave and Musgrave 1976). In a related sense, the typical treatment of allocation, distribution, and stabilization functions by economists addresses issues of public goods and market failure including issues of joint supply, externalities, and exclusion (Musgrave and Musgrave). But there has been relatively little direct treatment in a strict sense of government or public production. Production economics of firms is a well-developed subject-matter area by economists, but this does not carry over into public sector concerns. Hirsch (1970) is one economist who has addressed the government production issue directly, while others have studied the production function of single services such as police protection (Chapman, Hirsch, and Sonenblum 1975), schooling (White and Tweeten 1973), and solid waste (Savas 1977).

Noneconomic approaches to the organization facet of the delivery system have focused on the consequences of current trends in governmental organization or proposals for new organizational forms. Three major trends in state and local government to receive wide attention are the role of special districts in dealing with intercounty problems (ACIR 1973; Hawkins 1976, 1977), the organizational problems emerging from the spread of multicounty substate regionalism (ACIR 1973–1974; Christenson et al. 1979), and intergovernmental relations (Wright 1974; Duncombe 1977; Marando and Thomas 1977). (Many of the materials published by ACIR [Advisory Commission on Intergovernmental Relations] are of relevance as well as articles in journals such as *State and Local Government Review, Administrative Science Quarterly, Public Administration Review,* and *American Political Science Review.*)

Research has also centered on the development of new organizational forms. Numerous ideas regarding governmental reform are found in the literature. The ACIR (1977) has grouped the various reform ideas into five schools of thought: public choice, consolidation, federation, voluntary reorganization, and pragmatism. The growth of the public choice or polycentric school in recent years has created an interesting debate with the consolidationist school (Bish 1971; Bish and Ostrom 1973; E. Ostrom 1973; Bish 1977). Other research has examined the optimum jurisdiction for handling government functions (ACIR 1974) and other methods of restructuring local governments (ACIR 1976).

Most of the research on the organizational aspects has focused primarily on the form and function of the governmental unit. Other relatively unexplored issues are the comparative advantages of public versus private structures for delivering services and the relationships between sources of inputs and types of organizational form. Finally, centralization of functions within a single organizational framework, such as the negative income tax to replace most welfare programs, needs to be more carefully researched. As the cost of delivering services rises, new organizational forms may provide one method of maintaining the quality of services at a lower or at least stable cost.

Service Outcomes

Service outcomes involve the actual delivery of governmental goods and services including issues such as quantity, quality, efficiency, and equity. The literature in this area recognizes the difficult measurement problems regarding community services. Bradshaw (1974) has demonstrated the problems with the concept of social need by noting that four separate definitions of social need are used—normative, felt, expressed, and comparative—and they each have their difficulties.

Economists typically have tackled this area with the tools of demand theory. Economists have defined effective demand to be the situation in which people are prepared to back some want or need financially. But as

Bradshaw (p. 184) has noted, "This measure will not do for the social services, because there is normally no link between service and payment (though some economists think there ought to be)." Thus, the search for more refined measures of need and demand continues.

Economists also have been interested in the cost and efficiency of governmental service delivery, including various studies of cost-quality-quantity relationships (Levin 1974; King and Wall 1977; Stevens 1978). In discussions regarding the quantity and quality of service delivery in smaller communities, there is perhaps no more persistent theme than the need to achieve greater economies of size or scale. Size economies refer to the phenomena or considerations that cause average production costs to decrease as the size of the governmental producing unit increases (Fox et al. 1979). However it could be argued that the importance of size economies vis-à-vis other service delivery criteria has been oversold by many economists.

There have been advances in recent years in measuring the quality of community services by the use of multiple measures (E. Ostrom 1971, 1973; Parks 1976). However, such research is quite tedious, relatively expensive to carry out, and usually must be conducted on one service and in one locality at a time due to technological differences and regional variations.

Hatry and associates have conducted a number of studies recently with the aim of measuring the effectiveness of selected local government services (Hatry and Dunn 1971; Hatry et al. 1973; Webb and Hatry 1973; Hatry et al. 1977). A major focus has been monitoring the effectiveness of community programs and services for state and local officials by providing local leaders with some tools to evaluate their community's services; obtaining citizen feedback plays a major role in some of this work. Public participation in the assessment of the availability and quality of community services is discussed in the preceding section and has great potential for evaluating the delivery system, especially when used in conjunction with other approaches.

Research on service outcomes must also begin to address the relationship between who pays for services and the evaluation of the quantity, quality, and equity of services. For example, Kasarda (1976) indicates that as the size of the suburban population increases it affects the demand for central city services but frequently does not increase the resources available for providing the services. In other words, research on delivery outcomes must consider the cumulative effects of inputs and organizational forms on service outputs. Finally, the relationship between perceived quantity, quality, and equity of services and objective measures of outcomes must be clarified.

In brief, research on community services is important in the face of overall population growth and shifts coupled with changing service needs and service expectations. A systems approach to the study of the community services delivery system is used. The system is divided into four major components—resources, organization, delivery, and rules, each requiring a different orientation toward the service delivery system. This framework may facilitate the consideration of a vast literature and seem to imply a set of priorities, but it should serve only to illustrate the complex relations among different facets of the delivery system. While considerable research on particular components is available, more emphasis must be focused on interactive effects among the components to develop a greater understanding of how to most effectively improve the community services delivery system.

ECONOMIC ANALYSIS

Economic analysis is part of most community development research, but it is not neatly defined by standardized terminology or conventional usage in the literature. The wide range of research that can be, in whole or in part, considered as economic analysis makes any systematic discussion of previous research efforts difficult. A review of the literature reveals five principal types of research efforts that might be classified as economic analysis pertaining to community development questions: (1) a large proportion of community service research (including public finance); (2) economic base studies; (3) feasibility studies; (4) studies of the impacts of major community projects such as water, energy, recreation, or industrial development efforts; and (5) studies of the economic consequences of population growth or decline. These categories, while not comprehensive, do subsume the major research foci of most previous efforts.

Selected Approaches

From a historical perspective, an examination of early research efforts provides evidence that organization (and reorganization) and financing of local government have been critical issues. For example, calls for consolidation of governments or the development of regional special districts to achieve a more efficient government have been part of many research conclusions (President's Task Force on Rural Development 1970; Campbell and Dollenmayer 1975; Fitch 1975; Hawkins 1977).

During the fifties and sixties the federal government began to emphasize rural development. Early in the sixties a research workshop on rural development focused on economic research related to (1) the land resource, (2) the role of institutions, (3) the role of industry, and (4) outdoor recreation developments (Baum 1963). Most of the authors placed emphasis on the alleviation of the economic problems confronting rural communities.

The late sixties introduced a new facet to the economic analysis of communities—the stimulation of rural economic development as a mechanism for mitigating urban problems. Research in this area focused on the role of rural-to-urban migration in exacerbating urban ills and the need to reduce this migration stream by (1) increasing economic opportunities in rural communities, (2) improving community services and the living environment, and (3) raising the level of living of rural people (President's National Advisory Commission on Rural Poverty 1967; Southern and Huffman 1968). The results of these efforts provided a rationale for political support of rural economic development. These efforts reflected the assumption that the economic viability of urban and rural communities potentially depended on economic conditions specific to each area and the movement of people and employment opportunities between these areas. Hence, research activities focused on (1) mechanisms for stimulating economic activity in rural communities and the redistribution of population to these places, (2) methods for improving the quality of rural life, and (3) some attention to the consequences of economic development and population redistribution in both rural and urban communities.

These issues have been addressed with several different research orientations. Firm and budgeting analyses have examined mechanisms for increasing local government efficiency to improve the quality of rural life. The underlying assumption, of course, is that by making small communities attractive places to live, economic opportunities would be stimulated. Impact analysis has focused on the consequences of economic development.

Analysis of the firm has been one approach to economic analysis in community development. It assumes that most of the concepts and measures used to analyze the functioning of private sector firms also can be applied to the study of local government operations. Analysis of the firm has dominated much of the research on the delivery of community services and the operation of local governments (Willis and Engel 1973; King and Wall 1977). The record of firm analysis has been mixed. It has been most useful in cases where the goods or services examined are amenable to treatment as though they were market goods (such as some public utilities). However, on goods and services or in contexts where the research is focused on nonmarket phenomena (such as police or fire protection), its usefulness has been limited.

Another focus of economic analysis is the budgeting approach to determining the feasibility of certain community services, which often also includes information on optimum locations (Doeksen and Schmidt 1977). Budget analysis utilizes the basic budget to determine the net costs of different plans available to local decision makers (Doeksen et al. 1975; Schmidt et al. 1976; Childs, Doeksen, and Frye 1977; Doeksen and Schmidt 1977). It emphasizes the development of simplified models for evaluating the returns to a service area and the costs to the local government of providing a particular service or one form of that service as opposed to another. Table 9.2 is an example of an estimate of the costs and revenues of alternative forms of ambulance services for a community (Doeksen, Frye, and Green 1975). Budget analysis is frequently accompanied by a consideration of the optimum location of a service so as to minimize costs, yet maximize the service area. Since optimum location is included in a budget analysis,

TABLE 9.2.   **Summary Form of Alternatives Facing Local Decision Makers of Alfalfa County, Oklahoma**
(Form III.   Procedure used to compare estimated annual receipts and costs for alternative ambulance delivery systems.)

	1st Alternative (1)	2d Alternative (2)	3d Alternative (3)	4th Alternative (4)
I. Estimated receipt (potential receipts) equals				$19,870
Potential receipts × 60% payment rate =				11,922
Potential receipts × 70% payment rate =				13,909
Potential receipts × 80% payment rate =				15,896
Potential receipts × 90% payment rate =				17,883
II. Estimated costs: Specify vehicle, communication system and labor system				
A. Capital expenditure:				
Vehicle depreciation	$ 3,225	$ 3,225	$ 3,225	$ 3,225
Communication depreciation	800	800	800	800
Interest	1,440	1,440	1,440	1,440
Insurance	500	500	500	500
Subtotal	5,965	5,965	5,965	5,965
B. Operating expense:				
Vehicle	1,954	1,954	1,954	1,954
Communication	252	252	252	252
Medical	424	424	424	424
Subtotal	2,630	2,630	2,630	2,630
C. Labor costs: Subtotal	12,418	4,320	3,958	24,837
D. Other expenses: Subtotal	300	800	800	800
Total	21,313	13,715	13,353	34,232

Source: Reprinted with permission from Doeksen, Frye, and Green, 1975.

1 High-top van, new communication, hospital based.

2 High-top van, new communication, volunteer ($5 per night).

3 High-top van, new communication, volunteer 5 P.M. to 8 A.M. (paid $5 per call or 10¢ per mile).

4 High-top van, new communication, fully staffed system.

other objectives besides costs must be utilized in the analysis. As a result the optimum location, and hence costs, will vary with the objectives or criteria utilized in site selection. Table 9.3 illustrates these options based on a study of rural fire protection.

A third major thrust in economic analysis focuses on the feasibility or economic impact of major change. To some degree, impact research was stimulated by the legal requirements for economic impact statements for major government projects (U.S. Department of Transportation 1974; Northeast Regional Center for Rural Development 1975; McEvoy and Dietz 1977) and has focused on the economic impacts of major energy developments (Wieland, Leistritz, and Murdock 1977), recreational developments (Helgeson and Holte 1978), other federal projects (Coon et al. 1976), or private investments (Kale 1973; Scott and Johnson 1976). Most

Each Objective Function, Major County, Oklahoma

		Optimum Location		Response Time (mi)				Costs	
				1st choice		2d choice			
Objective Function	1st choice	2d choice		maximum distance	average distance	maximum distance	average distance	1st choice	2d choice
I. Minimize response time to get to:									
(a) All fires for location of:									
1. 1 truck	Fairview	Cleo Springs		34	12.2	37	15.8	$5,075	$5,284
2. 2 trucks	Ringwood, Orion	Fairview, Orion		24	13.6	26	9.9	7,363	7,193
3. 3 trucks	Ringwood, Fairview, Bouse Junction	Fairview, Ringwood, Orion		20	6.7	24	6.5	9,168	9,159
(b) Rural fires for location of:									
1. 1 truck	Fairview	Cleo Springs		34	17.0	37	19.6	4,161	4,251
2. 2 trucks	Ringwood, Orion	Fairview, Orion		24	11.7	26	13.0	6,267	6,314
3. 3 trucks	Ringwood, Fairview, Bouse Junction	Fairview, Ringwood, Orion		20	9.3	24	9.1	8,301	8,295
II. Minimize total miles:									
(a) To fight all fires for location of:									
1. 1 truck	Fairview	Cleo Springs		34	12.2	37	15.8	5,075	5,284
2. 2 trucks	Ringwood, Orion	Ames, Fairview		34	9.0	34	9.1	7,135	7,149
3. 3 trucks	Ringwood, Orion, Fairview	Ames, Orion, Fairview		24	6.5	20	6.7	9,159	9,168
(b) To fight rural fires for location of:									
1. 1 truck	Fairview	Cleo Springs		34	17.0	37	19.6	4,161	4,251
2. 2 trucks	Ringwood, Orion	Ames, Orion		24	11.7	29	12.7	6,267	6,303
3. 3 trucks	Ringwood, Orion, Fairview	Ames, Orion, Fairview		24	9.1	24	9.1	8,295	8,295
III. Maximum protection:									
(a) Per dollar's worth of burnable total property:									
1. 1 truck	Ringwood	Ringwood		34	12.2	54	20.9	5,075	5,466
2. 2 trucks	Fairview, Ringwood	Fairview, Ames		34	9.0	24	9.1	7,135	7,149
3. 3 trucks	Fairview, Ringwood, Orion	Fairview, Ames, Ringwood		24	6.5	24	7.8	9,159	9,214
(b) Per dollar's worth of burnable rural property:									
1. 1 truck	Ames	Ringwood		56	24.8	54	22.9	4,415	4,362
2. 2 trucks	Ringwood, Orion	Fairview, Ringwood		24	11.7	34	13.0	6,267	6,210
3. 3 trucks	Fairview, Ringwood, Orion	Fairview, Orion, Ames		24	9.1	20	9.1	8,295	8,295

Source: Reprinted with permission from G. A. Doeksen and R. L. Oehrtman, 1976, Optimum locations for a rural fire system: A study of Major County, Oklahoma, *South. Agric. Econ. J.* 8(2).

of the research in this area has been in the form of case studies (Northeast Regional Center for Rural Development 1975), others have summarized the results of earlier studies in an attempt to draw some generalizations on the consequences of various types of developments (Summers 1973; Jansen 1975), while still others have devised models for fiscal impact analysis (Goode 1975; McEvoy and Dietz 1977). Considerable study has been made of the impacts of industrial development and population change, which reflect the rapid changes in the geographical distribution of employment opportunities and population.

Economic Impacts of Development and Change

Events during the last decade indicate a major geographic redistribution in population and manufacturing industries. The nonmetropolitan population is now growing almost twice as fast (1.3 percent per year) as the metropolitan population (0.67 percent per year). Additionally, a decentralization of industries between 1970 and 1977 caused manufacturing employment in metropolitan areas to *decline* 7 percent compared to a 6 percent growth in nonmetropolitan counties; overall, rural counties exhibited a 22 percent increase in nonfarm employment compared to only 11 percent in urban areas.

Generally, growth in nonmetropolitan communities has been greeted enthusiastically for it has been assumed that growth stimulates the rural economy by realigning the balance between labor supply and demand or by increasing the flow of dollars. However, in recent years there has been an "increasing suspicion that in many areas, at many historical moments, growth benefits only a small proportion of local residents" (Molotch 1976, p. 318). More research is now developing to examine specifically our assumptions about the benefits of growth in order to clearly define who benefits, in what ways, and who pays, in what ways, for community growth and development.

It is also important to recognize that decreases in population and employment opportunities or simply reduced rates of growth can also have serious consequences. The research in this area is not as extensive, perhaps because growth is a significant tenet in the American ideology and communities find it difficult, if not impossible, to plan for decline or stability.

The efforts to encourage or induce the dispersal of employment opportunities to rural areas assume a geographic imbalance in the supply and demand for labor that has forced persons to leave rural communities in search of urban employment opportunities. It is further assumed that stimulating an increase in the number and types of rural employment opportunities will have a ripple effect on these areas, such as "income growth, population redistribution, housing improvements, better community services and facilities and other amenities" (Summers 1977). While the establishment of a new plant or business will generate jobs, the impact of this employment on the economy of the community depends on several factors.

The most extensive research efforts have considered the economic and social impacts of rural industrialization (Brinkman 1973; Scott 1973; Shaffer and Tweeten 1974; Summers 1977; Smith 1978; Smith and Summers 1978). Their conclusions vary, in part with the community or the particular industry under study, but some generalizations can be drawn from these diverse studies. The two most extensive reviews (Summers 1973; Smith and Summers 1978) analyze hundreds of case studies of single communities or geographic areas that have hosted new industries or whose existing plants expanded their operations.

These studies suggest that the decision to seek industrial development must be based on a careful assessment of a wide variety of factors that may affect the net gains to the community. The factors include: (1) the existing capacity of local facilities (how many additional users can be supplied public services without additional construction), (2) the particular labor force to be utilized (will women or men compose the primary labor force and will it be drawn locally, from within a larger geographic commuting area, or by in-migration), (3) incentives necessary to attract the industry (what public benefits must be offered and how they compare to the public costs of relocations), (4) the multiplier effect of the new industry for the local economy (how many dollars will be generated in the community for each industry dollar spent on public services, acquisition of raw materials, and payroll), and (5) changes in the local political and social structures that will result from the development of a new industry in the community. If a community decides the project can offer substantial benefits, a resource guide on how to foster industrial growth is available. Fernstrom (1973) has written a self-study course for community leaders or change agents. Remember that careful planning by the local community can help a new industry be an economic boom instead of a public burden.

Rapid growth in nonmetropolitan populations has accompanied the employment expansion in these communities and has been greeted with the same enthusiasm. Yet population growth, like industrialization, can have both positive and negative consequences for the community. Its impact depends on the rate of growth, the composition of the incoming population, and the structure of the local government. The area of community life that first and most visibly demonstrates the impact of population growth is the delivery of services. Watt (1974) points out that many people assume local growth will reap fiscal returns through a broadened tax base, yet this may not always be the case. Rapid population growth may strain the ability of local government to deliver essential services in a variety of ways.

A key axiom of industrial development is economies of scale; in other words, increasing size is directly related to increasing efficiency in the utilization of resources. Some have attempted to apply this assumption to cities, assuming that as cities grow public services will be more efficiently utilized at a lower cost per capita. However there are thresholds of size beyond which diminishing returns begin to operate.

The cost of public services delivery is influenced by the number of persons utilizing the services, the distance from and location of users, and the type and quality of services demanded by the users.

A hypothetical example illustrates. If a county (or community) has 1,000 persons spread over 100,000 acres (or 1 person per 100 acres) the cost per capita of providing sewage services will be $100, or the cost of the smallest efficient sewage treatment plant that can be built (one that will serve 2,000 people), the cost of sewer lines, and operating costs. If 1,000 new persons enter the community, sewage costs will be halved to $50 per capita, since the existing plant can process the additional sewage load, there is a fixed cost for operating the plant, and the new residents locate on pre-existent sewer lines. However, if an additional 1,000 persons enter the community, costs per capita of sewage services will jump, since the additional load will exceed the present operating capacity of the plant and require additional capital construction.

The spatial location of the users also influences the cost of the delivery services, as illustrated in the discussion of the community services delivery system (see Table 9.3). Research by the Real Estate Research Corporation (1974, p. 6) indicates that high density development patterns lead to "lower economic costs, environmental costs, natural resource consumption, and some personal costs for a given number of dwelling units" than would a low density sprawl pattern of development. Their analysis also suggests that for small communities, a high density pattern of settlement contributes to substantial savings to the public sector in reduced service costs.

Another factor to influence the delivery and cost of public services concerns the type and quality demanded by citizens. The services needed by a growing population depend on its characteristics. If the newcomers are primarily young families with school-age children, educational and recreational services will be needed. However, if the newcomers are primarily retirees, health care and social services will need to be expanded (Economic Development Division 1978; Ford 1979). The changing composition of the population will affect the type of services demanded from local institutions. However, demand is also influenced by the expectations of the population; and several researchers (Graber 1974; Morrison and Wheeler 1976; Ploch 1978) suggest there may be considerable differences in the service demands of old-timers and newcomers concerning the type, quantity, and financing of public services, which may result in shifts in the composition of local leadership.

Thus, an economic analysis of the impacts of population change must consider the effects on the community services delivery system and the changing demands of the residents. For some communities the newcomers permit the local government to realize economies of scale in the operation and delivery of previously underutilized services. However, too rapid growth, uncontrolled growth, or growth that exceeds the service capacity of local institutions can create more problems than benefits for nonmetropolitan areas. Some communities have devised programs to evaluate growth and its consequences with a systematic and consensual process (Tate 1978; Garkovich 1979), and their activities indicate that CD workers play a key role in ensuring that growth does not transfer urban problems to the countryside.

In summary, economic analysis research in community development encompasses a wide variety of perspectives and methodologies. Considerable attention has been devoted to the costs of delivering particular services or the costs of specific organizational forms, and recent consideration has also focused on the fiscal impacts of development efforts. The review of research on the economic impacts of industrialization and population change suggests that any evaluation of a proposed development requires a specification of the arenas of impact and the criteria for assessing the trade-offs involved. Many approaches are available to the CD specialist. Selection must be based on the development objectives and the resources of the specialist.

IMPLICATIONS FOR FUTURE RESEARCH

This review of three major areas of research is only a superficial examination of the possible relevant literature. However, it suffices to permit some conclusions to be drawn about the current state of the art and future directions for research.

Needs Assessment

Needs assessment research can be seen as the first step in any CD activity, for it is critical to know where we are before we initiate action for change. Needs assessments have been principally of two types: (1) those relying on subjective evaluations by community members and (2) those employing some type of objective criteria to measure community needs. Considerable attention has been devoted to developing techniques for general needs assessments; however, such efforts do not always produce information relevant to or useful in local decision making, and needs assessments have been haunted by a failure to integrate empirically defined needs into relevant decision options. In other words, sweeping generalizations about community needs have not always translated into community support for proposals to answer these needs. It is critical that more attention be given to the process by which perceived needs are transformed into demands, and ultimately, community programs.

Another problem in needs assessment research is the relative importance of various services or programs in the definition of needs or demands. The selection of one action involves trade-offs among other alternatives. Within a given budget the decision to spend more money on fire protection must mean less funding for other services or programs. Yet few, if any, needs assessments directly address the issue of trade-offs.

Finally, more attention must be given to the way in which results of needs assessments are provided to local leaders and how the results figure in the decision-making process. More consideration of the use of needs assessment will inform how they are designed and conducted. Needs assessments can be a key mechanism for citizen participation in community decision making only if they are designed to be an integral part of this process.

Community Services

The review of the community services delivery system provides a framework for studying different phases of the system. Much research in this area has focused on economic resources utilized in the production of services, organizational forms directing the delivery of services, and the evaluation of system outcomes.

The study of resources utilized in the service delivery system has tended to focus rather narrowly on economic inputs and has led to a rather myopic view of system capabilities, since human and informational resources may serve as the final limiting factors. Hence not only should fiscal resources be evaluated but also the quality and flexibility of the community's human capital and the quantity and complexity of information available to local leaders. For example, even if a community has the economic capital available from local or extralocal sources to establish an ambulance system, such a service may not develop due to the absence of informational resources to mobilize the pecuniary resources.

More attention must be devoted to an evaluation of how organizational structure influences the mobilization of resources and the delivery of services. For example, it has been suggested that counties as governmental and economic units are outmoded; yet we have not produced well-researched guidelines for developing alternative organizational units. Additionally, more comparative research is needed to understand why similar organizational forms produce different service outcomes.

Finally, consideration must be given to the feedback process. Little or no attention has been given to how service delivery system outcomes affect the quality and quantity of resources available or affect the organization and processing of these resources. Some needs assessment research addresses this issue, but more information is required if we are to understand the operation of supply and demand in the community services delivery system.

Economic Analysis

Economic analysis has tended to focus on the feasibility of action alternatives confronting local leaders and the economic impacts of action alternatives on social trends. Thus, the research has included budgeted costs and returns of specific programs, services, or organizational forms as well as economic effects of items or events over which the local community can exercise little control (such as migration patterns).

Much research in this area has had a growth orientation; that is, it has been focused on selecting the type of public investment that best stimulates further growth. As a result, there has been a tendency to emphasize the benefits of a particular action alternative almost to the exclusion of its costs. Additionally, the cost-benefit analysis has generally centered on quantifiable economic variables to the exclusion of sociopolitical effects that may eventually have fiscal impacts.

Greater emphasis in economic analysis also needs to be given to the effects of extralocal factors (such as national distributorships) on local action alternatives. This is especially apparent in the review of the research on economic impacts of industrial development.

On a more general level, this review of community development research illuminates some unexplored areas. It is imperative that more attention be paid to the population variable. We need to know the relevant population level for which development is to be considered as well as the characteristics of the human capital in a given area. This review strongly suggests that the human factor is a key in defining community needs, influencing the operation of the services delivery system, and the effective returns from public investments. The redistribution of population currently under way suggests we must begin to consider the consequences of population concentrated in a few areas while other regions are underpopulated. This redistribution also indicates a need to consider the developmental consequences of rapid changes in a community's size.

Another issue that needs to be examined is the role of energy in CD activities. The impacts of energy developments (such as fossil fuel generation or nuclear industries) on community life have been fairly well documented. However little or no attention has been given to the consequences of energy shortages on population redistribution, commuting patterns, and industrialization of more remote communities, all of which influence the process of community development in significant ways. For example, as the cost of transportation rises, what will become of industries in nonmetropolitan communities that depend on extralocal raw materials and a commuting labor force? The answer to this question will help CD practitioners give priorities to their future efforts.

Finally, there is a critical need to develop multidisciplinary research efforts. Given the complexity of the community system, it is absurd to operate as if we can understand the whole by decomposing the system into its smallest constituent parts. This review indicates that every aspect of community life requires the peculiar insights and methodologies of many disciplines. For example, a study of the need for and impact of a rural ambulance service requires an analysis of fiscal costs, optimum geographic location, consumer utilization rates, and the sociopolitical consequences of introducing either a new government service or a private entrepreneur into the community.

Simultaneously, we must begin to synthesize the conclusions of research efforts that are problem or development specific. An example of this is the work of Smith and Summers (1978), who have reviewed and distilled the research conclusions of hundreds of projects analyzing the consequences of industrial developments. Such efforts can provide the CD specialist as well as local leaders a set of generalizations with which to begin the decision-making process. Such efforts will also illuminate priorities for further research.

The body of research relevant to community development seems almost overwhelming. Effective community development demands that practitioners heed the problems of the sorcerer's apprentice and carefully call on that area of research that best suits the specific needs of the community and the resources of the practitioner.

REFERENCES

ACIR (Advisory Commission on Intergovernmental Relations). Washington, D.C.: USGPO.
    1973. Regional decision making: New strategies for substate districts, A-43.
    1973–1974. Substate regionalism and the federal system, vols. 1–5.
    1974. Governmental functions and processes: Local and areawide, A-45.
    1976. Improving urban America: A challenge to federalism, M-107.
    1977. Regionalism revisited: Recent areawide and local responses, A-66.
Alternatives for Washington, State-Wide Task Force. 1975. Citizen's recommendations for the future, vol. 1. Olympia, Wash.: Off. Program Plann. Fiscal Manage.
Aronson, J. R., and E. Schwartz. 1975. *Management Policies in Local Government Finance.* Washington, D.C.: Int. City Manage. Assoc.
Basson, P. 1970. Planning and perception of needs in five upstate New York counties. *J. Community Dev. Soc.* 1 (1):53–66.
Baum, E. L., ed. 1963. Selected topics on rural development research. USDA, Economic Research Service. Washington, D.C.: USGPO.
Bish, R. L. 1971. *The Public Economy of Metropolitan Areas.* Chicago: Markham.
    ———. 1977. Public choice theory: Research issues for nonmetropolitan areas. In *National Conference on Nonmetropolitan Community Services Research,* U.S. Senate Committee on Agriculture, Nutrition and Forestry. Washington, D.C.: USGPO.
Bish, R. L., and V. Ostrom. 1973. *Understanding Urban Government: Metropolitan Reform Reconsidered.* Washington, D.C.: Am. Enterp. Inst. Public Policy Res.
Blake, B. F.; N. Kalb; and V. Ryan. 1977. Citizen opinion survey and effective CD efforts. *J. Community Dev. Soc.* 8 (2):92–104.
Bradshaw, J. 1974. The concept of social need. *Ekistics,* Mar., pp. 184–87.
Brinkman, G. 1973. Effects of industrializing small communities. *J. Community Dev. Soc.* 4 (1):69–80.
Campbell, A. K., and J. A. Dollenmayer. 1975. Governance in a metropolitan

society. In *Metropolitan America in Contemporary Perspective,* A. Hawley and V. P. Rock, eds. New York: Halsted Press.

Chapman, J. I.; W. Z. Hirsch; and S. Sonenblum. 1975. Crime prevention, the police protection function, and budgeting. *Public Finance* 30 (Feb.):197–215.

Childs, D.; G. Doeksen; and J. Frye. 1977. Economics of rural fire protection in the Great Plains. USDA, Economic Research Service, Agric. Inf. Bull. 407. Washington, D.C.: USGPO.

Christenson, J. A. 1973. Through our eyes: People's needs and goals in North Carolina. Raleigh: N.C. Agric. Ext. Serv. Misc. Publ. 106.

_____. 1975. A procedure for conducting mail surveys with the general public. *J. Community Dev. Soc.* 6 (1):135–46.

_____. 1975–1976. North Carolina today and tomorrow. Raleigh: N.C. Agric. Ext. Serv. Misc. Publ. 141–49.

_____. 1976*a*. Public input for program planning and policy formation. *J. Community Dev. Soc.* 7 (1):33–39.

_____. 1976*b*. Quality of community services: A unidimensional approach with experiential data. *Rural Sociol.* 41 (4):509–25.

_____. 1979. Quality of life in Kentucky counties. *Community Dev. Issues* 1 (1):1–8.

Christenson, J. A.; P. Warner: M. Colliver; and R. Crouch. 1979. Are substate agencies adequately serving small towns? *Rural Dev. Perspect.* 1 (2):10–16.

Cocherhan, W. C., and A. L. Blevins. 1977. Attitudes toward land use planning and controlled population growth in Jackson Hole. *J. Community Dev. Soc.* 8 (1):62–73.

Cohen, M. W.; G. M. Sills; and A. T. Schwebel. 1977. A two-stage process for surveying community needs. *J. Community Dev. Soc.* 8 (1):54–61.

Coon, R. C.; N. L. Dalsted; A. G. Leholm; and F. L. Leistritz. 1976. The impact of the Safeguard Antiballistic Missile System construction on northeastern North Dakota. Fargo: North Dakota State University, Agric. Econ. Rep. 101.

Cordes, S. M. 1977. Needs assessment for medical services. In *National Conference on Nonmetropolitan Community Services Research,* U.S. Senate Committee on Agriculture, Nutrition, and Forestry. Washington, D.C.: USGPO.

Deacon, R. T. 1977. Needs and use assessment at national and local levels. In *National Conference on Nonmetropolitan Community Services Research,* U.S. Senate Committee on Agriculture, Nutrition, and Forestry. Washington, D.C.: USGPO.

Dillman, D. A. 1971. Public values and concerns of Washington residents. Pullman, Wash.: Wash. Agric. Exp. Stn. Bull. 748.

_____. 1977. Preference surveys and policy decisions: Our new tools need not be used in the same old way. In *National Conference on Nonmetropolitan Community Services Research,* U.S. Senate Committee on Agriculture, Nutrition, and Forestry. Washington, D.C.: USGPO.

_____. 1978. *Mail and Telephone Surveys: The Total Design Method.* New York: Wiley.

Doeksen, G. A., and J. F. Schmidt. 1977. Community service research needs of local decision-makers. In *National Conference on Nonmetropolitan Community Services Research,* U.S. Senate Committee on Agriculture, Nutrition, and Forestry. Washington, D.C.: USGPO.

Doeksen, G. A.; J. Frye; and B. L. Green. 1975. Economics of rural ambulance service in the Great Plains. USDA, Economic Research Service, Agric. Econ. Repr. 38. Washington, D.C.: USGPO.

Duncombe, H. S. 1977. Modern county government. Washington, D.C.: Natl. Assoc. Counties.

Eckstein, O. 1967. *Public Finance,* 2d ed. Englewood Cliffs, N.J.: Prentice-Hall.

Economic Development Division Staff. 1978. Rural America in the seventies. *Rural Dev. Perspect.,* Nov., pp. 6–11.

Fernstrom, J. R. 1973. Bringing in the sheaves: Effective community industrial development program. Oregon State University, Coop. Ext. Serv.

Fitch, L. C. 1975. Fiscal and productive efficiency in urban government systems. In *Metropolitan America in Contemporary Perspectives,* A. H. Hawley and V. P. Rock, eds. New York: Halsted Press.

Ford, T. R. 1979. The population shift to nonmetropolitan areas: A stituational assessment. Paper presented to South. Newspaper Publ. Assoc. Semin., Mississippi State University.

Fox, W. F.; J. M. Stam; W. M. Godsey; and S. D. Brown. 1979. Economies of size in local government: An annotated bibliography. Rural Dev. Res. Rep. 9. Washington, D. C.: USDA.

Garkovich, L. 1979. What comes after the survey? A practical application of the synchronized survey model in community development. *J. Community Dev. Soc.* 10 (1):29–38.

Goode, F. 1975. A framework for analyzing the fiscal impact of economic development on a community. In Evaluating impacts of economic growth proposals: An analytic framework for use with community decisionmakers, Northeast Reg. Cent. Rural Dev., publ. 8. Ithaca, N.Y.: Cornell University.

Gordon, R. L. 1969. *Interviewing: Strategy, Techniques, and Tactics.* Homewood, Ill.: Dorsey Press.

Goudy, W. J., and F. E. Wepprecht. 1977. Local, regional programs developed from resident evaluations. *J. Community Dev. Soc.* 8 (1):44–52.

Graber, E. 1974. Newcomers and oldtimers: Growth and change in a mountain town. *Rural Sociol.* 39 (4):4504–13.

Hagood, R.; D. Rankos; and D. A. Dillman. 1974. The future of the Pierce County area: Survey results. Unpublished report. Pullman: Washington State University, Dep. Rural Sociol.

Hatry, H. P., and D. R. Dunn. 1971. *Measuring the Effectiveness of Local Government Services: Recreation.* Washington, D.C.: Urban Inst.

Hatry, H. P.; R. E. Winnie; and D. M. Fisk. 1973. *Practical Program Evaluation for State and Local Government Officials.* Washington, D.C.: Urban Inst.

Hatry, H. P.; L. H. Blair; D. M. Fisk; J. H. Greiner; J. R. Hall, Jr.; and P. S. Schaenman. 1977. *How Effective Are Your Community Services? Procedures for Monitoring the Effectiveness of Municipal Services.* Washington, D.C.: Urban Inst.

Hawkins, R. B., Jr. 1976. *Self Government by District: Myth and Reality.* Stanford, Calif.: Hoover Inst. Press.

_____. 1977. Special districts in nonmetropolitan areas: Some policy and research issues. In *National Conference on Nonmetropolitan Community Services Research,* U.S. Senate Committee on Agriculture, Nutrition, and Forestry. Washington, D.C.: USGPO.

Helgeson, D. L., and G. J. Holte. 1978. A socioeconomic impact analysis of recreation at Lake Metigoshe, North Dakota. Fargo: North Dakota State University, Agric. Econ. Rep. 131.

Hirsch, W. Z. 1970. *The Economics of State and Local Government.* New York: McGraw-Hill.

Hitzhusen, F. J. 1977. Non-tax financing and support for "community" services:

Some policy implications for nonmetropolitan governments. In *National Conference on Nonmetropolitan Community Services Research,* U.S. Senate Committee on Agriculture, Nutrition, and Forestry. Washington, D.C.: USGPO.

Hitzhusen, F. J., and T. Napier. 1978. A rural public services policy framework and some applications. In *Rural Policy Research Alternatives,* D. L. Rogers and L. R. Whiting, eds., North Cent. Reg. Cent. Rural Dev., pp. 127–49. Ames: Iowa State Univ. Press.

Jansen, E. F., Jr. 1975. The impact of residential development alternatives: A case study problem. In Evaluating impacts of economic growth proposals: An analytic framework for use with community decisionmakers, publ. 8. Northeast Reg. Cent. Rural Dev., Ithaca, N.Y.: Cornell University.

Johnson, R. F. Q. 1976. Pitfalls in research: The interview as an illustrative model. *Psychol. Rep.* 38:3–17.

Jump, B., Jr. 1978. Public employment, collective bargaining, and employee wages and pensions. In *State and Local Government Finance and Financial Management: A Compendium of Current Research,* J. E. Petersen, C. L. Spain, and M. F. Laffey, eds. Chicago: Munic. Finance Off. Assoc.

Kale, S. 1973. The impact of new additional industry upon rurally oriented areas: A selectively annotated bibliography with emphasis on manufacturing. Lincoln: University of Nebraska at Lincoln, Coll. Bus. Adm.

Kasarda, J. D. 1976. The impact of suburban population growth on central city service functions. In *The Research Experience,* M. P. Golden, ed. Itasca, Ill.: Peacock.

King, R. A., and G. B. Wall. Estimation of cost-quality-quantity relationships. In *National Conference on Nonmetropolitan Community Services Research,* U.S. Senate Committee on Agriculture, Nutrition, and Forestry. Washington, D.C.: USGPO.

Koneya, M. 1978. Citizen participation is not community development. *J. Community Dev. Soc.* 9 (2): 23–29.

Levin, H. M. 1974. Measuring efficiency in educational production. *Public Finance Q.* 2 (1):3–24.

McCalla, A. F.; S. Cauchois; and P. Hackett. 1970. *Inventory of social services for the Stockton metropolitan area.* Davis: Univ. Calif. Ext., Cent. Community Dev.

McEvoy, J., and T. Dietz, eds. 1977. *Handbook for Environmental Planning: The Social Consequences of Environmental Change.* New York: Wiley.

Marando, V. L., and R. D. Thomas. 1977. *The Forgotten Government: County Commissioners as Policy Makers.* Gainesville: Univ. Presses Florida.

Miller, H. M.; P. L. Dressel; and H. L. Nix. 1976. Community social analysis of DeKalb County, Georgia. Community Soc. Action Anal. Ser. 11. Athens: University of Georgia, Inst. Community Area Dev. and Dep. Sociol.

Moak, L. L., and A. M. Hillhouse. 1975. *Concepts and Practices in Local Government Finance.* Chicago: Munic. Finance Off. Assoc.

Molotch, H. 1976. The city as a growth machine: Toward a political economy of place. *Am. J. Sociol.* 38 (Sept.):309–29.

Morrison, P. A., and J. P. Wheeler. 1976. Rural renaissance in America? The revival of population growth in remote areas. *Population Bull.* 31:1–26.

Musgrave, R. A., and P. B. Musgrave. 1976. *Public Finance in Theory and Practice,* 2d ed. New York: McGraw-Hill.

Nathan, R. P., and C. F. Adams. 1977. *Revenue Sharing: The Second Round.* Washington, D.C.: Brookings Inst.

Nix, H. L., and N. R. Seerley. 1972. *Dynamic DeKalb.* Community Soc. Action

Anal. Ser. 7. Athens: University of Georgia, Inst. Community Area Dev. and Dep. Sociol.

_____. 1973. Comparative views and actions of community leaders and nonleaders. *Rural Sociol.* 38 (4):427–38.

Nix, H. L.; G. S. Brooks; and B. L. Courtenay. 1976. Comparative needs of large and small communities. *J. Community Dev. Soc.* 7 (2): 97–105.

Northeast Regional Center for Rural Development. 1975. Evaluating impacts of economic growth proposals: An analytic framework for use with community decisionmakers, publ. 8. Ithaca, N.Y.: Cornell University.

_____. 1976. Priorities in community services research for the Northeast: A report of the ad hoc committee on community services. Ithaca, N.Y.: Cornell University.

Oates, W. E. 1972. *Fiscal Federalism.* New York: Harcourt Brace Jovanovich.

Ostrom, E. 1971. Institutional arrangements and the measurement of policy consequences: Applications to evaluating police performance. *Urban Aff. Q.* 4 (June):447–76.

_____. 1973. The need for multiple indicators in measuring the output of public agencies. *Policy Stud. J.* 2 (Winter):87–91.

Ostrom, V. 1973. *The Intellectual Crisis in American Public Administration.* University: Univ. Alabama Press.

Parks, R. B. 1976. Complimentary measures of policy performance. In *Evaluative Research,* K. M. Dolbeare, ed. Beverly Hills, Calif.: Sage Publ.

Petersen, J. L.; C. L. Spain; and M. F. Laffey. 1978. *State and Local Government Finance and Financial Management: A Compendium of Current Research.* Chicago: Munic. Finance Off. Assoc.

Ploch. L. A. 1978. The reversal in migration patterns: Some rural development perspectives. *Rural Sociol.* 43 (2):293–303.

President's National Advisory Commission on Rural Poverty. 1967. The people left behind. Washington, D.C.: USGPO.

President's Task Force on Rural Development. 1970. A new life for the country. Washington, D.C.: USGPO.

Real Estate Research Corporation. 1974. The costs of sprawl: Detailed cost analysis. Washington, D.C.: USGPO.

Rogers, T. F. 1976. Interviews by telephone and in person: Quality of responses and field performance. *Public Opin. Q.* 40:51–65.

Samuelson, P. A. 1954. The pure theory of public expenditures. *Rev. Econ. Stat.* 36 (Nov.):387–89.

Savas, E. S., ed. 1977. *The Organization and Efficiency of Solid Waste Collection.* Lexington, Mass.: Lexington Books.

Schmidt, A. R.; G. A. Doeksen; J. Frye; and J. C. Maxey. 1976. Analyzing the feasibility of rural rental apartments in the Great Plains: A guide for local decision makers. USDA, Economic Research Service, Agric. Inf. Bull. 397. Washington, D.C.: USGPO.

Schwebel, A. I.; D. A. Jones; J. W. Kaswan; and J. Napier. 1978. Developing a community concerns index. *J. Community Dev. Soc.* 9 (1):80–89.

Scott, J. T., Jr. 1973. Profile change when industry moves into a rural area. University of Wisconsin–Madison, Cent. Appl. Sociol., working paper R1D73.7.

Scott, J. T., Jr., and J. D. Johnson. 1976. The effect of town size and location on retail sales. Ames: Iowa State University, North Cent. Reg. Cent. Rural Dev.

Shaffer, R., and L. Tweeten. 1974. Estimating net economic impact of industrial expansion: An Oklahoma case. *J. Community Dev. Soc.* 5 (2):79–89.

Sloan, H. S., and A. J. Zurcher. 1970. *Dictionary of Economics,* 5th ed. New York: Barnes & Noble.

Smith, E. D. 1978. A synthesis: Industrialization of rural areas: Location and growth of manufacturing firms in submetropolitan areas. Rural Dev. Ser. 1. State College: Mississippi State University, South. Rural Dev. Cent.

Smith, E. D., and G. F. Summers. 1978. A synthesis: How new manufacturing industry affects rural areas. Rural Dev. Ser. 1A. State College: Mississippi State University, South. Rural Dev. Cent.

Southern, J. H., and R. E. Huffman. 1968. A national program of research for rural development and family living. Joint Task Force, USDA and state universities and land-grant colleges. Washington, D.C.: USGPO.

Stam, J. M. 1977. On the taxonomy of nonmetropolitan community services research. In *National Conference on Nonmetropolitan Community Services Research,* U.S. Senate Committee on Agriculture, Nutrition, and Forestry. Washington, D.C.: USGPO.

Stam, J. M., and T. F. Stinson. 1976. Voluntarism and revenue sharing: Considerations for local government. *J. Community Dev. Soc.* 7 (1):24–32.

Stevens, B. J. 1978. Scale, market structure, and the cost of refuse collection. *Rev. Econ. Stat.* 60 (3):438–48.

Stinson, T. F., and J. M. Stam. 1976. Toward an economic model of voluntarism: The case of participation in local government. *J. Voluntary Action Res.* 5 (1):52–60.

Summers, G. F. 1973. Large industry in a rural area: Demographic, economic, and social impacts. U.S. Dep. Commer., Natl. Tech. Inf. Serv. Washington, D.C.: USGPO.

_____. 1977. Industrial development of America: A quarter century of experience. *J. Community Dev. Soc.* 8 (1):6–18.

Tate, G. 1978. Small town values and the problem of growth. *Small Town,* Dec., pp. 4–10.

Twentieth Century Fund. 1974. *The Rating Game.* New York. Twentieth Century Fund.

_____. 1976. *Building a Broader Market.* New York: McGraw-Hill.

U.S., Department of Transportation. 1974. *Social and economic effects of highways.* Fed. Highw. Adm., Off. Program Policy Plann. Socio-Econ. Stud. Div. Washington, D.C.: USGPO.

Vintner, R. D., and J. E. Tropman. 1974. The causes and consequences of community studies. In *Stategies of Community Organization,* F. Lox, J. Erlich, J. Rothman, and J. Tropman, eds. Itasca, Ill.: Peacock.

Warner, P. D.; R. J. Burdge; S. D. Hoffman; and G. R. Hammonds. 1976. *Issues Facing Kentucky,* vols. 1–18. Lexington: University of Kentucky, Coll. Agric., Coop. Ext. Serv.

Watt, K. E. 1974. *The Titanic Effect.* Stamford, Conn.: Sinauer.

Webb, K., and H. P. Hatry. 1973. *Obtaining Citizen Feedback: The Application of Citizen Surveys to Local Governments.* Washington, D.C.: Urban Inst.

White, F., and L. Tweeten. 1973. Internal economics of rural elementary and secondary schools. *Socio-Econ. Plann. Sci.* 7:353–69.

Wieland, J. S.; F. L. Leistritz; and S. H. Murdock. 1977. Characteristics and settlement patterns of energy related operating workers in the northern Great Plains. Dep. Agric. Econ. Rep. 123. Fargo: North Dakota Inst. Reg. Stud.

Willis, C. E., and N. E. Engel. 1973. Economic theory and rural development, publ. 87. Amherst: University of Massachusetts, Coop. Ext. Serv.

Wright, D. S. 1974. Intergovernmental relations: An analytical overview. *Ann. Am. Acad. Polit. Social Sci.* 416 (Nov.):1–16.

Evaluation: A Typology and Overview

Donald E. Voth, Elizabeth Bothereau, and Richard Cohen

INTRODUCTION

What constitutes community development evaluation and what, if anything, is unique about it? There is little consensus. Community development is extremely complex and the evaluation literature is extremely diverse. When community development evaluation is defined broadly to include evaluation of its respective parts (leadership training, technical assistance, organizing, etc.), it is hard to distinguish it from social program evaluation in general; and probably more variability is present within community development evaluation than between it and the general field of evaluation research. On the other hand, if community development evaluation is defined more narrowly to be evaluation that focuses on some minimal part of the core content of community development (improvement in the ability of a community to establish goals, make decisions, carry out activities, etc.), the evaluation literature is very specialized and minimal indeed.

The accountability movement, which has lead to the current emphasis on evaluation, includes a strong and justified skepticism about social programs with "vague goals, strong promises, and weak effects" (Rossi 1972, p. 16). Horst et al. (1972, p. 302), in discussing the evaluability of social legislation, speak of "the vaporous wish, local project packaging, and how-to-do-it rule making." Community development is peculiarly susceptible to being characterized in this way because of the ambiguity of its targets (groups, institutions) and the developmental nature of its goals (Voth 1975*a*). At the same time, community development in practice has not yet reached such a level of development that it can take public acceptance and support for granted. Consequently, it may be a matter of survival for community development to deal with the accountability movement on the movement's terms. This will require taking the initiative in articulating the relationship between evaluation and community development in order to identify the role of evaluation in community development, to identify what is distinctive about community development evaluation, to show what community development can and cannot accomplish, and to contribute to the clarification of community development as a discipline and method.

Our objectives in this chapter are somewhat more limited. Using an inclusive definition of community development, we develop a classification of types of evaluation research based on two criteria; the general function served by the evaluation and the method of inquiry or research employed. It is our objective to illustrate simultaneously the wide variety of evaluation research approaches available and the manner in which two underlying issues, function and logic of inference, relate to these approaches.

COMMUNITY DEVELOPMENT

There appears to be widespread agreement about certain core objectives of community development. These objectives involve improvement in the ability of collectives to make rational decisions about things that affect them and to bring these decisions to fruition through various forms of collective action. Some place more emphasis on substantive achievements (improvements in economic well-being, services, etc.), and others place more emphasis on process aspects of community development. Nevertheless, the objectives above would probably be accepted by most community developers.

Analytically, however, this definition of community development still leaves a "black box." Some would fill it with the theory of social movements (Richmond 1974) or solidarity movements (Young and Young 1974). Others view the dynamics of community development primarily from the perspective of power and realignments in power relationships (Alinsky 1969; Clark and Hopkins 1969; Kahn 1970). Still others would use the logic of social relationships within the community (Wilkinson 1972; Warren 1973, pp. 161–66). Rick Cohen, in response to the many physically and economically oriented interpretations, has developed a scheme of several stages that is focused on change in the organizational capacity and institutional development of the community (1978, pp. 44–64, 1979). (See Rothman [1974] for a widely used classification of styles of community organization.)

Whatever community development is analytically, in practice it is purposive interventions that are designed to achieve some or all the goals identified above. A wide variety of interventions may be used; they vary in style and approach among agencies, among phases in the CD process, and among CD practitioners. The interventions are intended to influence generic community processes (black box), with resulting improvements in decision-making capability, quality of life, etc. Schematically this looks like Table 10.1.

In the context of a particular set of interventions, a particular view of the community processes, and a particular set of outcomes, the tasks of CD evaluation involve trying to answer the following questions:

1. Were the interventions actually carried out, and to what extent?

TABLE 10.1.   Schematic Diagram of CD Process

Inputs	Throughputs (black box)	Outputs
Interventions	Generic community processes	CD outcomes:
A	A	A
B	B	B
C	C	C

2. Did the interventions influence the community processes in the way expected or did they influence them at all?

3. Did the interventions and the ensuing community processes lead to the expected outcomes or to any outcomes of significance?

Many other questions about interrelationships among interventions, community processes, and outcomes can be raised.

Without being more specific about the definition of community development, several characteristics with profound implications for evaluation become readily apparent. (1) The processes whereby communities develop are evidently extremely complex and poorly understood. The black box is exactly that. (2) Community development, like many recent social programs, implies changes in values, attitudes, and behaviors of individuals, and even more, implies institutional and social structural change. Seldom have practitioners or community scholars been able to state with precision the operational measures of these changes or the processes whereby they occur. (An exception is the community development logic explicit in the CAP agencies of OEO [Vanecko et al. 1970, pp. 2, 3] and in Young and Young [1974, n.d.] as applied in the evaluation by Voth [1975*b*].) Nor have they been able to specify in operational terms how one would distinguish a developed community from one that is less developed. This raises the initial question of whether community development can be evaluated at all (Horst et al. 1972, p. 307) and justifies insisting on the need for basic analytic work on these community processes.

EVALUATION RESEARCH

The literature on evaluation research has grown tremendously during the last few years, with such important landmarks as the publication of the widely used two-volume *Handbook of Evaluation Research* (Guttentag and Struening 1975), the establishment of the *Evaluation Quarterly* in 1977, and the publication of the Quarterly's *Annual Reviews* (Glass 1976, Guttentag and Saar 1977). Excellent overviews of this literature with extensive bibliographic references can be found in Wholey et al. (1970), Caro (1971), Burton and Rogers (1976), Freeman (1977), Rossi and Wright (1977), and Cosby and Wetherill (1978).

Much of the impetus for the development of the evaluation research relevant to community development was the plethora of social programs of the 1960s. Community developers, of course, played key roles in the designs of those programs (Denise 1969; Rubin 1969) and many of the philosophical and operational tenets of community development were embodied in them. The literature on these programs contains important accounts of evaluation methods being devised and refined in turbulent social settings (Annals 1969; Clark and Hopkins 1969; Vanecko 1969).

Social program evaluation is not entirely new, however, as indicated by the widely referenced textbook by Suchman (1967) designed for use in evaluating public health work, the important work of Donald T. Campbell and his associates (Campbell and Stanley 1966, first published by N. L. Gage 1963), and less well-known works such as Hayes (1967, first published in 1959) in the field of international development.

Although there is disagreement in the literature about what evaluation research is or should be (cf. Scriven 1967, p. 39; Burton and Rogers 1976; Perkins 1977; Rossi and Wright 1977), we feel that most of it can be subsumed under a broad definition. We take as our definition the simple statement that evaluation research is scientific activity that is used to assess the operation and impact of public policies and the action programs intended to implement these policies. This definition follows Bernstein and Freeman (1975) closely, as quoted in Rossi and Wright (1977, p. 5). Rossi and Wright elaborate further that evaluation research is distinguished by use of the research techniques of the social sciences. We feel this is too restrictive. Certainly educational research techniques are included. In fact, we could as easily describe evaluation research as "disciplined inquiry" designed to determine the merit or worth of a thing—in this case community development or any of its elements (Worthen and Sanders 1973, pp. 11, 19–21). Evaluation research is not distinguished by a particular methodology but by the imposition of specific forms of discipline on the collection and interpretation of information. Cronbach and Suppes (1969, p. 12) discuss this discipline as follows:

> Disciplined inquiry has a quality that distinguishes it from other sources of opinion and belief. The disciplined inquiry is conducted and reported in such a way that the argument can be painstakingly examined. The report does not depend for its appeal on the eloquence of the writer or on any surface plausibility. The argument is not justified by anecdotes or casually assembled fragments of evidence.

Each subject-matter area has its own peculiar form of discipline. However, all involve the assumption that the argument must be susceptible to "painstaking examination" by others so that, using the same data and the same logic, others could be expected to reach the same conclusions. In the broadest sense, then, the "scientific" element in evaluation research is present to deal with the question of validity—validity of measurement and validity of the logic whereby conclusions are reached.

We add to this definition a normative criterion—evaluation research must be addressed to identifiable audiences that have a purpose for the research and can use it (Patton 1978). (We do not follow Worthen and Sanders [1973, pp. 14-39] in attempting to make a clear distinction between evaluation and research. Evaluation research, to us, is a subset of research, where research is defined broadly as "disciplined inquiry.")

Within this broad definition are many different types of evaluation research—indeed, many different ways of classifying the types (Forester 1975; Hudson 1975; Burton and Rogers 1976; Perkins 1977; Cosby and Wetherill 1978). The major methods of classifying evaluation research involve the dimensions of purpose or intent; design, including types of data and analytic techniques used; the particular phase of the policy process in which the research is imbedded; and finally, the level of abstraction or epistemological perspective. We have chosen to classify evaluation research along two dimensions as follows: (1) the function of research (what will it be used for, and by whom) and (2) the research method or mode (is it technically adequate and appropriate). Ultimately we create a matrix of three major research objectives by seven major research methods. Both of these dimensions could be divided into more categories with different titles. Space limitations prevent detailed classification and our objective of presenting the major categories of evaluation research can be achieved without it. (Two specific treatments of evaluation that imply different ways of classifying evaluation research are likely to be useful in community development—the inductive, system-process evaluation model [Burton and Rogers 1976; Burton 1978] and the combination of community development phases and levels of evidence of Bennett and Nelson [1975]. Since these are readily available we see no need to reproduce their logic here.)

FUNCTIONS OF EVALUATION RESEARCH

Evaluation research performs a number of distinct functions in the field of community development. Evaluation research (1) contributes directly to the CD process, (2) facilitates decision making about CD programs or projects, and (3) develops generalizations about the CD process. These functions are defined more clearly below.

Function 1: Contribute to the CD Process

In some instances evaluation research is an intervention or input used to achieve community development. The users of the research then are community leaders and the people themselves. An excellent example is given in R. Cohen et al. (1976), where simulation was used with community people to assist them in decision making. When performing this function, evaluation research usually includes engaging the community people themselves in research, perhaps in a process of self-study (Bruyn 1953; Poston 1953; Sanders 1953; Warren 1965). This function is also involved when the CD process is described in a series of phases as follows: (1) determining goals, (2) setting priorities, (3) assessing resources, (4) engaging in action, and (5) evaluation. This function of evaluation is implied by at least some examples of action research (Rapoport 1970; Lees and Smith 1975; Voth 1979). This function also includes much of what is referred to as the "process evaluation" of Rossi and Wright (1977, pp. 21–23). In this sense evaluation may occur constantly throughout the CD process.

One of the more influential writers to whom this function is particularly important is Paulo Friere (1970, 1973). His concept of "conscientizacao" epitomizes one of the goals of evaluation in this context. "The term 'conscientizacao' refers to learning to perceive social, political, and economic contradictions, and to take action against the oppressive elements of reality" (Friere 1970, translator's note, p. 19).

Horst et al. (1972, pp. 302–4) point out that many current social programs have specific goals and objectives that are characterized by uncertainty and discretion. This observation is particularly true of community development. Thus this form of research, where the target systems set their own goals, is important in community development, especially in the formative stages of projects. Thus "formative evaluation" may frequently be used to serve this function (Rutman 1977, pp. 57–71; Morris and Fitzgibbon 1978, pp. 24–68; Patton 1978).

Function 2: Facilitate Decision Making

Evaluation research generally, and in community development particularly, is concerned about whether programs or projects are achieving their objectives, how they can be improved, or whether they should be terminated or expanded. The users of such research are likely to be administrators, planner/evaluators, and CD practitioners. The research is sometimes internal, in which case it usually focuses on comparisons of different approaches or on the processes whereby a program is being carried out. When conducted or demanded by an external source, it may be concerned with evaluating program implementation or impact with a view toward making decisions about continuation, termination, expansion, etc. In terms of our scheme in Table 10.1, it is concerned primarily with the inputs and outputs and secondarily with the community processes.

Function 3: Develop Generalizations about the CD Process

Some evaluation research is focused on community development as a generic process and developing generalizations about this process. Thus it is primarily concerned with the throughputs of Table 10.1, their interrelationships, and the way they are related to interventions and to impacts. Users of this research are likely to be policymakers and academicians. This research has some unique characteristics—the concepts are more abstract and the populations to which generalizations are to be made are more ambiguous, leading to possible problems of external validity. Highly localized research becomes of questionable validity.

Some would not include this function in evaluation research at all. However, much of the frustration that has arisen about evaluation research results from the failure to distinguish this function from the preceding function. Furthermore, the interrelationship between these two functions is very close—without clear specification of CD dynamics it is extremely difficult to perform the evaluation that program and project administrators need (Horst et al. 1972, p. 303). At the same time, research to perform the second function can frequently contribute substantially to the development of generalizations about CD processes (Rossi and Wright 1977, p. 9).

MODES OR METHODS OF EVALUATION RESEARCH

The most frequently used typologies of evaluation research are based on the methods of research utilized. Burton and Rogers contrast the classical experimental design model with what they refer to as the inductive, system-process evaluation (ISP) model (Burton and Rogers 1976; Burton 1978), as have many others (Steele 1975; Scriven 1976; Perkins 1977; Patton 1978). Thus a major distinction is made between experimental or quasi-experimental designs and other methods. However, the other methods are very different. We suggest that evaluation designs can be arrayed along a continuum from hard, quantitative, classical designs to soft, intuitive, descriptive designs. The continuum has at least two distinct thresholds—the first as one moves from comparative to noncomparative designs and the second as one moves from goal-based to nongoal-based designs. Finally, a somewhat special category of designs, including policy simulations and cost analyses, are secondary or derived in the sense that they depend on use of known (exogenously determined) program or project effect parameters. Although not all designs suggested have been used in community development, there is no a priori reason to exclude any of them.

Comparative, Goal-Based Designs

Designs in which effect parameters are estimated by making explicit comparisons between experimental and control groups or across the range of independent variables are comparative, goal-based designs.

Experimental and quasi-experimental designs. As Rossi and Wright point out, the work of Campbell and Stanley (1966) on experimental and quasi-experimental designs is the bible of evaluation research. Since the work is readily available, the designs need not be defined here. It is important to point out some of their major characteristics. First, they deal explicitly with validity, particularly internal validity—providing the strongest basis possible for making causal inferences. They have weaknesses: The researcher often cannot exercise the control they require and they usually are planned to estimate only one parameter or a very limited number of parameters, which is unrealistic as a description of complex social processes. For example, they are frequently criticized for not indicating both beneficial and detrimental side effects of the processes of community development (Cohen 1976). The effect parameter estimates are available only after all the research is completed. Finally, they usually cannot be altered in midstream.

Multivariate designs and causal systems modeling. The solution to some of these problems from the comparative and classical design perspective is to include supposed confounding variables or side effects in the comparative design itself to effect the needed controls statistically (multivariate or covariance analysis) or to examine empirically the causal relationships among a wide range of variables (causal systems modeling) (Hawkes 1974; Cain 1975). Thus the evaluation of CD programs in Illinois by Voth (1975*b*) required a multivariate design. The researcher had no control over assignment of communities to experimental and control groups; consequently a number of confounding factors were present, most notably a correlation between community size and the presence of a CD program. The multivariate design also made it possible to separate process and content outcomes of the program.

Data requirements of causal system modeling techniques are so great and demands on CD theory (the throughputs of Table 10.1) so exacting that their utility in most CD evaluation is, unfortunately, not great at this time.

Some examples of these comparative designs in the evaluation of community development are Kaplan (1969), Clark and Hopkins (1970), and Vanecko et al. (1970). None are genuine experiments.

Noncomparative, Goal-Based Designs

Disillusionment with comparative designs—specifically experimental designs—has been widespread, especially in the evaluation of education and human services and in community development (Provus 1969*a*, 1969*b*; Burton and Rogers 1976; Cohen 1976; Burton 1978). In some contexts comparative designs, whether experimental or nonexperimental, simply do not fit. Therefore, a family of research designs has been developed that is not comparative but measures program or project achievement against specified goals or norms. We call these noncomparative, goal-based designs.

Discrepancy evaluation model. The discrepancy evaluation model (DEM) is a specific methodology developed by the late Malcolm Provus and his associates (1968, 1969*a*, 1969*b*) and elaborated in a manual by Yavorsky (1977). Conceptually it is very simple—although application is far more complex. Its essence is the establishment of measurable goals or standards and the measurement of achievement against these goals, from which comes the term "discrepancy." It usually also includes detailed specification of the project or program's "system" or chain of events that is designed to lead to the specified goals, and in this sense it is similar to the evaluation model for community development developed by Bennett and Nelson (1975).

Evaluation of implementation. Research designed to determine whether, and to what extent, planned inputs or interventions have in fact been carried out and whether they have reached their intended targets (Rossi and Wright 1977, pp. 23–26) is evaluation of implementation. The norms against which programs are to be measured are either specified in legislation or can be determined from program managers and administrators.

Freeman (1977) refers to this procedure as process evaluation and discusses it in some detail. He points out, for example, that faulty implementation is frequently the cause of no program effects. Much large-scale evaluation of programs is of this type, including evaluation of CD activities or programs (Madden 1977; Nathan et al. 1977).

Community development evaluation information systems. Program administrators frequently build evaluation into the design of various kinds of information systems. This activity is not so much a specific methodology of evaluation as it is an activity that can be engaged in while a methodology is being selected or in the absence of a clear idea of how a program is to be evaluated. One example of such an information system in CD literature is the Shared Process Evaluation System (SHAPES) of Mackeracher et al. (1976). The presumption is that information thus collected will contribute to evaluating the achievement of project or program goals.

Judicial evaluation. A technique developed by Wolf (1975), in which a project or program is evaluated using the advocacy style of judicial proceedings, is called judicial evaluation. Two opposing teams prepare documentation and elicit staff and participant observations and statements that will shed light on all aspects of the program. In essence, arguments for and against the program are presented to a "judge" or "judges," although the outcome may be a series of recommendations rather than an edict.

Noncomparative, Nongoal-Based Designs

As in the case of comparative designs, there has been dissatisfaction with some of the limitations of noncomparative, goal-based designs that has led to the second major threshold (or abyss, as some would suggest) in distinguishing evaluation research methodologies. Goal-based designs are criticized in particular for overlooking side effects, for bias resulting from attention to stated goals, and for inflexibility (Scriven 1972). In any case, this criticism leads to the third category, nongoal-based designs.

Goal-free evaluation. Weiss and Rein, in an old but frequently quoted article on community development (1972), and R. Cohen (1976) and Deutscher (1976), more recently, have advocated an intuitive evaluation methodology somewhat similar to the qualitative methodology of social anthropology or functional sociology. The same has been suggested by Patton (1978, pp. 220–28). Scriven (1972), the originator of goal-free evaluation, has taken perhaps the most extreme position by disregarding program or project goals on the assumption that attention given primarily and often only to stated goals leads to bias and invalidity in evaluation design. Scriven and other advocates of goal-free evaluation methodology suggest that the use of observation followed by the design of checklists, interviews, and other research tools will draw out information on all aspects of the program's effects and outcomes. They argue that a truer picture can be obtained than if attention is directed exclusively at stated goals.

Responsive evaluation. A similar position advocated by Stake (1975) is known as responsive evaluation. Stake, while not taking so extreme a position as Scriven, advocates the case study approach (1978) and the disciplined use of subjectivity.

Thus, a number of themes appear to characterize the noncomparative, nongoal-based designs. They include concern about the constraints imposed by focusing exclusively on stated goals, they view subjective judgments as being at least as valid as what they frequently refer to as "quantitative" assessments, and they advocate a kind of in-depth case study methodology.

Several other modes of evaluation are not concerned with estimating initial program effects as much as they are in using such effect parameters to reach conclusions about overall consequences. At least two are of particular importance to community development.

Policy simulation. Evaluation is not a part of the vocabulary of most economists. However, when it is explained to them they frequently think in terms of using known parameters (e.g., income multipliers) to estimate the effects of a project before it is even implemented. This policy simulation can play an important role in contributing to the process of community development. Some examples of policy simulation in CD literature are Awerbuch and Wallace (1976) and R. Cohen et al. (1976), which focus primarily on the impacts of housing development; Nelson (1977), which focuses on a range of rural development policy alternatives of the 1960s; and the growing literature on *ex ante* growth impact models (Clayton 1979; Darling 1979; Doeksen 1979; Morse 1979; Shaffer 1979; and many others). This evaluation is of quite a different sort from that discussed elsewhere. Since at its best it promises to be able to predict project or program consequences prior to program implementation, it has an obvious appeal to many CD practitioners.

Cost-benefit and cost-effectiveness analyses. These two modes of analysis are quite different; but both are concerned with attaching costs to program inputs (and outputs). Cost-effectiveness analysis is most likely to be applicable to community development (Levin 1975). In essence, it is a technique for determining, given a particular objective, which method of achieving that objective is the least costly in terms of staff time, money, and other resources. Obviously, effect parameters of the means for achieving the objective must be available—e.g., one must know whether development can be achieved and how much development can be achieved by the means being used. Cost-benefit analysis takes a broader approach to evaluating the outcomes from all of a program's inputs. Relative effectiveness of all inputs may not be derived.

IN DEFENSE OF AN ECLECTIC APPROACH

Table 10.2 presents an outline of evaluation research methodologies. It is a matrix of modes or methods by functions. Most of the types created are viable; some are not. It is hard to see, for example, how evaluation of implementation could be used to develop generalizations about the CD process. In general, the CD process is more likely to be reached by noncomparative methods and, perhaps, the special methods. All of them are likely to be used for facilitating decision making, whereas comparative goal-based methods are more likely to be used for developing generalizations about the CD process.

TABLE 10.2.   Classification of Evaluation Research

Model or Methods of CD Evaluation Research	Functions of CD Evaluation		
	Function 1: Facilitate CD processes	Function 2: Facilitate decision making	Function 3: Develop generalizations about CD processes
Comparative, Goal-Based Designs			
Experimental and quasi-experimental designs			Clark & Hopkins (1969)*
Multivariate designs			Vanecko et al. (1969)
and causal systems			Voth (1975*b*)
modeling			Kaplan (1969)
Noncomparative, Goal-Based Designs			
Discrepancy evaluation			
model and similar		Bennett & Nelson	
designs		(1974)	
Evaluation of imple-		Nathan (1977)	
mentation		Madden (1977)	
Community develop-			
ment evaluation in-		Mackeracher et al.	
formation systems		(1976)	
Judicial evaluation			
Noncomparative, Nongoal-Based Designs			
Goal-free evaluation		Cohen (1976)	
Responsive evaluation			
Special Evaluation Designs			
Policy simulation	Cohen et al. (1976)		
Cost-benefit and			
cost-effectiveness			
analysis			

*Examples of CD literature are placed in the approximate location of the perspective.

The illustrations in Table 10.2 show that community developers have used a wide range of evaluation research types. This in itself belies the sense one gets from much of the evaluation literature that there is a family of "correct" methods. The advocacy of a wide variety of methods is supported by the observation that evaluation research is and should be used by a variety of audiences with different objectives, different decision-making environments, and different criteria for the kinds of evidence they find acceptable. The most promising possibility for community development would seem to be the adoption of an eclectic approach, incorporating a wide range of methods suitable to the particular situation, function, and audience. Of particular importance in developing this position in the literature are Bennett and Nelson (1975), Burton and Rogers (1976), and Burton (1978). For general evaluation research, read Patton (1978). In fact, the Patton book should be the second piece a potential CD evaluator reads (after Campbell and Stanley [1966]).

This recommendation should not seem to lend too much credence to the criticisms of "hard" methodologies. From the perspective of disciplined inquiry, the classical requirements for validity that are presented so well by Campbell and Stanley cannot be overlooked (Bernstein 1976).

To return to an issue raised at the beginning of this chapter, there is also the question of public acceptance of community development as a discipline. It may appear attractive to adopt the "soft" methodologies of our friends in education. However, because of the great differences in public acceptance of the two disciplines, we can hardly expect to be given the freedom educational evaluators have enjoyed.

From the perspective of the CD evaluator the goal must be more than simply being able to show that community development activity has effects. No doubt random activity has effects of some kind. The goal of the evaluator must be to identify and measure the achievement of outcomes that the practitioner predicts. Otherwise neither the practitioner nor the evaluator is likely to be able to claim legitimacy very long.

REFERENCES

Alinsky, Saul D. 1969. *Reveille for Radicals.* New York: Random House, Vintage Books.

Annals of the American Academy of Political and Social Science. 1969. Evaluating the war on poverty, vol. 385 (Sept.).

Awerbuch, Shimon, and William A. Wallace. 1976. *Policy Evaluation for Community Development: Decision Tools for Local Government.* New York: Praeger.

Bennett, Claude F., and Donald L. Nelson. 1975. Analyzing impacts of community development. State College: Mississippi State University, South. Rural Dev. Cent.

Bernstein, Ilene. 1976. *Validity Issues in Evaluative Research.* Beverly Hills, Calif.: Sage Publ.

Bernstein, I. N., and H. E. Freeman. 1975. *Academic and Entrepreneurial Research.* New York: Russell Sage Found.

Bruyn, S. T. 1953. *Communities in Action: Pattern and Process.* New Haven: Coll. & Univ. Press.

Burton, John E., Jr. 1978. CD orientation to evaluation: Systems-process model for program evaluators. *J. Community Dev. Soc.* 9 (1):45–57.

Burton, John E., Jr., and David L. Rogers. 1976. A model for evaluating development programs. Ames: Iowa State University, North Cent. Reg. Cent. Rural Dev.

Cain, Glen G. 1975. Regression and selection models to improve nonexperimental comparisons. In *Evaluation and Experiment: Some Critical Issues in Assessing Social Programs,* Carl A. Bennett and Arthur A. Lumsdaine, eds., pp. 297–318. New York: Academic Press.

Campbell, Donald T., and Julian C. Stanley. 1966. *Experimental and Quasi-Experimental Designs for Research.* Chicago: Rand McNally. (Reprinted from N. L. Gage, ed., 1963, *Handbook of Research and Teaching.* Chicago: Rand McNally.)

Caro, Francis G., ed. 1971. *Readings in Evaluation Research.* New York: Russell Sage Found.

Clark, Kenneth, and Jeanette Hopkins. 1970. *A Relevant War against Poverty: A Study of Community Action Programs and Observable Change.* New York: Harper & Row.

Clayton, Kenneth C. 1979. The community economic growth impact model. Paper presented at Conference on *Ex Ante* Growth Impact Models, Columbus, Ohio, Mar. 6–7.

Cohen, Mark W. 1976. A look at process: The often ignored component of program evaluation. *J. Community Dev. Soc.* 7 (1):17–23.

Cohen, Rick. 1978. Partnership for neighborhood preservation: A citizen's handbook. Harrisburg: Pa. Dep. Community Aff.

——. 1979. Neighborhood planning and political capacity. *Urban Aff. Q.* 14 (3):337–62.

——. 1976. A test of an interactive community development impacts model in a rural environment. *Interfaces* 7 (1):51–56.

Cosby, Arthur G., and G. Richard Wetherill, eds. 1978. A synthesis: Resources in evaluation for rural development. SRDC Synth. Ser. 2. State College: Mississippi State University, South. Rural Dev. Cent.

Cronbach, L. J., and P. Suppes. 1969. *Research for Tomorrow's Schools: Disciplined Inquiry for Education.* New York: Macmillan.

Darling, David L., Jr. 1979. The Indiana experience with growth impact models. Paper presented at Conference on *Ex Ante* Growth Impact Models, Columbus, Ohio, Mar. 6–7.

Denise, Paul S. 1969. Some participation innovations. In *Citizen Participation in Urban Development: Cases and Programs,* vol. 2, Hans B. C. Spiegel, ed., pp. 7–19. Washington, D.C.: NTL Inst. Appl. Behav. Sci.

Deutscher, Irwin. 1976. Toward avoiding the goal-trap in evaluation research. In *The Evaluation of Social Programs,* Clark Abt, ed., pp. 249–68. Beverly Hills, Calif.: Sage Publ.

Doeksen, Gerald A. 1979. Community impact models and community service planning. Paper presented at Conference on *Ex Ante* Growth Impact Models, Columbus, Ohio, Mar. 6–7.

Forester, John. 1975. The practice of evaluation and policy analysis. Inst. Urban Reg. Dev., working pap. 257.

Freeman, Howard E. 1977. The present status of evaluation research. In *Evaluation Studies Annual Review,* vol. 2, Marcia Guttentag and Shalom Saar, eds., pp. 17–51. Beverly Hills, Calif.: Sage Publ.

Friere, Paulo. 1970. *Pedagogy of the Oppressed.* New York: Herder & Herder.

_____. 1973. *Education for Critical Consciousness.* New York: Seabury.

Glass, Gene V., ed. 1976. *Evaluation Studies Annual Review,* vol. 1. Beverly Hills, Calif.: Sage Publ.

Guttentag, Marcia, and Elmer L. Struening, eds. 1975. *Handbook of Evaluation Research.* Beverly Hills, Calif.: Sage Publ.

Guttentag, Marcia, and Shalom Saar, eds. 1977. *Evaluation Studies Annual Review,* vol. 2. Beverly Hills, Calif.: Sage Publ.

Hawkes, Roland K. 1974. Structural equations in evaluational research. Paper read at Institute on Methodological Concerns in Evaluational Research, Loyola University, May 31.

Hayes, Samuel P., Jr. 1967. *Evaluating Development Projects.* Paris: UNESCO.

Horst, Pamela; Joe N. Nay; John W. Scanlon; and Joseph S. Wholey. 1972. Program management and the federal evaluator. *Public Adm. Rev.* 34 (4):300–308.

Hudson, Barclay. 1975. Domains of evaluation. *Social Policy* 6 (2).

Kahn, Sy. 1970. *How People Get Power: Organizing Oppressed Communities for Action.* New York: McGraw-Hill.

Kaplan, Paul F. 1969. An evaluation of a Philippine community development program in the Cabanatuan marketing region of Nueva Ecija Province. Ph.D. dissertation, Cornell University.

Lees, Ray, and George Smith, eds. 1975. *Action-Research in Community Development.* Boston: Routledge & Kegan Paul.

Levin, H. M. 1975. Cost-effectiveness analysis in evaluation research. In *Handbook of Evaluation Research,* Marcia Guttentag and Elmer L. Struening, eds., pp. 89–112. Beverly Hills, Calif.: Sage Publ.

Mackeracher, Dorothy, et al. 1976. Community development evaluation and the SHAPES approach. *J. Community Dev. Soc.* 7 (2):4–17.

Madden, J. Patrick. 1977. Rural development and the land grant university: An evaluation of Title V of the Rural Development Act of 1972. Washington, D.C.: National Rural Center; and University Park: Pennsylvania State University.

Morris, L. L., and C. T. Fitzgibbon. 1978. *Evaluator's Handbook.* Beverly Hills, Calif.: Sage Publ.

Morse, George. 1979. With-without perspectives in growth impact models. Paper presented at Conference on *Ex Ante* Growth Impact Models, Columbus, Ohio, Mar. 6–7.

Nathan, Richard P. 1977. *Block Grants for Community Development: First Report on the Brookings Institution Monitoring Study of the Community Development Block Grant Program.* Washington, D.C.: Brookings Inst. (Prepared for HUD under Contract H-2323R.)

Nelson, James. 1977. A rural development policy simulator for teaching, research, and extension. Misc. Publ. MP-100. Stillwater: Oklahoma State University, Agric. Exp. Stn.

Patton, Michael Quinn. 1978. *Utilization-Focused Evaluation.* Beverly Hills, Calif.: Sage Publ.

Perkins, Dennis N. T. 1977. Evaluating social interventions: A conceptual schema. *Eval. Q.* 1 (4):639–56.

Poston, Richard W. 1953. *Democracy is You.* New York: Harper & Row.

Provus, Malcolm. 1968. *Discrepancy Evaluation.* Berkeley, Calif.: McCutchan.

_____. 1969*a*. Discrepancy evaluation model: 1969. Pittsburgh: Pittsburgh Public Sch.

_____. 1969*b*. Evaluation of ongoing programs in the public school system. In *Educational Evaluation: New Roles, New Means,* Ralph W. Tyler, ed., pp. 242–83. Chicago: Natl. Soc. Study Educ.

Rapoport, Robert N. 1970. Three dilemmas in action research. *Human Relat.* 23:499–513.

Richmond, Lynn. 1974. Active community thought: Myth and reality of a community development program. Master's thesis, Southern Illinois University.

Rossi, Peter, and Walter Williams, eds. 1972. *Evaluting Social Programs: Theory, Practice, and Politics.* New York: Seminar Press.

Rossi, Peter H., and Sonia R. Wright. 1977. Evaluation research: An assessment of theory, practice, and politics. *Eval. Q.* 1 (1):5–52.

Rubin, Lillian. 1969. Maximum feasible participation: Origins, implications, and present status. *Ann. Am. Acad. Polit. Social Sci.* 385 (Sept.):14–29.

Rutman, Leonard. 1977. *Evaluation Research Methods.* Beverly Hills, Calif.: Sage Publ.

Sanders, Irwin T. 1953. *Making Good Communities Better.* Lexington: Univ. Kentucky Press.

Scriven, Michael. 1967. *The Methodology of Evaluation.* AERA Monogr. Ser. Curriculum Eval., book 1. Chicago: Rand McNally.

_____. 1972. Pros and cons about goal-free evaluation: Evaluation comment. *J. Educ. Eval.* 3 (4):1–4.

_____. 1976. Payoffs from evaluation. In *The Evaluation of Social Programs,* Clark Abt, ed., pp. 217–24. Beverly Hills, Calif.: Sage Publ.

Shaffer, Ron. 1979. Estimating local income multipliers: A review and evaluation of the techniques for *ex ante* use. Paper presented at Conference on *Ex Ante* Growth Impact Models, Columbus, Ohio, Mar. 6–7.

Stake, Robert E. 1975. Program evaluation, particularly responsive evaluation. Kalamazoo: Western Michigan University, Eval. Cent., Coll. Educ., Occas. Pap. 5. Also in *Rethinking Educational Research,* W. B. Dockrell and D. Hamilton, eds. London: Hodder & Stoughton, in press.

_____. 1978. The case study method in social inquiry. *Educ. Res.* 7 (2):5–8.

Steele, Sara M. 1975. An emerging concept of program evaluation. *J. Ext.* 13 (Mar./Apr.):13–22.

Stufflebeam, Daniel L. 1972. Should or can evaluation be goal-free? Evaluation comment. *J. Educ. Eval.* 3 (4):4–5.

_____. 1974. Meta-evaluation. Kalamazoo: Western Michigan University, Eval. Cent., Coll. Educ., Occas. Pap. 3.

Suchman, Edward A. 1967. *Evaluative Research: Principles and Practice in Public Service and Social Action Programs.* New York: Russell Sage Found.

Vanecko, James J., et al. 1970. Community organization efforts, political and institutional change, and the diffusion of change produced by Community Action Programs, Rep. 122. Chicago: Natl. Opin. Res. Cent.

Voth, Donald E. 1975*a*. Problems in evaluating community development. *J. Community Dev. Soc.,* 6 (1):147–62. Also in *Community Development Research: Concepts, Issues, and Strategies,* 1979, Edward J. Blakely, ed. New York: Human Sci. Press.

_____. 1975*b*. An evaluation of community development programs in Illinois. *Social Forces* 53 (4):635–46.

_____. 1979. Social action research in community development. In *Community Development Research: Concepts, Issues, and Strategies,* Edward J. Blakely, ed. New York: Human Sci. Press.

Warren, Roland. 1965. *Studying Your Community.* New York: Free Press.

_____. 1973. *The Community in America,* 2d ed. Chicago: Rand McNally.

Weiss, Robert S., and Martin Rein. 1972. The evaluation of broad-aim programs: Difficulties in experimental design and an alternative. In *Evaluating Action Programs: Readings in Social Action and Education,* Carol H. Weiss, ed., pp. 236–49. Boston: Allyn & Bacon.

Wilkinson, Kenneth P. 1972. A field-theory perspective for community development resarch. *Rural Sociol.* 37 (1):43–52.

Wolf, Robert L. 1975. Trial by jury: A new evaluation method. *Phi Delta Kappan,* Nov.

Worthen, Blaine R., and James R. Sanders. 1973. *Educational Evaluation: Theory and Practice.* Worthington, Ohio: Charles A. Jones Publ.

Yavorsky, Diane Kyker. 1977. Discrepancy evaluation: A practitioners guide. Charlottesville: University of Virginia, Eval. Res. Cent.

Young, Frank W., and Ruth C. Young. 1974. *Comparative Studies of Community Growth.* Rural Sociol. Monogr. 2. Morgantown: West Virginia Univ. Press.

_____. (n.d.) Toward a theory of community development. In *Social Problems of Development and Urbanization,* Lowdon Wingo, Jr., ed., pp. 23–31. Washington, D.C.: USGPO. (Vol. 7 of Science, Technology, and Development, U.S. papers prepared for UN conference on application of science and technology for benefit of less developed areas.)

Building Theory for CD Practice

Edward J. Blakely

INTRODUCTION

The most important question confronting community development to-day is whether it is in fact an identifiable and discrete area of professional practice and scholarly inquiry. This issue is significant, both to individuals who earn their living in the field and to public policymakers, for several reasons.

First, in recent years, increasing attention has focused on community development. The Rural Development Act of 1972 and the Housing and Community Development Act of 1974 both contain assumptions regarding the efficacy of the CD *process* or *strategy* in addressing serious socioeconomic problems. Community development, according to its proponents, represents an integrated and coordinated national approach to socioeconomic planning and policy development for urban and rural areas (Hyde 1973). Second, the CD approach has formed the basis for so-called international development activities since World War II. The thrust of these activities has been the incorporation of villages, towns, and diverse economic and social groups into the economy and public life of developing nations. Finally, the advent of new groups of professional *change agents* (identifying themselves as community developers) in public and private organizations in both advanced and developing nations has raised questions about the scope of professional practice. This problem has sparked a debate within the Community Development Society over, as Duane Gibson puts it, "who is 'in' and who is 'out' " (1977, p. 37).

Clearly these recent trends are related. It is almost axiomatic that any new public policy and related government programs produce a corresponding group of specialists, consultants, and quasi-professionals available to manage them both within and outside of government. Besides, these trends suggest that the basic *concepts, principles,* or *notions* (theories) of community development have been sufficiently articulated to be incorporated into public policy and accepted by the populace. This is phenomenal in itself, since few active scholars or practitioners have attempted to codify or prepare a paradigm for the CD method. In fact, some writers have pointed to the singular lack of a clear conceptualization or theoretical foundation for the field (Sanders 1964; Eberts 1969, p. 234; Kim 1973; Christenson 1978). In spite of this lack, CD methods and practices have recently been adopted as public policy in many nations.

Is a theory necessary to support public policy? While there may be some debate on this subject, Kim (1973, p. 463) asserts, and I concur, that "in today's world, development, however defined, is a goal in itself. . . . were it otherwise, so many nations all over the world would not have made development their *raison d'être.*"

In government policy there is nearly always a presumption that the actions taken by the government will be beneficial. If government programs are of some benefit it can be argued that their proponents should be in a position to say why some programs succeed (by the developers' standards) and other programs fail (Voth 1979). One should be able to certify through theoretical hypothesis testing the fact that successful programs have accomplished intended objectives. Conversely, the same or a similar set of propositions should identify deficient efforts. As Spiegel (1979, p. 31) suggests, the absence of a substantive theoretical foundation for community development leads to "(1) much action (and social policy) proceed[ing] on the basis of presumed theory in the guise of unexamined conventional wisdom, and (2) much action casually pulled together into presumed theory that turns out to be self-serving."

Thus, theory is, or at least ought to be, the basis for relevant public policy. Theory in this sense is a useful measuring device for practitioners and policymakers. Theory serves as a guide to (1) policy formulation, (2) program design, (3) program implementation, and ultimately, (4) program evaluation. A complete theoretical construct for community development must therefore address each component of the development process. Whether such a theoretical framework exists is questionable. In the balance of this chapter, I discuss the basis for community development theory, how it might be formulated, what uses it can or should serve, and finally, what it might look like.

PERSPECTIVES OF CD THEORY

James Christenson, in reviewing articles appearing in the *Journal of the Community Development Society,* notes, "Few articles were found that might be grouped under the heading of theory. Few attempted to link theory to community development efforts" (see Chapter 3). The paucity of articles on theory is, I believe, related not so much to an absence of concern for it as to an inability to formulate it.

There is no single basis for formulating community development theory, partly due to the lack of a single disciplinary core for the field. Community development (see Chapter 1) is composed of several social, economic, and behavioral perspectives. Consequently, most of the notions underlying the field are linked to disparate conceptions of goals, intentions, direction, and definitions of the concepts of both community and development. However, all theory must proceed from a base. An operational definition for community development that can serve as a base for theory formulation might follow that provided by Speight (1973, p. 479):

Community development, as we see it, involves: setting priorities by external change agents in conjunction with people in the local community toward the ultimate goal of integrating the community into national life; combining what is rational to the community development expert and national planners and what is rational to the target population in such a way as to coordinate local programs and resources with national development goals; using specialized training techniques for development personnel to insure the attainment of overall goals and the coordination of activities; and fostering and maintaining community development as an idea with emotional attachment, value-infused with social value, i.e., institutionalized, so that it will tend to overcome resistance to change and set up self-perpetuating change.

This definition provides a potential conceptual framework for developing a model or paradigm from which theory might emerge. (Other definitions and more elaborate discussion are found in Chapter 1.) Developing a paradigm from this or similar definitions of community development is extraordinarily difficult. Nonetheless, a paradigm on which to articulate theory is advanced in the following section.

In Search of a Paradigm for CD Theory

A number of approaches can be employed to identify a CD paradigm. For example, one might follow the Picou, Wells, and Nyberg approach of theoretical sociological construct (1978, p. 560), which they borrowed from Ritzer (1975). This approach suggests three metatheoretical paradigms for sociology that are equally applicable to community development: (1) the social facts paradigm, (2) the social definitions paradigm, and (3) the social behavior paradigm.

The social facts paradigm is based on acquisition of data through surveys, questionnaires, or interviews. The social definitions paradigm is exemplified in the work of Weber (1964) and other classical social theorists who focus on social action. Within this stratagem, the researcher acts as a participant/observer, recorder, historian, etc. Finally, the social behavior paradigm emphasizes the notion of rewards and sanctions that relate to certain types of behavioral modification a la B. F. Skinner. To some extent each of these paradigms exists and has shaped CD scholarship and practice. A brief discussion of each follows.

Social facts paradigm. The analysis and assessment of community groups is fundamental to CD strategy. This approach emphasizes the collection of primary data on people within their cultural milieu. The literature on how data on the social environment are collected, which is quite extensive (Biddle and Biddle 1965; Cox et al. 1978), emphasizes every aspect of community-based data gathering—including identifying the social process (sociology); exploring social relationships (anthropology); and determining when, where, and how to induce (Blakely 1979, p. 135) or to introduce (Speight 1973, p. 481) change. The community developer (i.e., the change agent) identifies the total social environment and the forces or factors either promoting or limiting change (Lippitt, Watson, and Wesley 1958; Clark 1972; Ploch 1976; Warren 1977). The goal of the change agent is to discover community facts and alter the conditions in the community (human organizations) to a new *state*, one that is more satisfactory (Conrad and Field 1976). (*State* here means an altered sociopsychological condition, as in state of consciousness or state of awareness.) Thus the methodology emphasizes various forms of data gathering as part of the *process*. The social facts or descriptive materials relative to the community condition are not the property of the change agent but of the clients or community itself; hence these data are shared with the community (Schler 1970, p. 113; Blakely 1978). Unlike other social science disciplines (such as sociology and anthropology, which report their findings in journals) or public service professionals (such as planners, who develop reports to and for public bodies and bureaucracies), the CD scholar/practitioner provides data on the community to the citizens themselves as part of the process of promoting change.

    Thus, the data-gathering techniques of assessing social settings and environments set the stage for CD intervention. These methods are designed as part of the total strategy of the change agent to help social organizations, groups, and communities assess their needs for change and determine the direction of that change. Theoretical research in community development

focuses on the interplay between community and intervenor, and not on the community by itself or on the study of the intervening actor without the community context. The community development researcher *must* know about community and the intervening actor individually, but community development scholars must penetrate the process that brings them together. [Spiegel 1979, p. 29]

    The factors that separate CD data gathering from general community research are the intended use(s) of the information as well as the objectives of the process. The social facts paradigm states that *community data gathering is a basic component of the community development process and not the objective of it.*

    Social definition paradigm. One of the basic assumptions of the social- and community-oriented professions is that the socioeconomic-political environment can be altered. The supposition is that alterations in the social structure can improve the quality or quantity of life for a target population. In addition, it is assumed that the basic resources needed to achieve change are present within the social system itself (Hobbs 1971).

Community development scholars and practitioners have focused (Kim 1973, p. 466) on the ''type of structural change . . . essential to the alteration of a society's resource allocation or distributions [system]. Since the cores of development values all have something to do with society's resources and their distribution, it is logically consistent to conceive of the process of development in terms of structure of resource allocation.''

Altering social structure, social action, social change, conflict—these terms have come to be used interchangeably in community development. While other social scientists subscribe to various positive, neutral, or negative stances toward inducing or producing change, community developers are decidedly social change activists. Hobbs (1971) analyzes the stances toward social change in development as (1) functionalism—interdependent networks of institutions contributing toward the maintenance of socioeconomic order (the social system in this context transcends humans; in essence, it is not manipulatable); (2) modernism—the process of industrialization, urbanization, and growth (the central concerns in this context are the problems and dilemmas associated with either too slow or too rapid socioeconomic transformation); (3) conflict—the alternative view that social control and order are maintained through coercions and structural conditions that limit societal access (the interactive forces in the social structure that attempt to redistribute or improve access cause or result in conflict); (4) social behaviorism—the holistic orientation in which social groups (elites, media, etc.) determine socialization patterns (the behaviorist context provides for systematic ordering of social institutions to satisfy a given community order).

Basically, community development orientation is conflict oriented and modernist.

Social action has as its main objective the alteration of system attributes of society and its subsystems through the development of new systems, the alteration of old ones, or a combination of the two. . . . From the point of view of social action these systems are in a sense the targets for change. In another sense they provide the resources [italics added] and are the carriers of action. [Beal 1964, p. 242]

Community development research has consequently focused to some extent on studying the system itself, which might be a typical community, a set of institutions, or a particular disadvantaged community. For practitioners, the rich variety of case studies and success or failure stories portrayed in the Journal of the Community Development Society, the Community Development Journal, and other periodicals and monographs form a basis for theorizing about social action in various systems or subsystems.

In addition, the training of professionals recognizes the importance of keeping community profiles and personal diaries (Fujimoto 1972). This exercise is not merely an occasion for introspective reflection but is based on the recognition that systematic description and analysis form part of the development process. Practitioners are trained to assist the community and analyze its actions and reactions to internal and external events (Beal 1964). The social action strategies employed by CD professionals have been sufficiently articulated to be codified into a series of well-defined action steps and principles (see Chapters 2, 3, and 7). Society is viewed by community developers as dynamic rather than static and as undergoing some form of change internally or externally at all times; the community developer brings a certain order and impetus to this natural process. Thus, the social definition paradigm suggests that *CD scholars and practitioners recognize the community as a human creation and a human experience capable of being altered or changed in directions established by its own members.*

Social behavior paradigm. One principal obstacle to advancing theory in community development and related social action arenas has been the difficulty of determining cause and effect. The problems and promise of research in community settings go back at least as far as Kurt Lewin (1948). Cowen (1973) characterized community researchers as valuing *doing* more than *studying.* This occurs chiefly because developers are obliged to grapple with community forces in the natural process and to sort out cause and effect in vivo. It is a formidable task. However, if theory is to emerge, the various factors associated with practice must be dissected. Few community developers have embarked on this type of analysis. Community psychologists, somewhat distant cousins of community developers, have advanced most of the relevant research in this area, which has assisted in identifying such central issues as individual role behavior in small groups (Murrell 1973). Further, these researchers have advanced quasi-experimental research approaches suited to natural settings to measure such phenomena as status behavior, conflict origins and resolution, competition in group settings, gamesmanship (Nylen, Robert, and Anthony 1965; Schein 1969; Kelly 1977).

Such research offers a basis for understanding the dynamics of individual and collective behavior in both formal and informal settings. Community development practitioners are aware of the need to develop new institutional structures and to build them on the correct personality leadership base (Mitchell and Lowry 1973). However, the notion of social controls operating to stimulate or induce individual actions, rewards, or sanctions is only now being openly discussed in the literature. Speight's Machiavellian perspective development (1975) provides a macroanalysis of this concept, while other researchers are beginning to look at small groups and microbehavior. In the behavioral paradigm, *community change is based on individual behavior appropriately linked and directed to cause collective group action in a predetermined direction.*

This analysis does not attempt to provide a single broad integrated model of community development but advances a multiparadigm perspective as a base for analyzing community development to construct relevant theory.

BUILDING CD THEORY

Theory serves a useful purpose in every field. Economists, for example, advance concepts of monetary theory, micro- and macroeconomic theory, and the like to build various theories of collective management of resources. Community development theory requires the contribution of practitioners to the advancement of the body of knowledge related to collective social action. Unfortunately, many community developers, along with other applied social and behavioral scientists, have not actively engaged in theory formulation because they incorrectly assume that theory can only be generated from intellectually distant a priori assumptions and that what they do and observe cannot be categorized and classified to form theoretical or policy statements. As they see it, theory somehow emerges from books, articles, great thinkers, logic, or the wisdom of academicians—not from practitioners. Such a view of theory construction renders it of little use to active change agents. Further, community developers, like many social service and other professionals, are unable to perceive what kind of theory or theoretical constructs might be useful to them. Consequently, the rich descriptive case study materials in journals, books, or monographs are seldom organized or synthesized into usable observations or generalizations. Theory, in fact, can serve practitioners as the link between concept and action.

The process of arriving at community development theory is both analytic and synthetic. Theory building is an intellectual strip-tease in which the body of knowledge and practices in community development is openly and unmercifully scrutinized and analyzed to see what is underneath all the outer trappings. . . . Theory has to explain both the makeup of a single community development episode as well as the entire social fabric in which community development is embedded. [Spiegel 1979, p. 28]

Building on Spiegel, CD theory can take a useful form by (Blakely 1972):

1. enabling prediction and explanation of behavior
2. being useful in theoretical advance of the field
3. being usable in practical application—prediction and explanation—giving the practitioner understanding and some control over situations
4. providing a perspective on behavior—a stance to be taken toward data
5. guiding and providing a style of research on particular areas of behavior

Theory should provide a mechanism for handling research data and models of conceptualization for describing and explaining observed behavior. The categories and hypotheses provided should be clear enough that they can be verified in present or future research (Glaser and Strauss 1967,

p. 3). In this sense theory construction proceeds from practitioners' activities abstracted to a level of general application, although the degree of abstraction depends on the area of practice one is examining. Spiegel (1979, p. 36) has suggested at least ten levels of abstraction, ranging from a single practitioner's self-conscious examination (What am I doing here and now?) to general concepts that explain present and past behavior and are likely to predict future events as well. Every community developer engages in this kind of theory formulation at some level in daily work. The further articulation of observed behavior series of activities into a holistic concept that can be tested or replicated is the art and science of theory construction for the CD professional.

CD Theory

The principal activity of academic social scientists is not theory construction but theory verification. In community development, even the verification of concepts must derive from borrowed or converted theory. Clearly, the absence of both theory and theory-generating processes in community development impedes intellectual advancement in this field. Yet few community developers have addressed how theory might be formulated. In Chapter 1, Christenson and Robinson question the present status of CD theory by asserting that

community developers . . . stake a claim on "normative community development" on the one hand or on a group of "scientific principles of community action" on the other. Adherents to normative community development can create philosophical treatises on goals and guidelines for development. These will provide focus for CD efforts, though testing or measurement will be problematic. Adherents to the scientific principles of community action approach can define the variables in change and do carefully constructed experiments to test; for example, Are the community decision makers more likely to act in desired ways when conflict is intense?

However correct this statement is, it seems to beg the central issue of whether useful community development theory can be structured or, as Spiegel (1979) puts it, "teased out" of the community development process.

Several approaches might be considered for theory construction. First, CD scholars might put forward a set of assumptions about communities, social change, and institutional and individual behavior tailored to the CD process. This approach would follow the works on social action by Beal (1964) and Beal, Powers, and Coward (1971), which summarize various perspectives. The inherent problem with this approach is that identifying the threads that distinguish community development from other sociological theory can be difficult.

Second, the *great thinker* approach might well be used to advance a set of theories capable of testing. The works of intellectual pioneers such as

Biddle, Poston, Warren, Sanders, Sutton, Alinsky, and others might be carefully combed to isolate guiding principles and concepts that define and describe community development in theoretical terms. This approach has some promise; however, even these thinkers tend to rely heavily on the works of economists, sociologists, and social philosophers to derive their concepts. Determining where one writer's concepts (or someone else's) begin and end can be exceedingly difficult.

Third, the logicodeductive technique might be employed to generate theory. This process is already fairly well developed among the macrosocial accounting school of CD scholars, e.g., Eberts (1969), Young and Young (1973), and MacCannell (1979). Over the last decade this group has accumulated a significant amount of data on communities and the development process. They have advanced a paradigm for community development that emphasizes the concepts of solidarity (group standards and values), centrality (interactions of communities), and differentiation (varieties of groups and institutions in the social setting) (MacCannell 1979). While these concepts appear in various forms in other literature, this group has refined them to become the core of emerging theory by advancing a quantifiable intellectual construct. This approach is enormously useful in assessing which actions are more important to social change, although it brings with it the danger of screening out data and observations, as well as screening them in. The data-gathering and verification activity in this approach places great emphasis on identifying, labeling, and quantifying variables that act as predictors for development. However, common sense and some observed information may not be recorded or may be too filtered to determine its role in the process of generation theory.

Fourth, the grounded or comparative qualitative method provides a theory-generating technique open to every scholar and practitioner. It proceeds from the notion that theory is an ever developing entity and not a perfect product. The emphasis in comparative analysis is to develop *theory as process* (Glaser and Strauss 1967, p. 32). Grounded or comparative qualitative analysis allows the investigator to examine a unit of any size (organization, town, city, region, nation) and interpret recorded data into conceptual categories and properties, which form the basis for advancing theories. The approach depends on fieldwork and keeping accurate field notes on what has transpired in the natural setting (Strauss et al. 1964). These notes are carefully coded, analyzed, and cross-checked. This method is available to all practitioners and groups of practitioners, working either in concert or separately. The only requirements are good notes from the same field of practice (rural economic development, urban slum health, etc.). This approach has several advantages. First, it is available to the clients (community), practitioners, and scholars on an equal basis. Second, it does not require the use of sophisticated data-processing equipment or techniques unavailable in developing regions or areas. Third, it does not disrupt the natural setting or force ideas or categories on the natural phenomena. Finally, it treats theory as process, just as community development is viewed as *process*. Scant CD theory has proceeded from this approach (see Blakely 1972) because it is a little-known and novel methodology. In spite of this, it seems to fit well with the basic thrust of CD discipline.

Each of the methods outlined yields theory, but for theory to be valuable it must meet two tests: It must *fit* and it must work. Theory fits if it is readily applicable to and indicated by the data studied; theory works by explaining the behavior under study (Glaser and Strauss 1967, p. 3). Thus, community development (or any other applied social or behavioral science) theory cannot be esoteric; it must be useful.

Substantive and Formal Theory

Theory may be either substantive or formal. Substantive theory is developed from particular substantive areas (such as juvenile delinquency, urban renewal, or community mental health) or a particular geographic or subject-matter area (West African urban redevelopment or family planning and development in India). Formal theory, on the other hand, is developed for a broad conceptual area of inquiry, such as deviant behavior, socialization, or authority and power. Substantive and formal theory exist side by side in the literature. Formal theory is often reduced to substantive theory by community developers eager to offer proof of the validity and respectability of their observations. For instance, case studies frequently verify formal theories of race relations or political power by depicting conflicts involving racial groups seeking leverage or position in a community associations. In fact, racial conflicts within a community might well be incorporated into substantive theory about social status stress in new community-based organizations. Most theorizing is substantive as a precursor to a genuine formal social theory.

Both substantive and formal theory fall midway between the mere advancing of untested hypotheses and the grand theories of economic and social behavior (Merton 1968). In addition, community development as a field of inquiry occupies a midrange scholarly position. Therefore, at the current stage of theory formulation, CD scholar/practitioners might be well advised to move from prosaic commonsense hypotheses toward articulate midrange concepts based on comparative fieldwork.

Finally, for theory to serve practice, it may be either descriptive or prescriptive; that is, theory may serve to describe the phenomena under study or to provide a course or courses of action to alter observed conditions. As Brunner (1963) once put it, "A theory of learning [descriptive] is not a theory of teaching [prescriptive]." Community development clearly needs some of each. It is tempting for academic community developers to compile descriptive evidence and to neglect the requirements of prescribing better practices. The descriptive research trend in most social science and CD literature has led to a minicrisis in the journals. Unfortunately, the people in the best position to translate descriptive material into prescriptive theories, the fieldworkers themselves, do little writing for journals. As a consequence, the richest material and most insightful models for community development are confined to mimeographed or typed notes circulated among practitioners.

In summary, CD theory building is generated from field practice. Community development theory, therefore, should be substantive inasmuch as it is derived from and related to field practice. In addition, it should be expressed in the midrange concepts descriptive of the nature and process of CD interactions and should provide new prescriptive courses of action useful to current field practitioners. In this sense, theory is a living, moving, evolving part of a *process*. Theory building thus is one more useful tool for professionals and is central to their responsibilities to their communities and their profession. The next section articulates a set of categories on which academicians and/or practitioners might advance community development theory.

Articulating Theory

Theory does not emerge as a complete and self-contained body of knowledge. Rather, it is built on a series of smaller, identifiable building blocks, which are usually well-known, frequently expressed ideas or observations of practitioners regarding social behavior. Community development does not lack the necessary ingredients for theory formulation. "On the one hand, teachers, researchers and practitioners have recognized the need for a general theory of development; on the other, many of these individuals perpetuate the need by referring to 'community development' or other types of development while attempting to explicitly define the concept of development itself" (Oberle, Stowers, and Darby 1974, p. 69). While this observation is useful, it does not advance theory. Rather, theoretical advance is a painstaking procedure of ordering and organizing ideas gleaned from data into discrete and recognizable elements.

The two basic elements in theory generation are categories and properties of categories. A category is an idea that stands by itself as a central component of general theory, while a property is an aspect of a category. For example, two categories of community development are "analysis of community settings" and "action strategies." One of the properties of action is "group motivation," that is, the means used to stimulate action. The two categories and the property are interrelated, since the "analysis of community settings" provides information about *influentials* or *change transmitters* who form part of the "action strategy" for group organization. Research hypotheses can be derived from theory categories and properties.

The following outline provides an example of categories and their properties, with resultant hypotheses. The purpose of this example is to provide an intellectual template that can serve in the examination of the work of Oberle, Stowers, and Darby to "tease out" the building blocks for a theory of community development.

Categories: Social system flexibility allows development options.

Properties of categories: Differentiation in socioeconomic structures provides development opportunities.

Hypotheses: The more differentiated the community structure, the greater the potential for (1) professional community development intervention and (2) design of successful community programs.

No attempt is made here to provide the final or definitive theory for community development. Rather, the objective is to give form and order to what we know now about its practice. This framework for deriving formal theory is organized and presented as substantive descriptive theory categories and properties that might form the base for development theory and for the advancement of a science of community development.

Discovering and Stating Theory

Oberle and his colleagues (1974) did not produce theory, but they provided excellent elementary working concepts that might serve as the initial step in the organization of CD theory. These concepts may be divided into at least three broad categories: group and organizational behavior, planned social change, and the values and ethics of change.

Category 1. Group and organizational behavior. The unique feature of the CD method is its focus on group and organizational structure for collective action as a means to effect social change. Basic properties related to this process are:

Social structure: network of social interactions and behavior patterns that can be altered by professional intervention.

Social change: significant alteration (of a given social structure) that can be planned.

Social entity: individuals, groups, organizations, communities, or other recognizable social structures that have a "distinct" identity determined by geography and/or socioeconomic group.

Social interaction: two or more individuals in the same situation that take one another into account and meet mutually satisfying objectives.

Identification: externally verifiable group recognition that allows meaningful social units to act.

Social status: social structure positions that are capable of alteration or modification.

Social group: group cohesion based on sharing of awareness.

Interstitial structure: organizational form of human groups that gain social power with higher development.

These concepts clearly require further refinement and integration into existing principles of community development and prescriptive methods of professionals.

Category 2. Planned social change. The purposeful intervention into social organizations is the bedrock of CD practice. The means and purpose of intervention underlie much of the concern for a useful paradigm to guide responsible intervention. Among the properties of this concept are:

Goal: predetermined end or object that can be established by human groups.

Planned change: deliberate and conscious process that can be designed and articulated to reach a group objective.

Barriers: obstacles to change that exist within both the group desiring change and the targets of change.

Norm: behavior that defines group social controls.

Role: set of norms associated with an individual or group position that limits action.

Voluntary association: social entity that must be arranged for collective action.

Power: capacity to prevent or produce change in the face of opposition—critical measure of group's development capacity.

(Action) Organization: coordination of actions through institution building that provides a means to obtain and perpetuate a goal.

Leadership: impetus to group movement via individual or concerted capacities to mobilize people to act in the face of opposition or with few resources; depends on distribution of roles and responsibilities within the group.

Integrating concepts of planned change in social organizations and institutions is difficult. The most perplexing problem is how to build a theory of change in social institutions. A clear notion of what is progress or improvement is lacking. Community developers must come to grips with this vital issue in substantive/theoretical rather than philosophical terms.

Category 3. Values and ethics of change. Intervention into any social setting is extremely presumptuous. Who is to say what is good or bad? Who can make the best judgment about what means should be used to produce a change in any given direction? Some values or philosophical constructs, if not clear theories, are required to guide practitioners. These questions form the core of the values dilemma for community developers. However, valuation is central to understanding the desirability of development.

Efforts to run away from valuation are misdirected and foredoomed to be fruitless and damaging. The valuations are with us, even when they are driven underground, and they guide our work. When kept implicit and unconscious, they allow biases to enter. The only way in which we can strive for objectivity in theoretical analysis is to lift up the valuations into the full light, make them conscious and explicit, and permit them to determine the viewpoints, the approaches, and the concepts used. [Myrdal, in Kim 1973, p. 463]

The properties of values theory for community developers are:

Assessment: analysis of social action options using criteria or conceptions of group members to assess the impacts of altering the social order.

Zero sum situations: situations in which one person, group, or entity cannot gain at the expense of others.

Life chances: opportunities to gain valued goals and avoid misfortune that are implicit in all CD projects.

These are not the only value considerations, but they are central to a relevant values theory.

Community development theory then may be forged in miniconcepts that, when combined, form overarching or general theory. The miniconcepts can be assembled or disassembled into hypotheses for examination or reconceptualization or assembly into new forms or different ideological constructs.

Figure 11.1 shows an attempt to merge the broad intellectual concepts from this section with the theory components from previous sections. Though the arrangement is arbitrary, the figure is designed to help summarize the numerous ideas discussed, crystallize and integrate the relationships among the broad general concepts with potential theory building blocks, and stimulate theoretical advance by providing a matrix or template for scholars and practitioners to expand, criticize, or reformulate for CD theory.

Community development has been characterized as a *process;* its field theory is also described in process terms because the CD process must include theory construction as an underpinning for action. Normative theory for community development does not emerge from concepts or assumptions but from the interactive processes of social action and change. Therefore, the dichotomy that some community developers perceive between advancing theory and practice is not real. The core of the CD process is theory construction. In this sense, theory is emergent, changing, evolving, and integral with practice.

Community development theory emerges from *planned and organized* interventions into the lives of individuals and groups to produce socioeconomic change in a predetermined direction to enhance the quality of life in a defined area or the opportunities of an identified population.

This conceptual framework is the envelope for theory building that can provide a useful starting place for the next decade for scholars, researchers, and practitioners.

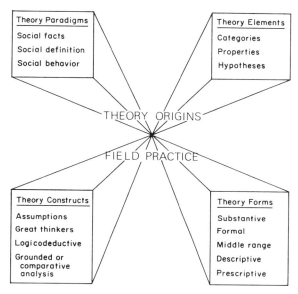

Fig. 11.1.   Theory building process for community development.

SUMMARY

One of the most urgent needs for community development is to design a way to arrive at meaningful theory for practitioners, policymakers, and the public. Attempts to state CD theory in some definitive manner are as yet embryonic. As a consequence, community developers, regardless of their roles or responsibilities, can significantly contribute to the theory building process with the concepts and methods outlined here. While some areas of sociology from which many CD concepts are derived are showing signs of theoretical closure or loss of vitality (Picou, Wells, and Nyberg 1978), community development is expanding its intellectual horizons. Theoretical advances require a conceptual framework for organizing and understanding theory, which this chapter attempts to fashion in broad outline. Scholars and practitioners have the opportunity to improve this framework as they advance the intellectual frontiers of the field.

REFERENCES

Alinsky, Saul D. 1972. *Rules for Radicals.* New York: Random House, Vintage Books.
Beal, George. 1964. Social action: Instigated social change in large social systems. In *Our Changing Rural Society: Perspectives and Trends,* James H. Copp, ed. Ames: Iowa State Univ. Press.

Beal, George; Ronald Powers; and E. Walter Coward. 1971. *Sociological Perspectives of Domestic Development*. Ames: Iowa State Univ. Press.

Biddle, William. 1968. *Encouraging Community Development: A Training Guide for Local Workers*. New York: Holt, Rinehart & Winston.

Biddle, William, and J. Louride Biddle. 1965. *The Community Development Process*. New York: Holt, Rinehart & Winston.

_____. ed. 1979. *Community Development Research*. New York: Human Sci. Press.

_____. 1978. Goal setting for community development: The case of Yuba City, California. Davis: University of California, Inst. Gov. Aff.

Blakely, Edward J. 1972. *Toward a Theory of Training People for the War on Poverty*. New York: Vantage Press.

Brunner, Jerome S. 1963. Needed: A theory of instruction. *Educ. Leadership* 20 (8):523.

Christenson, James. 1978. Community development: A decade in review. Paper presented at Annual Meeting of Community Development Society, Blacksburg, Va.

Clark, A. 1972. Sanctions, A critical element in action research. *J. App. Behav. Sci.* 2:78.

Clark, Peter A. 1972. *Action Research and Organization Change*. New York: Harper & Row.

Conrad, Jan, and Barry C. Field. 1976. Rural development: Goals, economic growth, and community preferences. Res. Bull. 634. Amherst: University of Massachusetts, Mass. Agric. Exp. Stn.

Cowen, E. L. 1973. Social and community intervention. *Annu. Rev. Psychol.* 24:423–72.

Cox, Fred M.; John L. Erlich; Jack Rothman; and John E. Trapman, eds. 1977. *Tactics and Techniques of Community Practice*. Itasca, Ill.: Peacock.

Eberts, Paul. 1969. Rural sociology's response to extension—Suggestions for action oriented theory. *Rural Sociol.* 34 (2):234–40.

Fujimoto, Isao. 1972. Reports on the community field experiences. Mimeographed. Davis: University of California, Dep. App. Behav. Sci.

Gibson, Duane L. 1977. Professional certification for community development personnel. *J. Community Dev. Soc.* 8 (2):30–38.

Glaser, Bernard G., and Anselm Strauss. 1967. *The Discovery of Grounded Theory: Strategies in Qualitative Research*. Chicago: Aldine Publ.

Hobbs, Daryl. 1971. Some contemporary sociological perspectives regarding social change. In *Sociological Perspectives of Domestic Development,* George Beal, Ronald Powers, and E. Walter Coward, Jr., eds. Ames: Iowa State Univ. Press.

Hyde, Floyd. 1973. Keynote address, annual meeting of the Community Development Society. *J. Community Dev. Soc.* 4 (1):5–13.

Kelly, James; Lonnie R. Snowden; and Ricardo Munoz. 1977. Social and community interventions. *Annu. Rev. Psychol.* 28:323–61.

Kim, Kyong-Dong. 1973. Toward a sociological theory of development. *Rural Sociol.* 38 (4):462–76.

Lewin, Kurt. 1948. *Resolving Social Conflict*. New York. Harper & Row.

Lippitt, R.; J. Watson; and B. Wesley. 1958. *The Dynamics of Planned Change: A Comparative Study of Planned Change*. New York: Harcourt Brace.

MacCannell, Dean. 1979. Elementary structures of community. In *Community Development Research,* E. Blakely, ed. New York: Human Sci. Press.

Merton, Robert K. 1968. *Sociological Theory and Social Structure,* enlarged ed. New York: Free Press.

Mitchell, John B., and Sheldon Lowry. 1973. *Power structures, community leadership, and social action,* publ. 35. Columbus, Ohio: North Cent. Reg. Ext.

Murrell, Stanley A. 1973. *Community Psychology and Social Systems: A Conceptual Framework and Intervention Guide.* New York: Behavioral Publ.

Nylen, A.; J. Robert; and S. Anthony. 1965. *Handbook of staff development and human relations training.* Washington, D.C.: Natl. Train. Lab.

Oberle, Wayne; Kevin R. Stowers; and James Darby. 1974. A definition of development. *J. Community Dev. Soc.* 5 (1):61–71.

Picou, Steven; Richard Wells; and Kenneth Nyberg. 1978. Paradigms, theories, and methods in contemporary rural sociology. *Rural Sociol.* 43 (4):559–83.

Ploch, Louis. 1976. *Community Action as Community Development—A Case Study.* Orono, Maine: Res. Life Sci. Agric. Exp. Stn. 23 (6):1–15.

Ritzer, George. 1975. *Sociology: A Multiple Paradigm Science.* Boston: Allyn & Bacon.

Sanders, Irwin T. 1964. Community development programs in sociological perspective. In *Our Changing Rural Society: Perspectives and Trends,* James H. Copp, ed. Ames: Iowa State Univ. Press.

Schein, Edgar H. 1969. *Process Consultation: Its Role in Organizational Development.* Reading, Mass.: Addison-Wesley.

Schler, Daniel. 1970. The community development process. In *Community Development As a Process,* Lee Cary, ed. Columbia: Univ. Missouri Press.

Speight, John F. 1973. Community development theory and practice: A Machiavellian perspective. *Rural Sociol.* 38 (4):479–81.

Spiegel, Hans B. C. 1979. Theoretical research and community development practice. In *Community Development Research,* E. J. Blakely, ed. New York: Human Sci. Press.

Strauss, A.; L. Schatzman; R. Bucher; D. Ehrlich; and M. Sabskin. 1964. *Psychiatric Ideologies and Institutions.* London: Free Press., pp. 18–36.

Voth, Don. 1979. Problems in the evaluation of community development efforts. In *Community Development Research,* E. J. Blakely, ed. New York: Human Sci. Press.

Warren, Roland. 1965. *Studying Your Community.* New York: Free Press.

———. 1977. *Social Change and Human Purpose: Toward Understanding and Action.* Chicago: Rand McNally.

Weber, Max. 1964. *Basic Concepts in Sociology.* New York: Citadel.

Young, F., and R. Young. 1973. *Comparative Studies in Community Growth.* Rural Sociol. Soc. Monogr. 2. Morgantown: West Virginia Univ. Press.

New Directions

Hans B. C. Spiegel

ROLAND WARREN once said that a community could be described as "a can of worms" (1971, p. 129); therefore, it may not be irreverent for me to suggest, in the light of the foregoing chapters, that community development is an elephant. This elephant (unlike the proverbial elephant with blind people feeling its trunk, legs, and tail) is surrounded by people who actually see the general contour of the animal and are, of course, most knowledgeable and enthusiastic about the part closest to them. It might be added that most observers of community development, including the present one, have a tendency to see the world through gray colored and short-range lenses.

The fact that there is at least *some* agreement about basic concepts is rather astonishing, considering that the practitioners and students of community development come to the field (still in its professional adolescence) from a variety of disciplines. Christenson and Robinson have done a signal service by pulling together many of the common threads of definitions, components, and functions. The long, gray vision of community development is still general, but it has shape and can be recognized. The profession, as one of its most endearing vital signs, also has enough elbow room for different approaches, programmatic disagreements, and ideological debates. In brief, community development, with its general boundaries staked out and its precise functions far from settled, should be an exciting field in the 1980s.

Making projections about *new* directions for community development is more than a little precarious when the *old* directions have hardly begun to congeal. Nevertheless, I undertake the risky task in the hope that it may add fuel to the debate. The following discussion is in two parts: The first deals with a number of possible future trends of the American community and the second with new opportunities that these projected trends present to the field of community development.

TRENDS IN THE EVOLUTION OF THE COMMUNITY

Community is the conceptual boiler plate on which everything else in community development rests. *Community* is the setting in which development is embedded. In writing about new directions, it behooves us to consider first what the likely community trends may be during the coming decade. Community development can successfully shove and tug at the evolutionary path and trends of the community but cannot fundamentally alter their course.

These attempts to discern the future for the community, even its near future, are speculations. They are informed but essentially nonquantifiable judgments. These projections are based on the assumption that there will be no major disruptions (such as wars) in the 1980s and that inflation, if it continues, will be moderate rather than rapid and uncontrolled.

In writing about the future of the American community, an introductory caveat may be in order: Whatever else may happen to cities, towns, and neighborhoods in the coming decade, the community will endure—and caring for the community will endure. Institutional forms, programs, and fads may come and go, but people will continue to look to the human community to meet human needs and will seek to sustain and preserve that community. In this generic sense, then, community development will survive the 1980s with more certainty than will the gold in Fort Knox.

Population

In the 1980s the United States will likely experience continued expansion of its population, but the rate of increase will slow. Some basic figures are shown in Table 12.1. The average yearly growth rate for 1960–1970 comes to 1.3 percent and for 1970–1975 to 0.8 percent. It may be instructive to compare population growth rates on a worldwide basis. From 1960 to 1970 the more developed regions of the world had an annual growth rate of 1.1 percent, a rate that likely will have decreased in 1970–1980 to 0.9 percent, while the less developed regions had increases of 2.3 percent and 2.4 percent, respectively. The United States is driving the population curve upward at a relatively modest rate while the developing nations will likely continue at a faster rate.

While the slower rate of population increase has consequences for community development, the shifting pattern of the U.S. population concentration is probably of more consequence. The spectre of the large cities and their metropolitan areas growing to ever more gargantuan proportions is going to fade during the coming decade. Indeed, from 1970 to 1976 all the central cities of the United States taken together lost more people than they

TABLE 12.1.   U.S. Population 1950–1990

1950	152,271,000
1960	180,671,000
1970	204,878,000
1975	213,540,000
1980	222,159,000*
1985	232,880,000*
1990	243,513,000*

Source: U.S. Statistical Yearbook, 1978, Table 5, p. 8.
*Series II, or middle, projection.

gained. Even though the metropolitan areas surrounding them became larger, the seven largest of the 277 standard metropolitan statistical areas together actually lost 1 percent of their collective central-city-plus-suburban populations. The regional population shift from the northeast and north central regions to the south and west, though relatively slow, is likely to continue; the sun belt will probably continue to grow more rapidly than other areas of the country.

Our country is thus slowing its total rate of growth; the population will continue to be overwhelmingly urban (73.5 percent in 1970), but there will be a shift away from the supercities and even their surrounding metropolitan areas to cities and suburbs that are somewhat smaller in scale.

Income and Discrimination

The elusive median family income, expressed in 1977 dollars, rose dramatically between 1950 when it was $8,356 and 1970 when it has almost doubled to $15,399 (U.S., Bureau of the Census 1978, Table 452). But after 1970 the income curve is almost flat; the increased dollar amounts were canceled by the parallel increase in the cost of living. A similar observation can be made about persons below the poverty level. In 1960 22.2 percent of the U.S. population was in this category, while in 1970 statistical poverty had been reduced to 12.6 percent (Table 754). However, since 1970 the percentage of the population below the poverty level has remained agonizingly constant in the area of 11 to 13 percent.

Economic projections are particularly precarious because of the unpredictable behavior of inflation. The Joint Economic Committee of the U.S. Congress (1978, p. 109) forecasts a growth in annual real gross national product of 3.5 percent for 1980–1985, with an inflation rate of 4.8 percent and unemployment at 5.0 percent. The days of galloping growth seem to be over for the near future. The present plateau of income can probably be maintained even though for the first time in many years we can speak of vulnerability on the downward side.

Statistics for the U.S. population as a whole and ''on the average'' hide serious discrepancies. The poor, regardless of race, are still very much with us and minorities generally are still lagging far behind majorities in earning power. These discrepancies should profoundly influence CD endeavors; even with median family income in constant dollars remaining at its present relatively high level, the unequal distribution of income will have unavoidable consequences at the community level.

For example, what city with a large black concentration can avoid the consequences of the fact that the national median family income in 1977 for whites was $16,782, while for blacks it was $9,485 (U.S., Bureau of the Census, Table 738)? Or, to put it another way, in 1977 only 7.6 percent of the white population had family incomes below $5,000 per year, while 22.8 percent or exactly three times as many blacks were in this lowest bracket (Table

279). The racial gap is likely to continue, especially for those minority groups that are the poorest and least educated.

It seems safe to predict that, regardless of race, the stubbornly consistent 12 percent of the population below the poverty line may continue and that working class income will not improve very much—unless, of course, welfare provisions are revised upward and employment programs, such as the Humphrey-Hawkins Act, can be drastically amended and adequately appropriated. Such potential lack of progress in alleviating conditions at the lower end of the economic scale becomes more ironically dramatic when it is compared to the relatively steady increase in financial benefits for the people at the upper end. In constant 1977 dollars, families who earned $25,000 or more constituted 18.2 percent of the U.S. population in 1970 and 22.4 percent in 1977 (U.S., Bureau of the Census, Table 279). Between a fifth and a fourth of all American families are now reasonably well off and can be expected to continue in this status in the near future.

School Enrollments

Because fewer people will be of school age, elementary and secondary school enrollments will decrease in the 1980s. Comparing actual enrollments of public and private schools in 1976 with projected enrollments for 1986, there is likely to be a decrease of 8 percent in elementary school students and a whopping 16 percent decrease in high school enrollment. Since many community development personnel are active in higher education, enrollment figures for colleges and universities are of interest (Table 12.2). The trend appears to favor public colleges, especially two-year institutions and those that can make part-time study available. The number of persons participating in adult education also has been growing for the past few years, increasing from 13 million in 1969 to 17 million in 1975. It seems safe to predict that growth of educational services will continue in the coming decade in postsecondary and adult education and CD educational services are likely to be part of this growth.

TABLE 12.2. **Projected Educational Enrollments in Higher Education**

	Fall 1976	Fall 1986 (proj.)	Percent Change
Total enrollment	11,012,000	12,903,000	17
Public	8,653,000	10,653,000	23
Private	2,359,000	2,250,000	— 5
Two-year	3,883,000	5,979,000	54
Four-year	7,129,000	6,924,000	— 3
Full-time	6,717,000	6,654,000	— 1
Part-time	4,295,000	6,249,000	45

Source: National Center for Educational Statistics, 1978, Projections of education statistics to 1986–1987, Table 1, p. 4, Washington, D.C.

Public Services and Expenditures

A plethora of services to improve the quality of community life is delivered either by governmental units themselves or by quasi-public or private organizations that frequently have considerable public regulations. The public has become accustomed to traditional governmental services (such as education, police and fire protection, and the judicial system) as well as related service areas (such as welfare, health, transportation, and public utilities). Major decreases in any of these services can be expected to result in considerable objection by affected constituencies, given the nature of special interest organizations, the perceived necessity of these services for an adequate standard of living, and a general reluctance to part with services once they have been locked into place.

Beyond these traditional services, the public will demand others with changing times. Environmental protection and natural resource management are recent examples. The public has seen these as areas that require increased governmental activity and appears ready to live with additional governmental control and regulations.

Juxtaposed against this demand for services is a growing sentiment to keep public expenditures from increasing at the rate they have since the 1930s. The recent public referendum in California (Proposition 13) and the consequent effort of public officials at all levels of government to outdo one another in cutting expenditures are probably significant. For the beginning of the 1980s this sentiment will probably continue to be a telling political force, especially if the public feels the pinch of inflation and lagging economic growth.

As a result of the demand for services on the one hand and the reluctance to pay for them on the other, public pressures for increased productivity in service delivery will be evident in the near future. There will, I think, be more rigid requirements to justify services at all levels of government. We have not seen the last of zero base budgeting and similar attempts to rationalize service performance.

As a result of this financial crunch a number of existing services and their organizational settings will be scrutinized by the public and found wanting. Health services, for example, will probably be attacked not only because they are exceedingly expensive but also because they may be overly specialized, complicated, and not sufficiently oriented toward prevention. During the 1980s, then, we may witness some profound challenges to the traditional services that previously appeared to be beyond such public examination. We will also witness accelerating growth of alternative institutions, especially those that provide services efficiently and with more control by their beneficiaries. Such alternative institutions have already been started in the public sector (neighborhood governments or external degree state colleges, for example) and in the private sector (buying clubs and prepaid legal services, for example). Other alternative solutions to service delivery appear to be waiting in the wings.

Citizen Participation

When, in 1964, the war on poverty was authorized by Congress with its provision for "maximum feasible participation" by the recipients of services, community development workers were in demand and some were asked to come to Washington. A number of hardened political observers believed, however, that the participatory emphasis and the CD personnel would evaporate with the next governmental program, or certainly with the next administration. Moynihan's *Maximum Feasible Misunderstanding* (1969) was deemed to be an appropriate epitaph.

But, somehow, citizen participation in both decision making and self-help has survived and become a household word in the lexicon of the citizen activist and the governmental bureaucrat. The concept of citizen participation has of late enjoyed an increased sense of legitimacy abroad, too. An observer of international development recently remarked:

The key to meeting basic human needs is the participation of individuals and communities in local problem solving. Some of the most important achievements in providing food, upgrading housing, improving human health, and tapping new energy sources will come not through highly centralized national and international efforts but through people doing more to help themselves. [Stokes 1978, p. 5]

Citizen participation can be expected to ride high into the beginning of the coming decade. Bottom-up as well as top-down participation will probably be endorsed; that is, the grass roots and its organizations will use the concept to justify their inputs to government and private enterprises, while the establishment will invoke citizen participation to gain popular support and functional assistance for its programs. The two parties will use the term with different connotations, of course, but like motherhood and apple pie, the concept will find broad acceptance.

It does not seem prudent to predict that the citizen participation wave will crest beyond the first part of the eighties. The bifurcation that is envisaged will, I fear, result in two forms of citizen participation: an autonomous one sponsored and guarded by the grass roots and one sponsored and sanctioned by government. The very term *citizen participation* may fall into disuse in the late 1980s, and new terms and concepts (and their institutional forms) may take over.

The central function of participation in organizational life will, however, remain through the end of the decade and beyond. The participatory imperative will surface in human organizations of every stripe; the rank and file will seek involvement in the affairs of religious organizations, consumer groups, trade unions, recreation associations, political action, and so forth. Citizen participation will probably also have an impact on the workplace in the form of demands by both union and nonunion labor for a greater role in decisions concerning workplace services and amenities and even in selected management functions.

Inténsifying concern about service delivery will be another reason for the continuing demand by ordinary people to be heard in public and private enterprises. We may well experience a backlash against elitist and over-professionalized services (medical, legal, educational, for example) that rob persons receiving such services of consequential voice in and power over them. As a handful of CD educators pointed out a decade ago:

> The creation of specialized competence and the placing of this competence in organizations and agencies . . . has led to three classical forms of isolation and estrangement: the separation and isolation of agencies from each other; the separation and isolation of specialized agencies from the community; and the estrangement of agencies from both the people they serve and those they might potentially serve. [National University Extension Association 1971, p. 2]

Still another indication that citizen participation is coming of age will be the increasing importance of local institutions and neighborhood decision making in the coming decade.

Stature of the Neighborhood

Americans are rediscovering their neighborhoods. A variety of books, newsletters, organizations, governmental offices, and the Congressional Neighborhood Commission testify to this fact. The new localism is upon us. In Janice Perlman's (1976) terms, we are witnessing the "grassrooting of the system."

The local neighborhood can provide an outlet for participation for many persons who find involvement in large, bureaucratic structures more cumbersome and perhaps less rewarding. The local neighborhood, neighbors, and neighboring (though the concepts are not identical, as Keller [1968] has shown), provide the active participant with a number of concomitant physical, economic, and psychological rewards. It is an arena that can be understood; self-help efforts have results that often can be quickly seen and touched, and the targets and goals of a protest can be identified and even personalized. In a world where governmental and corporate decisions and policies are centralized to a considerable degree, the person on the periphery of these structures can find consequential participatory opportunities at home.

It is reasonable to expect, therefore, that during the 1980s neighborhood organizations will increase and by the end of the decade there will be vastly more private block organizations, neighborhood councils, tenant groups, suburban civic associations, local beautification and ecology groups, etc. Also, municipal government is likely to continue to decentralize parts of its planning and service delivery function from city hall to the neighborhoods—utilizing such mechanisms as community planning boards, "little city halls," neighborhood cabinets, and redevelopment area councils (Spiegel 1974). These private and public neighborhood organizations can be expected to gain political muscle, especially in local decision making. Of special interest to the CD specialist is the prediction that technical assistance will continue to be available to these groups through increasing levels of public and private support.

Lagging behind in the development of these neighborhood groups will be the people who may need them most—the poor. Lacking massive governmental commitment and funds, organizational efforts in slums and poverty areas will have a difficult time. Poor neighborhoods will not be totally unorganized; there will be tenant organizations within public housing projects and instances of militant welfare rights organizations. But the bulk of neighborhood self-help action will occur in moderate income and middle-class areas where households have been able to develop a financial and psychological stake that is worth enhancing and defending.

THE NEXT DECADE

In view of these possible developments, what are some fruitful new directions for community development? What are some strategic interventions that CD workers can make to respond creatively?

As I attempt to answer these questions, it is only fair to state once more my bias that community development *by itself* cannot redirect macrosocietal trends. Far from succumbing to historical determinism, however, community development can and should try to support, oppose, or influence these trends with integrity, intelligence, and at times more than a little indignation. Efforts in the following areas will, I believe, make telling contributions to the development of communities during the coming decade; they are opportunities for community development.

CD Roles

It is proper to infer from trends previously cited that community development will be a growth industry in the 1980s. By the same token, it should be no surprise that growth in a given field will attract people from adjacent territories. Community Development Society types may have been among the first to champion the humanized, participatory, community-improvement process, but they will certainly not be the last. Many other professionals are now crowding into this turf—in most cases, quite appropriately. They include planners, public administrators, political scientists, consumer advocates, social workers, community organizers, union organizers, volunteer administrators, antipoverty workers, members of the clergy, and many others with and without collars.

A major opportunity for community development in the coming decade, therefore, will be to explain itself to a larger audience—to articulate the mission of traditional community development. Not only do present CD workers require larger perspectives and increased clarity about goals and roles, but this understanding needs to be communicated to colleagues in related fields and to others who make decisions about community endeavors. This should greatly facilitate the creation of teams for comprehensive community building tasks and the development of political coalitions among concerned professionals to affect public policy.

I trust that this process will avoid professionalism in the overly parochial sense and, instead, CD workers will identify roles and functions that distinguish themselves from and at the same time lend support to their colleagues from related fields. Such role clarification will revolve around the issues raised in this book; particularly suggestive should be the inquiry into the unique "honest broker" role of community developers as they attempt to link a wide variety of community needs that they have helped to elicit from the grass roots with resources that are lodged within and outside the particular group.

Such role clarification is essential not only for self-identification but also for justifying public and private expenditures for community development. The public purse will be opened grudgingly and any vaguely defined function in the public sector will be especially vulnerable to budget cuts. A rather compelling case must be made for housing, economic development, and energy conservation programs that require more than casual public relations for the public to become meaningfully involved.

Failing such articulation, community development units in government, education, and the voluntary and private sectors will be severely handicapped in responding to inquiries from budgeting officials, in dealing with federal requests for proposals, or in joining comprehensive teams of citizens and professionals.

Program Evaluation and Organizational Development

With increasing competition for limited public and private funds for CD programs, evaluation of program results and the correlative development of capacities of the organization delivering the services will attain still more attention than today. (See Chapter 10 for present evaluative efforts.)

It does not seem necessary to discuss the generic value of these procedures. It will suffice to underline the need for relatively objective and, if possible, quantifiable means of judging program results and organizational capabilities. Officials who control public and private purse strings will insist on such hard-nosed data, and any field that continues to rely on soft procedures may well find itself shortchanged in the 1980s. Even churches are in the process of toughening their approach to organizational effectiveness. A desirable activity may thus become a necessity that, like it or not, will be forced on most CD projects.

Transcending Limited Community Interests

With many organizations active in specialized community and neighborhood activities, who speaks for the whole community? Everybody and nobody. Everybody speaks for a particular aspect of the community—

health, education, housing, or a given neighborhood—but hardly anybody is functionally committed to climb above these legitimate interests to view the interests of the community as a whole. Even politicians and public administrators are often governed by parochial considerations.

A new direction for community development, then, might be the further development and insistence on procedures to assure due consideration of development issues that transcend special interests. This task is enormously difficult. The overarching interests of a community are not easily enumerated and the process poses philosophical and operational dilemmas.

Philosophically, how can one best formulate a functional definition of the elusive "public interest of the community as a whole"? It appears that today "the public" resembles a multiheaded beast whose various heads whimper and roar according to their own agenda. One shudders to think about the problems of devising firm criteria that are applicable to a specific community. Nevertheless, it should be possible for trained CD workers not merely to understand the agendas of the various interests and, at times, to seek *modus vivendi* among them but also to advance the interests of unrepresented groups and, to the extent possible, of the community as a whole.

Operationally, the challenge is how to devise indicators to measure community needs and interests—even when these have been successfully defined. It is encouraging to know that environmental impact statements have been utilized for a number of years now and that several attempts have been made to create social impact statements. It is interesting that such social impact statements have been pioneered by the Department of Transportation to assess the social consequences of highway construction (U.S. Department of Transportation 1975, 1976; Christensen 1978).

Creation of a workable and accurate community interest assessment will be a long time in coming. Some progress will likely be made in the 1980s by CD theorists and practitioners. In the meantime, perhaps it would be realistic to expect that CD workers will help the people and groups with whom they are working to enlarge their vision to include the larger community. This larger community should, at the very least, include the needs of often overlooked segments of the community, expressed through their own spokespersons. Some of these groups include Hispanics (who will soon constitute America's largest minority), youth between the age of leaving school and approximately 22 years, institutionalized persons (who numbered over 2 million in 1970), 90 million workers, uncounted recent legal immigrants and illegal aliens, and (always) the very poor in both urban and rural areas.

The CD Profession
Just as the 1960s helped workers from various CD traditions to come together, the 1980s may see some strains in professional relationships. Social upheavals and corresponding governmental initiatives in the 1960s helped workers from university extension units, trade unions, the civil rights movement, overseas development, social services, etc., to discover one

another. The planners of the war on poverty began to discover unexpected battalions and regiments who had been struggling against the same enemy rather effectively for years. The Community Development Society, founded in the late 1960s, was able to incorporate rural and urban, governmental and private, and confrontational and collaborative styles under one professional roof.

In retrospect, the 1960s and early 1970s were times of relative sufficiency of resources for community development. Now that governmental commitment and dollars have grown scarce, there may be more cause for retreating into parochial havens of relative safety. Radical may become less chic in the 1980s, and Alinsky-type organizers and governmental citizen participation specialists may become more aware of the ideological chasm that is part of the bifurcation of community development. Similarly, CD workers employed by public utilities and organizers of antinuclear and lifeline protests may find it more difficult to march under the same professional banner.

The strains will show more clearly in the years ahead, I believe, and the field will be challenged to seek ways to keep the various clans of the CD family talking together.

Self-Reliance and Decentralization

The trend toward more decentralized and neighborhood-oriented programs presents a golden opportunity for community development. Specialists can become indispensable at the microlevel to breathe operational life into cold organizational charts of bureaucratic decentralization that now show more boxes on the lower levels. Perhaps more than any other professionals, CD workers should be able to help organizations become self-reliant, to "think small," and to conduct their affairs, in the memorable phrase of E. F. Schumacher "as if people mattered."

This opportunity can be enhanced as CD training supplements the teaching of the CD *process* with the necessary *substantive* knowledge of concrete resources, programs, and procedures. Economic neighborhood development, for example, will not move forward simply by gathering affected residents into a determined action group; someone needs to inform residents about concrete options for economic development. This may mean, as Congressman Henry S. Reuss has pointed out, that people must be able to explore alternative economic institutions, such as neighborhood credit unions, consumer cooperatives, food buying clubs, community development corporations, local business development companies (Reuss 1977, pp. 44–45). Community development workers must be intimately acquainted with these possibilities.

Here is a challenge for preservice and in-service training institutions continually to update their knowledge about concrete development resources. A closely related challenge concerns not only *what* knowledge to impart but *who* should be trained. It seems to me that the requirements of effective neighborhood-based programs make it mandatory that a whole system, rather than a few functionaries, be trained, including the grass roots, government service providers, private corporations, and the professions that have an impact on a given geographical area. It seems almost self-evident, for example, that CD workers should be the key trainers for the Community Development Block Grant program. As defined and as in practice, community development is at the core of this large-scale, HUD-sponsored program—which is unlikely to be dropped in the coming years. Intriguing opportunities are presented by programs such as these that require training efforts to reach people who heretofore have not been exposed to community development.

The cause of community self-reliance was espoused by Morgan, one of the founders of the American CD movement, during a long life in which he championed the spirit of the small community in an urbanizing world. "Attention should be given," he wrote more than two decades ago, "to the need for maintaining community self-reliance and autonomy in as many respects as would be feasible" (Morgan 1957, p. 60). But community self-reliance will not come about merely because the present energy-scarce times make it seem appropriate. Rather, it can be increased through deliberately planned projects that are guided by sophisticated and well-trained community developers.

User-Oriented Information Systems

The filtering-down process of technical assistance information from a central source to the eventual beneficiary may not work very well; a plethora of information destined for the grass roots never gets there. The information pipeline eats it up; technicians, middle-level bureaucrats, and leaders of large organizations sitting in air-conditioned offices may receive the information, which is often written in such a way that even if it reached the intended consumer it could not be comprehended or acted on. Turner (1976, p. 157) claims that

data banks tend to be counter-productive . . . the user is overwhelmed with facts that obscure as much as illuminate. Furthermore, data banks are technologically opaque to all but the experts, most of whom are employed by agencies that flout all the principles the network supports.

It seems to me that community development has a unique opportunity to deal with Turner's charge. First, it should be determined what CD information penetrates to the grass roots and how it is used and what never makes it. For example, it might be useful to examine a number of CD handbooks that have recently been issued (Davis 1976; Carlson 1977; Nebraska Department of Economic Development 1977; Cohen 1978; Warford 1978; Andersen et al. 1979). Second, it might be helpful to examine the information needs of citizens engaged in community improvement activities. Third, a series of information-giving devices (from illustrated booklets to recorded messages) might be tested with the people engaged in various tasks. Fourth, it might also be important to look at the information carrier who can or cannot use the message creatively. How can CD workers who are sensitive to the needs of the grass roots best utilize such information? What existing networks that effectively reach people can be utilized to help deliver such technical assistance data? And how can grass roots feedback best climb the hierarchical ladder of the help-providing organization?

In this connection it might also be intriguing to ask experienced community developers from third world countries to come to American urban and rural settings to give technical assistance. The information and the information carrier might both find an unusually receptive audience. And anyway, is it not about time to reverse the one-way flow of technical assistance from the first world to the third?

Creative Risk Taking

Community development has opportunities to move in many new directions in the 1980s. I have outlined some of the areas in which it can take place. I would like to end with one caveat about too much caution. Community development, it seems to me, can afford to take creative risks. During the next few years the conditions seem ripe for innovative ventures that entail stepping beyond the safe and well-tested projects: Demands for CD services appear to be increasing, alternative educational programming (especially in higher and adult education) seems to be increasingly accepted, and problems such as the energy shortage have forced us to seek solutions beyond the traditional ones.

Some of these calculated risks at the outer edges of CD practice might include the entry of community development into the world of work—experiments with in-service training of CD operatives in business and government, exploitation of the energy crisis for CD consciousness-raising (for example, by using community windmills to generate both energy and neighborhood collaboration), stepped-up political activity for desired federal legislation, exploration of self-generating funding for community development through direct operation of local businesses and service enterprises, new ventures for community cable television, experiments with neighborhood-based tax levying and budget-making decisions, etc.

A foundation executive put it well when, on examining the organization's domestic grant-making policy, he said, "A foundation that has the capacity to bring about more bountiful seeds of rice and wheat may also, on occasion and inadvertently, sow a crop of dragon's teeth." I am not advocating that American community developers deliberately sow unexamined seed, but I accept the premise that in community development it is far better to endure a few counterproductive results than never to take a risk in reaching for new achievements.

REFERENCES

Anderson, William G.; Hans B. C. Spiegel; Terri A. Suess; and William K. Woods. 1979. *Profiles of Participation: A Workbook on Citizen Organization and Action.* New York: Natl. Munic. League.

Carlson, Karin. 1977. New York self help handbook. New York: Citizens Comm. New York City.

Christensen, Kathleen. 1978. *Social Impacts of Land Development: An Initial Approach for Estimating Impacts on Neighborhood Usages and Perceptions.* Washington, D.C.: Urban Inst.

Cohen, Rick. 1978. Partnerships for neighborhood preservation: A citizens' handbook. Harrisburg: Commonwealth of Pennsylvania, Dep. Community Aff.

Davis, Susan. 1976. Community resource centers: The notebook. Washington, D.C.: Natl. Self-Help Resource Cent.

Keller, Suzanne. 1968. *The Urban Neighborhood.* New York: Random House.

Morgan, Arthur E. 1957. *The Community of the Future and the Future of Community.* Yellow Springs, Ohio: Community Serv.

Moynihan, Daniel P. 1969. *Maximum Feasible Misunderstanding.* New York: Free Press.

National University Extension Association. 1971. *Our Urbanizing Society: A Search for Perspectives.* East Lansing, Mich.: Community Dev. Div.

Nebraska Department of Economic Development. 1977. *A Community Development Process.* Lincoln.

Perlman, Janice. 1976. Grassrooting the system. *Social Policy* Sept.-Oct.

Reuss, Henry. 1977. *To Save a City.* U.S., House, Committee on Banking, Finance, and Urban Affairs. Washington, D.C.: USGPO.

Schumacher, E. F. 1973. *Small Is Beautiful.* New York: Harper & Row.

Spiegel, Hans. 1974. *Decentralization.* Citizen Participation in Urban Development Series, vol. 3. Fairfax, Va.: Learn. Resour. Corp./NTL.

Stokes, Bruce. 1978. *Local Responses to Global Problems: A Key to Meeting Basic Human Needs.* Washington, D.C.: Worldwatch Inst.

Turner, John. 1976. *Housing by People.* London: Marion Boyard.

U.S., Bureau of the Census. 1978. *Statistical Abstract of the United States.* Washington, D.C.: USGPO.

U.S., Congress. Joint Economic Committee. 1978. *U.S. Long-Term Economic Growth Prospects: Entering a New Era.* 95th Cong., 1st sess., Jan. 25.

U.S., Department of Transportation. 1976. *Social and Economic Effects of Highways.* Washington, D.C.: USGPO.

_____. 1975. *Social Impacts: A Guidance Manual for the Assessment of Social Impacts Due to Highway Facility Improvement.* Washington, D.C.: USGPO.

Warford, Ann Ritter. 1978. *Handbooks for Community College/Community School Cooperative Relationships.* Washington, D.C.: Am. Assoc. Community Junior Coll.

Warren, Roland. 1971. *Truth, Love, and Social Change.* Chicago: Rand McNally.

LIST OF CONTRIBUTORS

EDWARD J. BLAKELY is professor of community development, University of California, Davis and Berkeley. His work has focused on public policy and community change; he is author of three books on community development and has advanced a new theoretical model for rural development in the United States.

ELIZABETH BOTHEREAU is director, Community Services and Community Education, St. Louis Park, Minn. She was formerly assistant professor, human services planning and administration, Mankato State University, and she has been involved in a variety of human service planning, delivery, and coordination efforts.

LEE J. CARY is professor, Department of Regional and Community Affairs, University of Missouri, Columbia. He has published directories on the status of graduate education in community development; his particular interest is the CD process, and his book, *Community Development as a Process,* is widely used both here and abroad.

ROBERT C. CHILD is president of Central Development Associates, a private consulting company in Carbondale, Ill., that provides management training, and planning support for development organizations at the regional, local, and national levels. He has been engaged in CD programs for more than a quarter-century.

MARK W. COHEN is director of the family mental health program, Oklahoma City Veterans Administration Medical Center, and assistant professor of psychiatry and behavioral sciences, University of Oklahoma Health Sciences Center. He has worked for community change through the voluntary participation of area residents, and he has published articles on citizen participation, program evaluation, and methodology for conducting household surveys.

RICHARD (RICK) COHEN of Rick Cohen and Associates is a community development consultant in Hoboken, N.J. Currently he is evaluating 5 neighborhood preservation projects for HUD and 15 neighborhood improvement demonstration projects for the Community Services Administration.

RONALD T. CROUCH is legislative analyst, Legislative Research Commission, state of Kentucky. His principal focus is providing staff assistance to the General Assembly, drafting legislation, and researching issues in the area of health and welfare. He has done research on care of the mentally retarded, neonatal care of sick infants, provision of emergency medical services, and provision of services to the aged.

BOYD FAULKNER, professor emeritus, was on the staff of the Department of Regional and Community Affairs and directed the annual International Seminar on

Community Development, University of Missouri, Columbia. He served the Agency for International Development for 13 years as a CD advisor in Afghanistan, Iran, and Tanzania, and for 13 years he was an extension agent for the Bureau of Indian Affairs.

FREDERICK FISHER teaches community development and directs the Community Consultation Laboratory, College of Human Development, The Pennsylvania State University. His work experience includes 7 years as city manager, 8 years with Washington public interest groups, and consultation with many public and private agencies in this country and abroad.

LARRY GAMM is associate professor, Community Systems Planning and Development, and chairman, Center for Community Research, The Pennsylvania State University. His research and publications have focused on intergovernmental programs and community decision making: he has provided consultation to national, state, and community organizations.

LORRAINE E. GARKOVICH is assistant professor of sociology, University of Kentucky. Her research has focused on migration and its consequences on communities of origin and destination.

VANCE E. HAMILTON is extension associate professor and district program leader for community development, North Carolina State University. He has served as a county CD agent and a state CD specialist, and he has authored a number of extension publications in the areas of leadership development and in extension's role in health education.

IAN HARRIS is assistant professor of community education, University of Wisconsin-Milwaukee. He is a trained Alinsky organizer and has helped create alternative schools and food coops in Philadelphia. He is active with the New American Movement and has helped establish community-based day care centers in Milwaukee.

JOHN M. HUIE is budget director for the state of Indiana. He was a CD specialist on the Cooperative Extension Service staff at Auburn University for 2 years and on the agricultural economics staff at Purdue University for 8 years; he was project leader for the Community Development program in Indiana while at Purdue.

E. FREDERICK LIST is associate professor and state extension CD specialist, University of Missouri, Columbia. He has served as a community consultant at Southern Illinois University and is particularly concerned with small group process as it applies in CD work and in the design and implementation of community attitude surveys.

DONALD W. LITTRELL is state extension CD specialist and assistant professor, Department of Regional and Community Affairs, University of Missouri, Columbia. He is widely known for incorporating theory and practice and has been a consultant/trainer for state, regional, and national groups. He is author of *The Theory and Practice of Community Development: A Guide for Practitioners,* which is used around the world.

PALMER E. McCOY is professor, Department of Community Affairs, University of Wisconsin-Extension, Hayward. For most of his professional career he has worked in or with the private sector; he has published and worked in the areas of growth strategy, rural development, small business development, economic planning and development, and downtown analysis and development.

ERNEST E. MELVIN is professor of geography and director, Institute of Community and Area Development, University of Georgia, Athens.

BRYAN M. PHIFER is professor, Department of Regional and Community Affairs, and director, Community-Public Sector Programs, University of Missouri, Columbia. He formerly served as assistant director of the Division of Community Resource Development for the Federal Extension Service in Washington, D.C.

HANS B. C. SPIEGEL is professor of urban affairs and director of the graduate program in urban affairs, Hunter College, CUNY. He was Deputy Assistant Commissioner of U.S. Urban Renewal Administration, on the planning team for the War on Poverty and Model Cities programs, and consultant to the Carter urban policy planning group. He has trained CD workers for Kenya, trained PCVs, has been UN consultant on human settlements, and chaired the 1978 UN Expert Group on Participation in Development.

JEROME M. STAM is leader, State and Local Government Program Area of the Economics, Statistics, and Cooperative Service, USDA. He is directing research activities in community development and local government with a focus on finance.

DONALD E. VOTH is associate professor of rural sociology, University of Arkansas, Fayetteville. He has been involved in CD research and education for about 20 years; he is particularly interested in citizen participation in rural development and community development evaluation.

PAUL D. WARNER is associate extension professor of sociology, University of Kentucky, where his principal focus is in the application of sociology to community development. He has piloted new approaches in the delivery of manpower services in rural areas, in the use of paraprofessionals in small Appalachian communities, and with computerized informational delivery systems for communities and individuals.

INDEX